Layla Masters!!
Enjoy reading!
May the Lord bless you!..
♡♡ Veronica :D
July 2018

I Can Only Hear God

My Journey As a Deaf Person and My Personal Relationship With Jesus.

Veronica Dunnington

Contents

Foreword

By Reuben Dunnington

Consider it pure joy, my brothers and sisters, whenever you face trials of many kinds, because you know that the testing of your faith produces perseverance. Let perseverance finish its work so that you may be mature and complete, not lacking anything.

James 1:2-4 (ESV)

I cannot think of any other person that I know this scripture applies to more than my mom. She is an incredible, enduring person who has not only struggled through many difficult times throughout her life, but had to do it while being deaf on top of it all! I, like many of us, am not deaf and can't even pretend to know what it's like to live in a world primarily designed for hearing people, and to be left on the outside. But my mom, through her relationship with the Lord, has come out of the other side of each misunderstanding, interpersonal conflict, and inner struggle with a stronger faith, deeper wisdom, and a maturity that has enabled her to love everyone she knows—even those who have hurt her the most.

So often we hear stories about famous "super" Christians whose lives appear void of the often seemingly weekday difficulties and struggles everyone faces. But hearing her often funny, sometimes serious, and always inspiring stories (that I have often heard more than once!), it is clear to see God involving himself in all the little aspects of her life, and that He alone is the source of her strength and capacity for grace. Her heart to know Jesus and make Him known is the driving force behind this book, and His presence shines through her life and these stories in a way that inspires me to lay my life down again for the sake of the King. I hope it does for you as well.

My heartfelt thanks to those who contributed to my book:

Lord Jesus Christ

Reuben Dunnington

Tiffany Dunnington

Gar-Yun Ho

Patti and Dick Meredith

Guy Noel Ganados

Lisa Sheets

Julie Quandt

Joyce Sheets

Matt Saettler

Jim Bryson

My deaf Friends

Introduction

It took me years to think about writing a book about my life experiences, inspiration, and God. Many have encouraged me to write, but I hesitated because English is my second language. I was born deaf and grew up in an oral school. Last year we went to a home meeting at our friends' house where there was a guest speaker whom I had never heard of. When he got up, he pointed his finger at me and said, "You are going to write a book. Don't be afraid and God will help you. So no more excuses!"

"Aahhh. Who me?" I thought. I brainstormed what I was going to write about. I got stuck and put it on hold because I kept asking around for an editor for my book. A year and a half later, I found out that my long-lost cousin Patti moved to Harrisburg (where I was flying into to tend my elderly parents in Jersey Shore.) When I contacted her, immediately she invited me to stay overnight and offered me a ride to my parents'. She and her husband Dick, a writer, were great inspirations and motivated me to get started with my book. Patti proofreads, so she offered to edit my book. All fell into place, definitely the Lord's timing. I had been thinking of the title for the book for about a year, and I couldn't figure it out. Dick asked me what I wanted to write about. I told him and a couple of minutes later he said that he thought of a title for my book. Here it goes: *I Can Only Hear God.* I knew that I had hit the pot of gold. That was it. I had goose bumps and whoa, praise the

Lord! Lord, bless Dick and Patti. They motivated me and I began to write.

Growing up as a deaf person, I developed my own phrases, idioms, and sayings that may sound different than what you are used to.

For your information, all the people here in the book are hearing unless I mention that they are deaf (to avoid confusion). I changed some people's real names just to protect their identity in this book. The situations and experiences are real. I wanted to share real-life experiences with you. Why? To empower, encourage, and exhort you spiritually as they did me.

Chapter 1

The Early Days

My dad was in the Air Force. Yes, I was a military brat. He was in the service for 20 years and we had moved around a lot and lived in the United Kingdom where my sister and I were born. I was born in a small town on the west coast of Scotland called Prestwick that was once an Air Force base. My parents had no idea that I was deaf until I was taken to the doctor at the age of 18 months. They assumed that I could hear. I fooled them maybe because I felt the breeze, vibrations on the floor, and I saw the moving shadows. They thought I was a stubborn and rebellious child. Who knows how many spankings I got for not listening to them?

The doctor in England tested me and found out that I was born profoundly deaf so he recommended my parents get mail education from Tracey Clinic in California. It was discovered that hands-on education was working for me. I was told that I was a natural lip reader understanding my mom who worked with me exclusively.

While living in England where my dad was stationed in the Air Force, we lived in a farm house with my older hearing brother Jim and my baby hearing sister Janette along with one cat. It multiplied to 12 cats and they were everywhere. I remember one day very clearly, maybe I was two. I crawled under the bed trying to get the cat out of there, and it scratched me. I had eye contact with that cat with my declaration it was my rival from day one. Sorry to the cat lovers.

After our big move from England to Florida, I got really sick

When I was five, living in Florida.

with a high fever and had bronchitis. I was sent to the hospital for a few days and placed under a plastic tent. My mom stayed up all night to watch me since there were no night shift nurses. She went home during the day to tend to my other siblings. I thank the Lord for wonderful parents who cared for us.

When my Dad was stationed in Orlando, Florida, I was sent to a multi-handicapped school that was called Forest Park School

for the Handicapped. There was a small deaf program. Actually, it was supposed to be an oral training program separated from the integrated programs for those who were blind or had cerebral palsy and other disabilities. At that time I was three, and I recall the torture of learning to speak... by saying "aaaaaaaaaaa, eeeeeeeee, oooooooooo" for at least a minute until I was out of breath. I remember that very clearly to this day. However, my mom said that I had always wanted to talk like Mama or Dada. I even lip read before I had all the training.

4

The Early Days

When I was either five or six years old, there was a teacher in training from Clarke School for the deaf, a private coed school in Massachusetts, who taught me. My first two words that I was able to pronounce clearly were "purple" and "apple". My sister recalled that I kept repeating "purple" and "apple" all day long. That drove her nuts even though she was about four years old then.

I have two other brothers who were born deaf while we lived in Orlando, Florida. They were a handful and I remember playing in the small, blown up swimming pool and stepping on an upside-down tin tub to jump in. We went around and got in line taking turns jumping in the pool on hot tropical days. My brothers worked together getting the back door unlocked and climbing our house's glass louver windows without breaking them. We had a German Shepherd puppy, and they were so afraid of it.

I was 6 1/2 when I started my first year of Clarke School for the deaf.

My parents came to a decision that I be enrolled in Clarke School after passing the test and being accepted even though I missed the first two years of school there. We relocated to Granby, Massachusetts, in 1961. Trying to fit in at a new school and my small class of eight wasn't easy. I had speech therapy and lip-reading lessons every day as well as a spelling bee every Friday. I loved spelling. I enjoyed the challenge, and I went home every weekend to be with my family. Every Sunday before returning to school, I had to write the news about what I did over the weekend and I had my faithful mom go over the news

5

that I wrote. That was practice and exercise to improve our English structure.

Speaking was the hardest learning process for me...holding the teacher's throat to feel the vibrations for me to imitate her sounds. She wound hold a strip of paper or feather to distinguish between the breath and voice sounds by the movements of the paper or feather. It was painful learning to speak. I recall in my last year, we had a speech test by speaking in front of the teachers-in-training. I got about 30% understanding while others had 90% comprehension by the teachers. "Ugh, no fair," I said to myself. What a humiliating experience. There was always silent competition among the peers. I hated that.

I loved playing with my deaf brothers when we got home from school on the weekends. We were at the same level communicating and we developed a special bonding. They really looked up to me as a deaf role model.

I was born after my hearing brother Jimmy who was 13 months older. He was pretty active in sports at home and at his school. I was in competition with him in kickball games and even touch flag football in the neighborhood during my summer break from private school. He twisted my arm to play touch football. He always challenged me in racing, running and bike riding around the circle drive where our house was located.

My sister Janette is two years younger, and we shared the bedroom all of our lives until I moved out for college at age 20. We were close and at the same time we had cat fights. In the winter time, it took a while to warm up the bed as Janette and I shared a full-size bed. She would put her freezing feet on my warm body, and I always got mad at her. We took turns massaging each other's backs before sleep. I would go first then she said she would do it the next day. I called her cunning. She seemed to be older than me and I seemed to be stronger than her. I looked so young. Even when I was 25, a fifteen-year-old was flirting with me as I was on staff for a campout for troubled teens. The other staff members told him that I was staff, meaning I was at least 21.

Hey, no fair... but I can't complain that I still don't look my age. Anyway, Janette always strived for attention while all the boys were clamoring for me I didn't want the attention. I didn't understand why they wanted a deaf girl like me. I felt like some kind of outcast of the hearing world.

For 10 years, that school was full of life and activities like skiing, splash parties, sledding, ice skating, and Sunday closed-captioned movies. I preferred to stay behind with my deaf peers rather than challenge myself in the total hearing world at home. I didn't realize that my parents sacrificed a lot for the sake of our future. I could feel their pain but they were overjoyed that I was to succeed in life.

Dad and I at the Clarke campus.

When I was eight, I was moved when I was reading about Jesus healing people, performing miracles, dying on the cross for our sins and rising from the dead, it moved me. Since my parents raised us in the Catholic Church, I asked my mom if I could become a nun and get married. She exclaimed I could not do both. I was determined to serve the

Lord and get married. It has come to pass. The Lord saw my desires of the heart.

Around that time, sharing with three other girls (age from 5-10) in the "Magna House" dorm bedroom in the deaf private school, there was a routine every morning to go to the bathroom and wash up, make the bed and go to the playroom before breakfast in the dining room. Each table was seated by class level. So I grew up with my classmates at the same meals throughout the years. The dorm was very strictly organized, and the routine was never broken.

Every morning after breakfast, we were all lined up to go bowel movement as required. There were four or five stalls with toilets but no doors. There was a housemother sitting in the front of us watching us like a hawk to make sure we go BM. Whenever one of us had done, the housemother came to see the toilet to see if we did it. If we did it, she checked off the box of the chart that we each did it. I was such a rebel, I was so uncomfortable for her to watching me and I was never able to go BM. She always was scolding me. I had seen my empty boxes in the morning, but usually checked off in the afternoon when no one was around. Again the housemother scolded me for not be on the schedule. I was not afraid to dare to be different from others.

One night I was dreaming that evil spirits were taunting me when I woke up seeing three demons' faces up in the ceiling corner speaking to me, "You cannot swallow the saliva or you will die!" So I kept drooling out the saliva and the pillowcase was wet, thinking that I was surviving. It went on and on for a couple hours. So finally I had to call the housemother named Mrs. Daniel, the mean one, in the middle of the night. She was puffing, huffing, and yelling at me. I told her the story and it made her madder. She told me to go to sleep; I didn't see any more demons and went to sleep.

The next morning Mrs. Daniel wrote on the board, "Ronnie is very foolish!" I was stunned with some laughing at me. Sometime later, the incident happened again but worse. So I was sent to the

My class with Miss Pike at CSD at Lower School (I'm front, second from left).

infirmary across the campus. The nurse was very supportive and told me to call her if I needed her. It happened again, so I cried out and she was there for me. It didn't happen again.

When I was about 12 years old, I went to see the priest for my first confession outside the confession box. Since I could not hear the priest, I had to face him in the open. I came out crying with frustration because of the communication barrier. That was just before the day of my First Communion. Mom was always there to comfort me.

For about ten years, we grew up in Granby, a country town in farmland. We always went tobogganing on our hill and went ice skating on the pond. We made huge snow forts and had snowball fights. One winter that I will never forget, there was a bad storm and there were snow drifts everywhere. There was a drift at least 12 feet high reaching almost to the two-story house's roof. We were jumping from the roof into the drift of powdered snow. It was one of the most fun experiences I ever had. I loved that home as my stomping ground. Our neighbors were always friendly and made effortless communication with my deaf brothers and I. We had our community there. Every year, we as neighbors got together for a BBQ party.

Michael, Nelson, Jimmy, Veronica and Janette.

Every summer my family faithfully took a two-week vacation in a campground by a lake in Cape Cod. We camped out in a huge canvas family tent that fit seven of us. (Paul was not yet born.) We had a propane stove to cook pancakes, eggs, bacon, and other home-cooked food. Every night, we had campfires to roast marshmallows for s'mores. We went boating, swimming, sunbathing, fishing, and water skiing.

Niagara Falls was another place we went for a spring break. It was awesome and majestic to see roaring falls. We went across the border into Canada to the Skylab the majestic tower overseeing Niagara Falls. We went outside on the tower. The wind was so strong that it made me feel like I was being swept away. It was scary; my heart was beating fast. I wanted to go inside so I wouldn't worry about being carried out in the wind. I went into the bathroom and someone turned the lights off. It was pitch black. I screamed loudly. The light was turned on. Janette was laughing so hard since she did that on purpose. With an upset face, Mom ran up and asked what was wrong. I said, "Janette turned the light off on purpose." Mom said that the lady down the hall thought I had the most powerful lungs she ever heard in her whole life. I guess that the Lord made my voice loud for His purpose.

I roomed with Pam most of our school lives. She visited our family every weekend because her family lived out of the state. My family lived only 20 minutes away. She was like a sister to me. She had everything that I didn't. When I was 13, she came to school from home flaunting her new fake sheepskin hat. I thought, "Oh, I am tired of her having everything she wants. I am going to get what I want--a real sheepskin hat." So I told Mom what I wanted for a Christmas gift...a REAL sheepskin hat! She hadn't the slightest idea who I was competing against.

Mom said that she couldn't afford one, but I kept bugging her to get me one for Christmas. At that time, my dad had two

My sheepskin hat.

jobs and Mom was a housewife. On Christmas Day, I opened one of my gifts and there was a REAL, beautiful, big, furry sheepskin hat with fluffy balls. It was just beautiful and bigger than Pam's. I wore it out on the wintry cold day and it turned out that it was too hot to wear. I never wore it again. Mom was furious, took it away from me and kept it until two years ago. It was well-preserved when she gave it back to me. I realized back then I was being selfish and thoughtless while my dad was working hard with two jobs. The moral was to be content with what I had.

Although Pam had to put up with me as a drama queen, I

always expressed myself strongly. She was a very devoted student studying hard and faithfully doing her homework thoroughly. My desk was right by hers, and I kept nagging her for attention, since I was bored with school.

I was never fond of school. I was boy crazy and an athletic jock. I just couldn't keep still, always on the go. There were a lot of girls watching TV and dreaming of the movie stars. I had no interest. I loved ice skating, sledding, skiing, water skiing, swimming, bicycling, family sports, even real football that was kind of rough. I was too proud to admit that I was hurting. Those guys were bigger than I was. Once or twice, there was a long line of boys trying to beat me at arm wrestling. Only one boy beat me. That is how I was tough like a tomboy, and I loved the physical challenge.

In the middle school level when I was about twelve, I tap danced steps that I learned from Laura. She took tap dance class at home during the weekend and brought whatever she learned and taught me. The bonding between us developed. She moved up to another level where I didn't see her anymore. However, a classmate named Leah was a new student at Clarke. She went through our playground to go to class on another side of the campus, and we were captivated by each other. We always talked even when she was running late for class or heading back to her dorm.

Pam growing up with my family

Chapter 2

Teen Drama

The next fall, I moved up to Upper School level. Both Leah and Laura were there. We always got together to talk. Leah and I had more things in common. We liked playing sports, ice skating or even just being outside sitting on the big pile of leaves and talking. We were seen together a lot and made some girls very jealous. Some told lies to the teachers and housemothers about us. I didn't understand why they would do that; I guess they didn't understand the value of the relationship. Maybe they didn't know how to maintain a good relationship. I am thankful to my parents who taught us to communicate when we got into fights with our siblings. We had to work it out and make up.

My family had been calling me by my nickname Ronnie since birth. As a carryover, the teachers and the peers called me Ronnie, too. I got tired of being teased. My name was too boyish for me. Everything built up to the point that I had enough. One day I came home from school for the weekend announcing that I had a new name. I declared to my parents that I wanted to claim my real name back and use the name of Veronica from that day on. That was when I was 15. They understood, but even my siblings still call me Ronnie today. However, at school, the teachers and my peers respected me by using my new name.

I was growing up and got into trouble in that school. I had a controlling boyfriend to whom I was too afraid to say no. When I was 14, he came to me one day and proclaimed that I belonged to him. I felt powerless when he approached me and he was the most popular boy in middle school. I didn't know any better. He was good looking and I was dating him for 2 to 3 years.

Cheerleading squad (I am 2nd from left)

One time he wanted to make a plan to sneak up to my 2nd floor dorm room in the mansion with his buddy in the middle of the night and I was too afraid to object. I knew if I got caught, it was to be a scandal and we would be expelled. He wanted to be intimate with me, I refused him and was so scared of being caught. Nothing happened. Whew, I thought. However, 2 months after Thanksgiving, I was called in to see the head manager of the dorm and I somewhat knew I was caught somehow. Mr. Head said to me that I was lucky that I didn't get too intimate. I was told that the watchman, who had been on duty, was on the top of the roof watching over the 22-acre campus for the deaf students' safety. That was where he saw the whole incident and reported us right away, but the head manager didn't want to ruin our holidays, so he waited until our return from vacation. I was punished by eating with the cooks in the kitchen for one month. It was one of the most humiliating times in my life because of all the attention I had from the school and my peers. Some looked down on me. However, I got to know those cooks and become friends with them as they showed me compassion. That made me stronger because I had to stand (face) it alone. I realized that there was power to say no, but I didn't have the courage. It was a lesson and it was by the grace of God that I didn't get expelled or get seriously in trouble.

When I was fifteen, I begged my parents for me to join the ski club at Clarke. Even though it cost our poor family money, they were still happy to help. On my very first day, on the ski slope of Mt. Tom in Holyoke, Massachusetts, I was taking a beginner's lesson with my other deaf peers. The instructor taught us how to ski on the small slope, and we practiced all day. I was excited to try skiing from the top later that day. When I got to the top, I was a little nervous while looking down the slope - it seemed steeper than before. Once I started skiing, I was very focused, and only looked up when I was partway down the slope. I realized I had gone on the expert slope and it was too late to go back. I prayed that the Lord would help me through the endless snow moguls. I kept aiming at one bump at a time, going very slowly. Eventually, my legs were tired, and I was caught off guard; I lost control and I found myself skiing straight down at top speed. Finally, at one big bump, I flew way up the air and I cried out to the Lord, "My life is over! Help!" I remember looking down at how high I jumped and saying to myself, "That's it!" Then I crashed and rolled down the hill. I was knocked out and several people came to see if I was OK. I remember faintly that I was carried on the stretcher to the ambulance and taken to the hospital. I slowly awakened and my mom was already with me in the emergency room. I had no idea how long I was unconscious! The doctor said I was fine; my mom was upset, worried, and expressed how I need to be careful. I nodded. I felt strange for the whole time since the impact of the fall. I felt a calming spirit had overtaken me, keeping me in some kind of trance. I had my eyes closed the whole time. I didn't even have any broken bones, bruises, or sprains! I was whole just as before I skied. I could not explain the phenomenal experience, but I knew that the Lord was with me for the whole time. I continued skiing for the next fifteen years!

One of the worst situations that really influenced me was in my second to last year of school. When I was walking to Catholic Church one Sunday morning on a beautiful spring day, I was asked to accompany a senior named Chris who was the most feared and popular guy at school. We walked through Smith College campus on a beautiful trail with flowers blooming everywhere on our way back to our school campus. Since he had a girlfriend who went on her senior trip that week, he tried to make bad moves on me but I resisted him and left him there. I really stood up to him and didn't care what he thought of me. The very next day, the rumor was going around fast, spreading false stories about me to get revenge on me. No one wanted to talk to me or be friends with me as they feared that big shot. A few girlfriends did stand by me and supported me throughout the horrible ordeal. I was 16 and, as you know, that kind of peer pressure was really killing me as a teenager. After five months of persecution and silent treatment, I couldn't take it anymore and spilled my guts to my wonderful teacher Mrs. Pratt and her husband, the school principal. They listened passionately and said that they would see what they could do. Actually, they really couldn't do much.

Finally, one day in class, a classmate was mean to me saying, "Don't look at me." Those on the other side of the room said the same thing. Wow, was I supposed to look up at the ceiling? Mrs. Pratt saw the whole situation, and she stood up and said, "Let's stop the class right now. I want to share something with you." She shared the biblical story about how the townspeople including the Pharisees, the religious leaders, brought and threw the prostitute down to Jesus' feet and wanted to stone her to death. Jesus said to them, "Who has not sinned will have the right to stone her," and slowly one by one, they left Jesus and the prostitute. Jesus said to her, "Sin no more," and she was free to go. That powerful parable impacted the stunned and silent class. There was silence in the classroom and the class went on as usual. The silence broke and caused ripples throughout the whole campus. That rude classmate apologized, and heaven broke loose. Everyone apologized to me and gave me a chance to explain what really happened to me and that big shot. It took Chris about a month to humble himself before me. God is all-powerful, and He took care of the whole situation. Hallelujah to this day. The big shot is now a faithful servant to the Lord, although he has cancer to fight against. Keep him in your prayers.

When I had one more year left to graduate from Clarke School, my parents got a letter from the Upper School supervisor. The correspondence advised that I had not been doing well in school for the past year. I was given two choices: either be demoted to the less advanced class or go to summer classes to catch up. I was devastated. Of course, I didn't want to stay another two years at school. Since it was a big wakeup call, I decided to shape up and chose the summer classes. I had a tutor who was my teacher Mrs. Pratt who happened to be one of my favorites. We had a great time, and I caught up with no difficulty. She said that I was smart but lazy. She encouraged me to make good use of what I had to succeed in life.

Upon returning to school in the fall for my last year, I was determined to be a good student once for all. I had no boyfriends to deal with after a few years flirting with the guys as I had been boy crazy. My ex-boyfriend was out of the picture. I dedicated the whole year to study, improved academically and prepared for the transfer from Clark School to public high school.

At graduation, surprisingly, I received an award for the greatest academic improvement. "You reap what you sow" is one of my favorite scriptures that truly applied to that situation.

Dressing time of Romans for Dinner (Mrs. Pratt with my class of 1971, I'm far right in the front)

My graduation day from Clarke in 1971.

Senior class 1971 on Washington DC trip with Ted Kennedy (I'm front fifth from left)

I Can Only Hear God

Chapter 3

The Hearing World and My Friend Carolyn

We were uprooted from our home in Massachusetts to move close to Erie, Pennsylvania, when my dad got promoted at General Electric. I was enrolled in high school in Girard, skipping 9th to 10th grade. Little did I know that it was going to be the toughest year of my life.

My mom and I met with the guidance counselor, and Mom wanted me to take a public speaking course. I had terrible speech only 30% was understandable. No way. Mom persisted and encouraged me to take the opportunity to improve my speech through that class. I took another humiliating trip with everyone glaring at me speaking garbled speech. Oh no. I couldn't stand it. I told the teacher that it was not working. She said that I should not give up even though the other students were not used to my raw voice (deaf voice). It was a one-year class with one-minute to 45-minute presentations. It was an amazing class that gave me confidence, and the whole class loved me and cheered me on. I gave a 45-minute presentation as my final exam, and it turned out to be a Hollywood moment. I got videotaped as I shared about my life at deaf school and how I learned to speak, lip read and use the hearing aid. The class was so captivated with my improved speech. That was a reward that I worked hard for. I was a movie star that day.

On the very first day of public school, my sister was in the 11th grade, and I was in the 10th even though I was two years older. After riding a bus together, of course, I was really scared like a kid going to kindergarten for the first time. She pulled me aside and spoke to me, "From this day on, I don't want you to follow me around or ask me to help you. You are on your own!" I was freaking out inside and didn't want to show her how cowardly I was. You know I was older and was supposed to be in control. I was losing it when I entered the big hallway with lockers on both sides with all the students there staring at me. My legs felt like rubber. I had to go to the bathroom to regain my composure, but I went to the guys' bathroom instead. They were laughing at me. Oh, oh, oh. I was about to faint. I had to rush to the girls' bathroom and looked at myself in the mirror. My face went white like I had seen a ghost. A girl came to me recognizing me as the new girl in the territory and asked me if I needed help. So I yielded to her guiding me to the homeroom class, and I was already late. When all the eyeballs were glaring at me, I felt worse and tried to look for an empty desk. The teacher welcomed me, and Carolyn Bovaird, the girl in front of me, greeted me. She became my best friend, tutor, and note taker. How blessed I was to have her throughout three years of high school. At that time I had no interpreter. The teachers expected me to sit up front so I could lip read all the teachers. The teachers were asked not to face the blackboard and talk, but instead turn around and face the class speaking so I could lip read.

I took a biology class with the world's fastest speaking teacher, and he acted like a college professor whom no one could understand. I was in the same boat as the rest of my class. Wink, wink. My classmate next to me named Chris was aware of my lip reading situation. The "professor" had a black beard so his lips were hardly visible and moved what seemed a million miles an hour. Chris took advantage of that situation using me as a scapegoat and raised her hand. The professor said, "Yes?"

Chris said, "Veronica couldn't lip read you because you talk too fast, so please slow down for her."

He said, "Huh, OK," then went on with speeding lips.

The very next day, he walked into the room and I was stunned.

His beard was shaved. Oh no, he went on with speeding lips and asked me if I understood him. I had to sink below the desk. I wanted to strangle Chris. She was full of fun and laughter all the way through high school.

Chris hung out a lot with my sister. One time as they were peeking through the store glass windows with all the equipment for smoking pot, she asked my sister, "Which stuff should I buy Veronica for her birthday?"

My sister laughed out loud and said, "Veronica is a straight girl!"

Chris said, "Oh really? How come she hangs out with me at school? She accepts me the way I am." At that time, I didn't know anything about diverse group of people. I interacted with anyone from nobodies to jocks. I loved people, and the division had never entered my mind. How naive I was. My heart was full of excitement and willingness to associate with people who accepted me.

My mom was in her 40s when she bore my baby brother Paul who is 17 years younger than I am. I went straight home to take care of him, and I loved him. I always looked forward to coming home to be with him. I helped Mom by watching and playing with him after school every day. He always looked forward to my coming home from school. I had almost

Slumber party in high school (I'm on the bottom left with Carolyn on top of me)

no social life in high school outside of school. For three years, I learned how to take care of him as a baby, then as a toddler. It was a rich experience and most rewarding that I had a great relationship with him. I loved hosting his birthday party for him and his little friends. He was about four when I went to art school. I usually came home on weekends from art school to be with him as well as to be close to my mom. I could talk to her about anything.

The history class in the first year was beyond my understanding, and my vocabulary couldn't match it. I was overwhelmed and even cried every day when I tried to study and understand what was being said in the history book. Dad was there to help me every night reading word by word. He explained and I had the dictionary at my side to look up every word I didn't know. It was an everyday thing. Dad was there faithfully all the way through. Fortunately, my vocabulary tripled and I was able to comprehend what was being said. It was the biggest jump in my entire life. My brain had literally expanded, and my speech had improved dramatically from public speaking. That sophomore year was incredible, and it was the grace of God that helped me through. I couldn't believe that I made the honor roll for two years. I was immersed in books. During my senior year I became more lax, took it easy, and got a social life.

I got my first job as a dishwasher for a small diner in Girard and got paid $1.10 an hour. I had to wash a big pile of dishes all night for two weekends. I was mistreated by the demanding and rude boss, so I quit the job. I felt unappreciated, and he took advantage of my handicap with his cruel treatment of me. I got a housecleaning job for one year from a thin lady in her 50s.

Then I had a strange experience with that client. She told me that she had some kind of sickness or cancer. (I don't remember which.) I recall that she had some kind of surgery. She asked me to help her take a bath. She was naked and she wanted me to help wash her. I felt so awkward. I had never seen a naked person in my entire life except for my sister. It was not in my job description at all. I told Mom about it. She thought it was strange, too, so I quit that job. Some people viewed me like I had no brain because I was deaf. In the third year of high school (my senior class), my mom said that there was a job opening at the pie factory only on Saturdays. I worked on an assembly line of different pies. It was a fun place and I had a wonderful supervisor with a great sense of humor. He looked Italian. He was short in height, thin, with dark skin and black, short hair tucked behind his ears. He had a long, big nose with smiling, white teeth that always lit up the room.

One spring day I went out with a friend and went to New York's border past Erie, 45 minutes from my hometown. We wanted to buy Boone's Farm wine, and 18 was the legal drinking age in New York. I brought the wine to my close friend and "right hand girl" Carolyn who helped me through high school. She invited a couple of guys to join us. We drank the cheap wine. I loved strawberries so I bought strawberry flavored wine, and I drank two whole bottles because it was sweet. The next thing I knew I blacked out and could not remember anything. Carolyn didn't drink much and said that we needed to sleep in the tree house out in the back of her house because we didn't want to get into trouble with her religious parents. We slept in the tree house in the cold night. I remember throwing up all over the tree house and dozing off and throwing up again. The red color was all over the outside of the tree house. Early the next morning, I realized I was covered with vomit and got up to see my friend's glaring mom with an angry look. Oops. I had to come down and walk through the woods the back way which was a shortcut to my parents' house.

As I was wandering in the freezing cold creek, I tried washing the vomit off of myself and my hair. I felt numb not feeling the coldness of the water and I was soaking wet. It was an early, misty morning with heavy dew on the long grass as I dragged myself through our eight acres of land across the racetrack and up the hill past a variety of fruit trees. I rang our doorbell because the door was locked. I dreaded facing my parents anticipating a great punishment. The door slowly opened. Mom saw me in a big, wet mess like a drowned rat. She hugged me with relief as she was worried and up all night. I said to her, "I am sorry that I got drunk and will never do it again!" She smiled and said not to drink out, but only at home. She swore that she would not break the news to my dad, so he would not punish me. I was surprised because

I expected punishment but I didn't get it. Mom said I already punished myself. She showed mercy and grace.

There was always a choice between mercy and condemnation, that would push one away from God. It took me more than one week to recover from the hangover that lingered a long time. For a whole month, I wanted to vomit after smelling all the strawberry pies where I worked. It made me feel sick, and my supervisor showed mercy with understanding and let me go home. He didn't condemn me either. I learned that wonderful lesson of mercy and love.

One summer before my senior year at high school, I was enrolled in a summer program for speech therapy at Edinboro State College in Pennsylvania. I was the only deaf student enrolled there, and the others were hearing people who had speech impediments. It was a challenge to interact with them daily, and I lived in the dorms with college students. We had all kinds of activities like volleyball, swimming and picnicking. There was a guy there named Dave who liked me. I was ignoring him because he was kind of nerdy to me. I had a bad attitude towards him since I thought that I was better than him. Then the Lord spoke to me of my pride. Oops, I had to humble myself, and all of sudden I felt love toward Dave like a brotherly love. Wow, we became good friends. My lesson was to never judge people but to love them.

Since the small town we lived in was not updated like the town I came from, I wanted to focus on improving the school class image. I decided to run for president of the senior class along with the party of my own including vice president, secretary, and treasurer. I had to practice making my speech (thanks to public speaking) and spoke in the front of the whole high school. There were five other candidates running against me. At the very last minute, my best friend jumped in to run against me as president. What a challenge. She had more experience being in the office so the votes came in very close. Although I was winning, at the end my friend won. That was close and yet a great experience. She did a good job as senior class president. She came to me saying that she wished she had not taken the office. I was glad she did because I would have had trouble following the group meetings. So it worked out just fine. I knew the Lord's favor in my life; since I won people's hearts and gave them hope for the impossible to be done.

The spring before I graduated, I decided to take up a challenge to ride my ten-speed bike to Edinboro about 25 miles one way. Going down the steep hill for more than one mile was pretty scary. Since my ten-speed bike had really thin tires, it was really dangerous if it went over one stone, even a pebble. At about 25-35 miles an hour, the bike could easily flip over. I held the bike handles really steady, praying that I would not slip. I didn't have protective gear at that time; it was not required for regular bikers. It was a beautiful country of rolling green hills. I enjoyed the quiet scenery. On my way back, I had to ride back up the steep hill. I went huffing and puffing with each stride. I overcame the challenge and didn't want to do it again. I knew that the Lord's hand was on me. As I look back, if I did it again, I would go with friends, wear protective gear and ride on thicker tires. I would be crazy not to take those safety precautions.

On my 20th birthday, with two months left to graduate, I heard the sad, tragic news that two of my classmates were killed by a train right up the hill from our farmhouse. I was saddened to hear that. I always crossed that railroad track with extra caution. I dreaded crossing it because there was no signal to warn of the train approaching. Since I was deaf and not able to hear the train coming at all, it was always spooky to cross there.

I made it through high school in three years, and it was tough. I earned it because I did it even without interpreters. All the teachers were asked to face me when they used the blackboard so I could lip read. Besides that, several of my classmates were note takers who offered support. I heavily depended on textbooks and notes.

My friend Carolyn tutored me through three years of the high school. We did everything together. She helped me transition from the deaf school to the hearing public school. She was at her best with me. She always smiled and was never angry or impatient with me. She was God sent and I was truly blessed. I thank the Lord for allowing us to have a decent conversation a week before she passed away of cancer. What touched me the most was that she said, "I will look for you in paradise." Hats off to Carolyn Bovaird.

I felt my life had been truly stretched out in intelligence, mentally, emotionally and spiritually. I finally broke through my potential level; I used to think that all hearing people were better, smarter and more advanced than I was. Then I realized that I was an individual who aimed to accomplish much in life, and no one could stop me. I set high standards, expectations and goals. Yes, I did and I am still aiming today. I am able to accomplish anything I desire, and deafness doesn't stop me. So my horizons have expanded, and I am seeking more.

I have always felt the Lord's presence and favor in my life. I was raised Catholic, and I always talked with God about stuff I had to go through. During high school days, I recall when I was around seventeen, my sister loaned me all kinds of books including The Cross and the Switchblade by David Wilkerson about a street gang in New York City finding God. My sister Janette was involved in Young Life, and sometimes she took me without an interpreter. I got the idea that the teens loved Jesus. I was consumed with the love of Jesus through Young Life. It impacted my life even though no words were understood.

Chapter 4

Life After High School

A few weeks after graduation, I attended summer school at Edinboro before the fall enrollment, and I took college algebra. I was surprised that class was fun and easy. There were about 30 students at the beginning of the class, and at the end there were only two of us. I realized that quitting class could lead to a habit of quitting life altogether. That really hit me hard. I kept telling myself that they were hearing, and I was the only deaf person in that class. They had more advantages. That really stunned me, and I made a vow to never give up on anything in life. I wanted to be thoroughly done so I could accomplish my goals or whatever my tasks were. Anyway, the summer program was supposed to help the pre-freshmen become fully prepared to be enrolled in the fall. It did help me as I was really scared of the word "college." That seemed very advanced, out of my league.

When I enrolled in college, majoring in Fine Arts, I took the basic courses including Art History. I found myself in the dark classroom every week staring at the white slide projector screen with all the pictures of art subjects that were hardly from the textbook. The "Women's Lib" lady professor was speaking about the slides, and I just glared at the slides not knowing what they were all about. Whenever I took a test, I almost flunked. I approached the liberal lady and asked if any of the information was from the textbook and she replied, "No. All is from the slide presentations."

I asked to get information from the slides. She said, "No." I went to see my guidance counselor and asked him how to deal with the situation. He suggested that I ask her if I could write a thesis instead of going through the silent slide presentation. I tried but to no avail. I realized that left me no choice but to leave college after the first semester. I felt hopeless and moved back in with my parents.

My parents moved to Connecticut from Pennsylvania due to my dad's promotion in his company. I worked as a maid for a hotel. Out of despair, I was thinking of becoming a model because Connecticut was full of modeling agencies. When my dad heard of my intentions, he challenged me (like always) to do something better, to use my brain instead of using my body. So we went to the Division of Vocational Rehabilitation to see the counselor about what I could do with my future. My parents noticed that I was talented in art so the counselor said that there was an art school close to New Haven that offered a four-year program. My reaction to the idea was, "Yes, let's go for it." How little I knew about how much I had to learn. So, taking the plunge, I enrolled in the Paier School of Art.

My first experience with income tax was frustrating yet liberating. My dad first gave me the income tax return form and said, "Fill it out." I stared at the form like it was foreign, and my mom read my facial expression which said, "I don't know how to do this. I need help." Mom mentioned to Dad that he needed to show me how to do it. Grunting, Dad sat down with me and explained it to me, but I still had to fill out the form. He was known to be short on patience, and corrected it afterward. It was my first step toward independence. How little I knew about how the Lord used Dad to prepare me for the world and shape me to be fully independent.

My experience of seeking the Lord was so intense. I started to question if God was alive or dead when I joined Buddhism, one of the modern branches in which you didn't need to shave your head. I was struggling with the Catholic Church because the people in church never smiled or talked about God or their faith in Him. Actually, I was frustrated with the same routine and I didn't understand the meaning of it. One day, my sister Janette invited me to visit the Buddhist meeting. The people were friendly and reached out to me. I thought it was strange. I was again invited to attend. I remembered that people there said that I should commit to sign the contract to become Buddhist. I felt incredible pressure to do it. I asked them if I could still believe in God while being Buddhist. The answer was, "Yes." So I signed up and I was given a piece of paper that was like a short scroll that had Japanese writing in symbols meaning that when you chant, you reap benefits. I thought it was cool and my sister and I shared chanting in front of the scroll for things that I wanted. I got what I wanted. It was a boyfriend. It was kind of spooky. The more I chanted, the more things happened. In the meantime, I felt a great struggle inside of me. I had a spiritual war going on inside of me for a month.

Then one night I had a powerful dream as if it were real. It was very vivid up to today. In that dream, I was standing at home facing the open basement door. I looked down the stairs and there were walls all the way down so I could not see what was down there.

There was a lady at the bottom of the stairs. I knew her as Janette's friend who brought her to become Buddhist and worked with her at the motel where I used to work as a maid. I recalled seeing her as the receptionist at the motel. She was the friendliest lady, and she had the most smiling face I had ever seen. I was very impressed by her. Anyway, she was that lady in that dream. She said to me, "Come on down," with her famous smile and welcoming gestures. I felt uneasiness in my spirit. I couldn't put my finger on it. I kept searching her to see if there was anything wrong with her before I made a decision to come down the stairs. I didn't know what to expect at the bottom of the steps. I couldn't see what was down there, and I didn't know why she wanted me to come down. I was intensely searching her over and over before I decided to go down. Finally, I saw something in her eyes. I flipped out, screamed and slammed the door. Then I woke up from my deep sleep. I found myself soaked with heavy sweat all over my body and even on the bed as if I had taken a shower. I was really shaken up. Her eyes revealed to me an evil spirit glaring at me despite her smiling face. I realized that it was a real window to her soul. I felt that good and evil were battling. Finally, I said to God, "Okay, I am going to challenge you to see if you are alive, not dead!"

I decided to quit my job as a maid at the Stratford Motel in Connecticut just before college in the fall. I felt compelled to hitchhike to Ohio to see my college friend. I said to God, "I want to know if you are real and alive and will protect me and bring me to my girlfriend Becky's home in Cleveland, Ohio. I expect to arrive just before the sunset!" I wanted to arrive before sunset because I couldn't lip read in the dark. So it was about 13 hours to drive straight but hitchhiking would take much longer. It was my very first time to do that. I asked Janette if she would take me to the freeway in Connecticut that leads to Ohio and she gladly accepted since she had experience thumbing. I asked Janette to call Becky telling her that I would arrive at her home the next day. There was no TTY (teletype device for deaf communication) or video phone at that time. That night I packed an Army bag and went to see Mom who was sleeping in the TV room. I woke her up and told her that I was planning to hitchhike to Ohio the next morning. She pleaded for me to take a bus instead. However, I was firm with my decision. I had important business with God.

The sun rose and it was a beautiful, sunny summer morning. At 5 A.M., I was ready to go. Janette drove me up the countryside north about 30 minutes. Dew was on the grass, a very pretty morning. There I was waving goodbye to Janette. I stood looking up, "So here I am, God." Alone with my green Army bag, I declared, "I am ready and from here on, I want you to protect me from the police arresting me." I was breaking the law hitchhiking and expecting Him to get me over to Ohio by nightfall. I was really nervous as I didn't know what to expect. I was risking my life. I asked myself, "Am I crazy to do this?" I had to remind myself that I had to find out about God. I walked down the long ramp that seemed forever. Oh boy, I was really nervous. I was anxious to get my first hitch ride. I felt silly sticking out my thumb asking for a ride. The first one was a pickup truck. Just an ordinary man picked me up. I felt relieved. He said that he needed to get off at the next exit. Oh, only a mile. How disappointed I was. I had to get off then waited for a ride for about ten minutes. I said, "God, where is the ride?" A beat-up car stopped. I opened the door and I smelled trouble. The heat hit my face. What was the heater doing on in the summer? Oh no. There was an old man in his late 50s whose two bottom teeth were knocked out so his smoking pipe could fit in nicely. He was puffing and huffing smoke from his grinning mouth. He had a white T-shirt on with a huge belly popping out, drab pants and a belt over his belly. He invited me in.

I kind of hesitated and got in. I saw clothes were thrown in the backseat, and it looked like he had been living in the car. I was kind of nervous. He asked me where I was heading to. I said, "Ohio." He grunted and said that he was heading south to Virginia. So we went on riding. I felt uneasy about him. The heater was blasting, and the car was smoke-filled because the windows were closed. I was coughing and opened the window to breathe fresh air. I commanded him to turn down the heater and leave the window opened. He grunted, "Okay."

Then I noticed that he was taking the exit. I asked him where he was going as we entered the country road with all the trees. He said that he was out of gas and needed gas. We were going nowhere in the woods with no sight of civilization like living souls, homes or buildings. I asked him where he was going. He said, "Oh no, I am not gonna rape you!" as he was rocking himself. I had to yell at him to turn the car around to go back to the freeway. He repeated that he needed gas. We were at least five miles out of the way in the woods. I cried out to God. A gas station appeared out of nowhere. He pulled up. I had to get out of the car quickly and went into the restroom to relieve myself. I was trying to figure out what I should do. I decided to go back to the car. There he was washing the window. The car already had a full tank of gas so he had never filled it up. I ordered him to get back to the freeway. He said, "Okay, okay."

We went back to the freeway, and I had a map in my hands in case he tried any tricks on me. I watched the road closely and I was acting like a tough tomboy chewing gum and sticking my elbow out on the window sill. I said to him if he tried to trick me again I was getting out of the car, period! He said he was going south. We only went on about 20 miles after stopping a few times. He stopped again in the rest area. I had to be bold not to be intimated by him. Wow, I was a nervous wreck inside. Was he trying to look for excuses to get what he wanted? Believe me, I was scared to death. I kept crying out to God for direction. Finally, he steered quietly to the right on the freeway. I noticed that it was a wrong way and he was trying to deceive me. That was the last straw so I boldly blurted out, "I am getting out of the car now." I was opening the door while the car was still moving.

He said, "Oh no, I don't want you to get hurt." I stepped my foot out, and he stopped the car. He showed his true colors as he was furious, became violent and waved his arm down at me. I said goodbye and smirked at him. He was gone in a split second. I was alone and did not know where I was. I was discouraged that I had to walk down the ramp again. A car came with a young man and his five-year-old son. The man stopped asking if I needed a ride. To my surprise, I was gleefully hopping in, and we sped away back to the freeway. We had a nice conversation. He had to drop me off on the freeway before he got off the exit. There I went again. I said to God, "I need a ride," as I was getting close to the turnpike to cross New York, New Jersey and Pennsylvania. Minutes later, there was a pickup truck swooping me up and I hopped in. There was a happy guy in his 40s. He was telling how he had gone to beaches where people sunbathed or went swimming naked so he confessed to being one of that kind. He was super friendly and he took me all the way across three states then dropped me off before the Pennsylvania Turnpike that stretched across the whole big state. It was about a straight six-hour drive. I said to God, "I need a ride all the way across Pennsylvania." I was getting tired. Then a tiny car pulled up, and I jumped in the back of the car and it sped away. I told the driver who looked like a friendly hippie that I needed to go to Ohio. There was a young lady sitting in front and a large guy sitting in the back of the small, cramped car. Well, I needed the ride. I fell asleep for the whole trip across Pennsylvania. They woke me up to get off on a very busy freeway close to Pittsburgh. There were about five lanes during the 5:00 PM rush hour. I was getting close to Ohio. I prayed to God, "Please get me out of here." That seemed impossible. There were many avenues in and out of the city. I was standing there looking for any car that would stop for me. No police, please. I said, "Hey, God." All of sudden, a car from the furthest lane pulled all the way over to me. The door popped open, and I jumped in as I didn't have time to check out the driver. He asked me where I was going. When I told him Cleveland, Ohio, he said that he was on his way there. Yay! I happened to have a bad headache that was throbbing badly. I asked the good-looking guy in his 30s to wake me in time for me to get off before Cleveland. I fell asleep, and he covered me with his coat. What a gentleman. Two hours later, he tapped my shoulder, and it was time for me to get off on the specific ramp that led out off the toll exit. I knew I was in trouble because if I walked to the toll exit, I would be arrested for hitchhiking. I was nervous and kept nagging God, "Hey, what shall I do?" I stayed where I was just before the ramp of the toll exit. All of a sudden, a bright yellow Cadillac appeared from heavy rush hour traffic on my right side. The door popped open; I dove into it and I noticed the tall, black guy who dressed like a pimp from the seventies who asked rudely with an upsetting attitude where I was going. I said, "Mentor." That was the town where Becky lived in suburban Cleveland. He said, "What? I don't understand. What's your problem?" As he paid the toll and pulled over, I said that I was deaf and I lip read. His attitude changed as if he melted instantly, and he became very nice. He said that he was not heading that way but that he would drop me off on the outskirts of Mentor. I got off and I was in the little countryside town, and the sunset was almost over. I said to the Lord, "You promised to take me to Becky's before sunset."

There was a car pulling up with an elderly father and his son in his 30s who waved me into the back seat with his friendly gestures. I told them that I came all the way from Connecticut. They couldn't believe that I came out there so fast. They were willing to take me straight to my friend's home. They were so kind to me and were happy to be part of my journey. Finally, I arrived at my friend's house standing quietly with the sun still peeking out. As I climbed up the entrance steps, I rang the doorbell, and Becky came out and greeted me with a warm hug. She saw the car pulling out of the driveway and realized that I didn't drive but got a ride. She said," No, you didn't thumb all the way here, did you?" I smirked. She went into fits. "Something bad could have happened to you!" she exclaimed.

I said, "I FOUND GOD!" She looked at me in disbelief. I told her how the Lord orchestrated that trip on a nice summer day so I would know Him personally. I arrived just in time as the sun faded away. I humbled myself and repented that I had challenged the big God and I felt foolish, but now I knew Him as He is Alive, not dead. He is so real. Imagine that I had slept twice with total strangers in a deep sleep. I was completely in the Lord's hands and no harm had touched me. I was in awe, and I was completely transformed from my one-day experience with Him. He answered every single request and demand.

Of course, I called Mom that night to let her know that I got to my friend Becky's safely. Mom was sure worried all right! She said to take a bus home. I told her that the trip was the best thing that ever happened to me. It was like I was reborn in Him. That established my first walk with Him. I knew He was always there for me. Even if I was unfaithful, He was still faithful. What an amazing God I serve.

Chapter 5

Art School and Summer Jobs

I was majoring in the Art Advertising four-year program at Paier Art School. Before I arrived, I was assigned to live with seven other roommates at a duplex home. All of them were ladies and there was a "queen" who had her own room. She was a senior at our school named Gail. She was actually a hippie.

My roommate, also a freshman like me, wore heavy makeup and always looked at herself in the mirror. She seemed very insecure. She did have amazing talent in painting but it was farfetched since she had been taking LSD or some kind of acid. Her boyfriend always came over during the weekends, and they took advantage that I couldn't hear them. That was disgusting. I had to sleep against the wall on my bed to avoid the embarrassment. It was a culture shock for me.

There were four other roommates in one of three bedrooms. They were always out and I hardly saw them. I was always the one to cook for myself. One time I was really broke and I had no food except for some bouillon cubes and a little rice so I made soup.

I enjoyed every minute of learning different aspects of art:

drawing naked, real-life models, oil painting, acrylic painting, water color painting, color pencil drawing, pencil drawing, pen and ink drawing, package designs, charcoal drawing, photography, darkroom, paper sculptures and graphic design. I had no interpreters. Fortunately, they were small classes up to fifteen students I had more time to converse one-on-one with the teachers so they could explain things to me.

Anyway, when I decided to stay with my roomies during the weekend, we would go out to bars or go to friends' houses. It was hard to carry on normal conversations as I could not follow what was being said. I had to drink to break the ice and get into the center of attention. It became a habit almost every weekend. I experienced blackouts many times, and it was scary as I didn't remember what really happened. I always asked my roomies if I did anything out of ordinary and they said I was just fine. That crept on me as Thanksgiving was around the corner. I started buying liquor to bring home to drink in the evenings and a few days more in a row.

One day I just blew up at my roommate, and I realized that it was uncalled for. I felt the Holy Spirit speak directly to me to stop drinking altogether. I stopped cold turkey and it was hard. I pressed through Christmas without a drop. I felt better as I had almost become a raging alcoholic. I thanked the Lord for saving me from falling into a trap that could cause problems in my life. That was a close call.

That same year I used to ride my bike to school and to work cleaning homes. At that time there was no protective gear so I always rode without it. One sunny spring day, I was riding on the right side of the road on my way to my apartment. I was riding fast on my ten-speed bike about 20 miles an hour. In a split second, a car cut in front of me with no warning. I used both brakes to fully stop but it was too late. I hit the back of the car, flew up and fell back on the hard pavement head first. I got up fast and felt no pain. Over and over I yelled at the guy, "Why did you cut in?"

He took off. I went back on my bike to continue. I was in total shock and got home. A witness followed me home. He told my roommates that I was hit by a car, and he was taking off to find the hit-and-run driver. My roommates called the hospital and asked for advice. They were told to look at my injuries and my eye pupils for a while. They made sure that I didn't sleep in case I bled inside of my head. I felt pain eventually, and they took me to the hospital despite my objections. The doctor examined me and the X-rays that they took of my head. I was cleared, and the doctor said that I was lucky. I believed the Almighty God was there to protect me. However, that guy who hit me was never found. I had to let him go and forgive him for what he did to me. The vengeance belonged to the Lord.

The summer after my first year of art school, I got a job as an artist working for the City of New Haven. I also got a position as a part-time live-in maid in a suburban town so I didn't have to pay for rent or food. I took the bus downtown every day to paint two posters for the city. It was my first experience being in a real city as I grew up naively in the country.

One day I walked on the street towards the town center, and I saw a guy hitting another guy's head with a baseball bat. The victim was bleeding badly. I wanted to rush to put a stop to the violence, but something stopped me and I heard a voice say, "No. Stay where you are." At that time, there were no cell phones. I had no means of communication. I was in shock. I couldn't believe that someone dared to hurt someone like that. Then I realized I should never be involved in things like that because I would get hurt, too. The wisdom of the Lord was given to me by His grace.

It was a humbling experience to be treated like I was a nobody when I lived with a family of four. I had obligations to do the housework, laundry, and house sit while they were out of town. The summer air was hot and humid, and the house was partially air-conditioned. My small bedroom didn't have air, not even a fan but just two small opened windows. I remember clearly that every night my room was hot like an oven and I had to lie still not moving trying to stay as cool as possible. Then I would drift into a fitful sleep. I chose not to complain and went with the flow. I accepted the hardship and trusted that it would turn out to be okay. It did.

I met a hard-of-hearing guy named Dave at the city where I worked. I thought that he was friendly, and we became friends. Later in the springtime of the second year, my friend Bud wanted to introduce me to the deaf culture that I had never been exposed to. I thought that I was successful in the hearing world, and he wanted me to understand the deaf manualists (the deaf, raised and taught to use American Sign Language (ASL), who didn't speak but only signed) compared to us as deaf oralists (the deaf who were raised learning to speak and were strictly taught not to sign ASL). I wanted the challenge to learn something.

When we got to the deaf club in Hartford that had The American School for the deaf close by, there were deaf people signing. It was a completely different world. I didn't understand any of the American Sign Language. It was like committing a sin to sign as I was brought up in The Clarke School for the deaf, a strictly oral school for the deaf. It was a new world that I wanted to explore. Later when I ran into Dave by surprise, he didn't greet me but instead he was signing in a flash. I said, "Hey, I never knew sign language." I didn't know that he knew how to sign when I first met him at work for the city.

He said, "Too bad," with a cruel response. I was stunned to see a different person than the Dave I knew at my work. I tried to persuade him to be reasonable and talk to me instead of signing but with no avail. I walked away ignoring him, still feeling betrayed and shocked. I tried to forget him by meeting other deaf people but it was difficult. I thought the deaf manualists were uneducated.

All of a sudden, I was alone in the room with Dave, and he called for the crowd's attention. The deaf people began circling around us, and he prodded me with a chair like I was a lion. Then he proclaimed signing with both of his arms folded and moving his lips, "You are oral." He mocked me in front of everyone, and they laughed. I was so humiliated, I walked away and asked my friend Bud to take me home and I never looked back. That deepened the hurtful scar in my heart. I made myself a vow never again to be friends with the deaf manualists. I declared them as disrespectful, uneducated low lifes. That is how I felt back then.

Later in the spring, I made friends with Beth Ottenstein, a tiny Jewish lady, who wore unmatched clothes like a mixture of hippie and gypsy. From Boston, she was full of creativity and intelligence, but she had manic depression. She was in one of my classes. I was looking for a roommate for my second year, and she mentioned to me that she had been looking for a roommate too. We lived in a two-bedroom apartment (duplex home) so I had my own bedroom.

She was darling to me. She didn't have friends from our school. Her dad was a psychiatrist and he also suffered from depression. I thought it was strange. I always encouraged her and shared my faith with her about the Lord even though I didn't know the Word. She dramatically improved and she felt good about herself. She

shared some Jewish food like lox on cream cheese and bagels with me. She was a vegetarian and made one of my favorite recipes, cottage cheese loaf with walnuts. It was amazing. So I explored healthier food. It was my awakening time about health consciousness. Eventually, Beth stopped taking antidepressant pills because she felt good about herself and was no longer

Beth and Arlene trip to Charlottesville, VA

depressed. We parted our ways as she graduated and went to college, and I continued my third year and moved back home for one year.

That same year I hung out with my old friend Laura from Clarke School for the deaf, who lived in Massachusetts. We got together often and met oral friends from Clarke and one guy named Ryan from Yale University. Yale was located very close to where I used to live. I also met other hard-of-hearing people. We enjoyed hiking, camping, skiing, canoeing, picture taking and hanging out. One of the most exciting events was our trip to New York City for the bicentennial celebration in 1976. We saw tall ships sailing, long parades and ate great food. We reclined on the grass in Central

Park looking up at the starry night watching incredible fireworks displays of actual pictures of presidents and many other sparkling pictures. It was a special celebration of America's freedom. It was peaceful although thousands of people crowded Manhattan in New York City! The thought of danger never entered our minds like today.

For two years, I had special relationships with my friends. I learned more about myself freely expressing who I was: a free spirit loving people, having fun, enjoying life. I was proposed to by Bud whom I helped draw out of loneliness. I felt that we were just good friends, nothing more. I was too strong of a leader type, and I preferred a man to lead me.

Laura and I hanging out.

After my second year of art school was over, I didn't want to stay at home for the summer since I had an adventurous spirit to explore outside of my comfort zone. I took the map of the east coast out, I prayed, asking God where I could work for the summer as a live-in housekeeper. Then I closed my eyes and had my finger pointed to the map. It said Charlottesville, Virginia. I didn't have the slightest idea what that town was and who lived there. It was about a ten-hour drive.

On a leap of faith, I put an ad for a live-in housekeeper job in the mail and sent it to the Charlottesville newspaper. A phone call came in. Of course, Mom had to answer for me and told me that I would have to go down to Virginia for a job interview. You would think I was crazy! Yet, I was determined to have someone drive me down during the Memorial Day weekend. Beth was willing, and it was a long drive. Before we got there, I knew that I had taken a risk for just one interview. I had faith that I would get that job. A fragile, tiny elderly lady welcomed me, and she was very nice and offered me the job right away. We understood each other. After the interview, I don't recall if we stayed at the hotel overnight. I remember a long drive. When school was out for the summer,

Mrs. Small

Beth, my faithful friend, was willing to drive me down again, but this time, Arlene, a hard-of-hearing lady, came along and dropped me off. How little I knew that summer was going to be a great adventure.

I was working as a live-in housekeeper. I cooked meals for Mrs. Small with her cocker spaniel puppy, cleaned the house and kept the yard clean. I drove her car to go shopping, and sometimes she drove. I didn't realize that she was an alcoholic. She always included some wine or liquor on her grocery list. She demanded I run to the store to buy some more for her whenever she ran out. I refused because I didn't want to enable her to drink because of my own past. It was not my responsibility for her drinking problem. She could be Jekyll/Hyde; she could be very sweet, and another day she could be very mean. No wonder no one wanted to work for her. She was becoming impossible. I told myself if I could get along with her then I could get along with anyone in the world.

The second week I was there, I was walking up the hill for exercise not knowing that my deaf brother's classmate Matt lived up the hill. I just ran into him. That was strange. He asked me what I was doing in town. We become acquainted. Later, I discovered he was a devoted Mormon. He invited me to visit his church with him. It was different from the Catholic Church. He gave me his Mormon Bible. I felt it wasn't right; I even cried. Matt couldn't understand why I was crying. Maybe because I was ashamed that I felt that I should be reading the Bible instead of the Mormon Bible. We visited each other for a little while, although I tried to keep a distance.

I was looking for a church where the deaf went. I ran into some lady who knew sign language that I still didn't understand. She was a church interpreter for the deaf, and she invited me to visit her Baptist church. It was another church different than my Catholic background. I enjoyed it. I met the deaf people there. A cute hillbilly guy named Ronnie who reminded me of "the Fonz" with a convertible car from Happy Days always drove me around and introduced me to the deaf. Most of them were raised oralists with signing abilities. They always welcomed me into their homes and served me meals.

I later learned that Thomas Jefferson had his home in that town. We visited Thomas's gorgeous estate and learned that he was a genius. Ronnie took me all over the Blue Ridge Mountains where the hillbillies lived their simple lives. I really loved that guy Ronnie who had a big heart although he was not very educated and again he was no leader.

I had to say goodbye when the summer was over. Mrs. Small had grown fond of me even though we had some clashes. She said to come back again the following summer. I thought it was a very special time, but I wanted to move on. How little I knew that the town of Charlottesville with its rich history would have people I was familiar with. The Lord actually handpicked that town for my personal growth.

Having no car for two years, I didn't go home much on weekends to visit my parents, two deaf brothers and one hearing brother. That led me to my decision to move back home for the third year of school for one year. I bought a used Maverick and commuted every day to school through snowstorms, falling asleep at the wheel several times. Eventually, I carpooled with Gloria and Brian who were in my class and lived in the next town. They were willing to share the carpooling. I developed a friendship with these people through that year.

I thought I was friends with Gloria. I wanted to buy her a birthday gift during our senior year of art school, even though I barely had any money. I knew her favorite store was The Casual Corner so I bought her a skirt and a blouse. I was so excited to give it to her. I never heard a response from her. She completely ignored me for the rest of the year. It was a mystery that was never solved. I even dreamed of seeing her again to resolve it. I thought our friendship was special. I just gave it up to the Lord. It still remains a mystery today.

Back then, my mom was telling me that I was the one who

always made the calls. (I had no choice but to rely on my mom to make the phone calls since there was no TTY, video phone or cell phone at that time.) Mom kept saying a one-way street isn't good because I was the one who made the calls. Gloria rarely called me. Maybe she was afraid to say no to me, and it was the final straw when she got the gift. Who knows? Since that time, I made sure that there were two-way, accountable friendships.

Actually, when I was living at home for the third year, I was able to maintain a relationship with my little brother Paul. He was amazing. One time my parents were working in the garden when I came home from school, and I saw him carry out sandwiches for their lunch. I was blown away. He managed to cut homemade bread all by himself, four slices for two sandwiches with a stack of meat, cheese, and lettuce. He was five then. I couldn't forget that one. Today he's a great chef at home.

My dad usually came home late as he was the manager for General Electric, and he worked hard and got a lot of recognition for his work. He had been losing his temper for whatever reason. Whenever he was home, I had to walk on thin ice. One day, he said something that was uncalled for, and I talked back for the first time in 21 years of my life. He slapped my face really hard and pushed me down the basement stairs. I got hold of my fall. That anger gripped my heart against my dad whom I resented. That resentment went in deeper as the years went by without my realizing it. Forgiveness came much later.

During the third summer of the school year, I decided to explore the West. I applied for a job in Yellowstone National Park and got accepted. I wanted to experience the West by hiking, backpacking, and most of all seeing the Rockies. The unknown adventure began when I took a Greyhound bus with a big box and a bicycle. My dad said to me, "Ronnie, are you moving to Yellowstone?" He suggested I pack lightly. I had to bring a backpack, equipment, sheets and a pillow. I didn't know that bike riding in the national park was dangerous because RVs or vehicles with stand-out mirrors for hauling campers could hit the bicyclist's head. So instead I just rode my bike in the village where I lived and worked.

There was an employee dorm in each village of Yellowstone. I was drafted to work at the Grand Canyon village with its breathtaking view. There were many bears roaming around there especially at night. I met a wonderful, bubbly roommate Elliot from Spokane and she accepted me as a deaf person. She was easy to communicate with, and she was a born-again Christian. I worked in the cabins as a maid. There were about 25 cabins. I cleaned five to six cabins every day. I kept receiving large tips of $20-$50 even from one-day guests. No one in town had received tips this big. I asked my peers if they had received the tips like I did, and they asked me how I did it. I said I just kept the rooms clean and was faithful with small things, and the Lord blessed me. I was called the "BEST TIPPED" in town, and the word got around. Employees kept coming to me asking me how I did it.

Elliot and I backpacking.

During the evenings, the employees gathered around for socializing in the employees' pub. There was a pool table there.

I'm in the meadow of Yellowstone National Park.

Men were competing, so I joined in. They were looking at me like, "What's she doing here?" I was always friendly to them, beat them all and left them as upset individuals. That made me feel good. I didn't know that I was resenting all men because of my unforgiving attitude toward my Dad.

I went hiking almost every weekend and sometimes backpacking. There were all kinds of wild animals like elks, moose, bison, black and brown grizzly bears, deer, and all kinds of birds. During one of our backpacking trips, we went round trip for 22 miles on one of the most beautiful treks that summer. I had to put bells on my boots and backpack to scare the bears away since the grizzly bears usually didn't show their mercy when encountering any humans. I heard many stories about how the tourists or employees got mauled to death or seriously injured. Yeah, it was scary to go on an adventure in the wild and expect the unknown.

Story about the cabin and bison.

I was with eight other employees taking two days off trekking through beautiful, flowered meadows with the gentle breeze in the dense forest. We stopped and looked over to the right side at a herd of bison and elks really close by. We were in awe and observing them quietly grazing in the meadow where we were at just near the entrance of a forest. All of sudden, we looked to our left about 25 feet. We saw a black bear sitting and looking in our direction. While we were trying to escape the bear's presence, I looked at my peers, then down at my buckle for my brand new backpack. I tried to unbuckle it, but it was STUCK! I was too late, then I looked up and the bear disappeared as it left in a hurry. It was as scared as we were. The most amazing thing was that one of the guys from our group took off his backpack and climbed a tree in a split second. We were told not to climb trees or run, but to take off our backpacks and play dead in a fetal position on the ground. What a scare. I knew the Lord's hand was with us. We continued trekking and arrived where the cabin was. After 11 miles, we decided to camp there for a night. Everyone wanted to sleep in the one-room cabin instead of pitching our tents because we realized that we were in bear country. That following morning I got up early just at sunrise. Being a morning person, I snuck out quietly while the rest of the gang was still sleeping on the hard floor. Who knows if I made any noises without my knowledge? I didn't have my contact lenses in yet for my nearsightedness. I was stretching out and enjoying the peeking sun beaming through the dense forest. Out of the corner of my eye, I caught a glimpse of something moving toward me. I was startled when I saw a bison trotting on a path right by the cabin. I jumped, screamed, and climbed the ladder that was leaning on the cabin. Then I realized that it was not attacking me, but it was just passing by. I ran down and yelled trying to tell everyone that the bison was out there. They were groaning and went back to sleep except for one guy who joined me taking pictures. We returned to the village full of tales.

Back then in 1978, I had a cheap instant camera with four blue flashbulbs. That was before I bought my Pentax 35mm camera for my photography class in my fourth year of art school. I wish that I had that camera then. I would have had great shots of the park. Since I wanted to practice my art skills through the summer, I asked the resident assistant for permission to paint a wall mural in our bedroom. I brought the acrylic paints with me in case I needed them. It took me one week to paint Yellowstone National Park's raging geysers and rolling meadow with a big head of an elk on my wall. I felt quite accomplished and it was a unique, flavored addition to the plain dormitory room.

I had always wanted to see the West. I even dreamt about it before I actually did it. When I got to see it, I fell in love with the different culture of the West. It was more relaxed, friendly, open, and fun. The East was more reserved, serious and traditional. I wanted a change in my life as well as my environment. I am a friendly and outgoing person who loves meeting people with their acceptance. That is how I fell in love with the Western culture. I didn't want to go back to finish my fourth year of school. I was actually planning to venture to Denver, Colorado after my contract was over with the park. When my dad found out about it, he wrote me a long, lecturing letter and asked me to come home to finish school. He said I could do whatever I wanted after I was done with school. It was very hard to execute the whole plan for Denver. So I decided to go ahead and finish school.

Near the end of the summer, I heard through the grapevine that someone was looking for a person to join their ride to back East. His name was David, and his home was in Maine. He was planning to leave early with another guy before my contract ended. My boss was never nice to me the whole time even though I was the best maid in town. I guess that she didn't accept the fact that

I was deaf and maybe she had a sad life. She got really mad that I gave notice to leave a few days early. She threatened me that if I broke the contract I would not be allowed to work there again. It was okay with me.

When it was time for us to leave, these two guys couldn't believe that I actually had a bike and a big box to transport in his small car. We had to cram the box in the back seat. David was so upset and had to keep his word that I could go. He said that he didn't want to drive all the way from Wyoming to Maine alone and wanted us to share the driving. The other guy named Doug freaked out and didn't want me to drive because I was deaf. David said that he was the owner of the car, and he could decide who drove. Doug got mad huffing and puffing. When it was my turn to drive, I was filled with excitement as it was something to do. I drove all the way through Wyoming then to Nebraska. Doug was hovering over me and yelling how bad and what a slow driver I was. I said nothing and ignored his ramblings. Next, it was his turn to drive. He drove at night, and I went into a deep sleep in the back.

All of a sudden, the car swayed and bumped all over the place because the car went off the freeway and hit a grassy median. I was rudely awakened from my beauty sleep and got out of the car fast. I was hoping that the car and my bike were not damaged. Everything was okay. David yelled at Doug and he was humbled. What had happened was that he fell asleep at the wheel. What he sowed, he reaped. Doug later apologized to me for his bad attitude toward me, and he had to swallow his pride. He realized that he was the one who almost got us into a terrible accident. The Lord had mercy and protected us. David continued to drive the rest of the way and dropped me off in Connecticut where my parents lived. My parents liked David and they fed him a meal before he took off for his home in Maine. He was well remembered.

I saw him again many years later when my husband and our two children went to Yellowstone for a vacation. I kept asking to see if David was still around working in the park. The funny thing was when I saw him at Old Faithful village and called out to him, he saw me with delighted surprise and ran to hug me. He had never forgotten about me. I introduced my family to him. We learned the fact that he had never gotten married and remained single. He continued working in the national park. The moral is that he did respect me as an individual regardless of my deafness and strong-willed, independent spirit. The Lord was faithful to see me through.

Upon my return to school for the fourth year, I decided to move into a house with thirteen people from different colleges.

Graduation Day from Paier Art School.

I was much less motivated and less focused. I got myself into astrology, not knowing that it was unscriptural and not aligned with the Word of the Lord. Back then, I didn't have a Bible and I was still going to Catholic Church. I studied the horoscope that represented the people's lives according to their birth time frame. Eventually, I realized it was so unfair to judge people according to their astrology personalities. When we receive Jesus as our Savior, our personal relationship with Him grows. Our old lives pass away, and we become new in Him. So He gives us a chance to be who He helps shape us to be for the better. Discovering more of the Lord in that year was challenging and inspiring. As the time went on, I wanted to stop compromising my faith. As a result, I didn't do much homework in the first part of the fourth year. I abandoned my focus on school. I was struggling with school, and I was getting behind. I was planning to drop out of school. Again, my dad kept challenging me to continue and finish since I only had a few months left. Man, it was the hardest thing I had ever done. I accepted the challenge to catch up on all projects before graduation. I had about three months to do the catching up. My teachers agreed to give me the grace period of time for me to finish. I had the cheering going on until graduation day. My family came to the graduation. When I got the diploma, I yelled, "I made it!" with such great pride in my accomplishment. The moral is to never give up or give in before finishing what you start. It is the way of life. That helped me to grow and overcome any obstacle that came my way. ("I can do all things through Jesus Christ who strengthens me.") I am an overcomer with the Lord's help.

Visiting my parents during winter break brought me to a new perspective of my spiritual level. I had a vivid nightmare and felt an evil presence. I saw a person in a black hooded cloak so I didn't see who it was. I felt strongly that it was an evil spirit trying to seduce me physically. I tried to wake up. Finally, I woke up sweating. It was horrifying and chilling. Then I went back to sleep and it tried again to come to me. I struggled to get up and got away from it. I woke up distraught. I went to my mom and asked her what it was. She had no idea. I went to ask the priest who worked with the deaf in New Haven, and all he said was that it was nothing, and evil was like air. I disagreed and he left me frustrated and determined to search for the truth. Eventually, I found out that Satan literally came to me and tempted me. I realized that the spiritual battle was real. Satan and demons are spiritual beings that constantly torture people who don't know to take the authority to rebuke them. A real spiritual journey had begun.

My dad wrote a poetic letter to the president of Clarke School expressing how hopeful he was for his three deaf children's future that depended on their drive in learning and success. He showed bursting pride in us and gratitude for all the dedicated teachers working tirelessly with us in the sixteen-year span. His letter went viral and that impacted the campus of Clarke. That influenced the board of trustees to decide to pick me and my two other deaf brothers to be in their film to promote awareness of Clarke School for its education and oral program. It showed our successes, and our futures were bright. The film was named The Gallaghers Three. Wow, the Lord gave us favor and promised us that He was to take us to the next level for His glory.

During my last year, I was intrigued with health food ever since I met my old roommate Beth. I decided to stop eating white bread and started making honey wheat bread. I had fun sharing and introducing new health food trends to my friends and family. To my surprise, many thought that I was crazy or a health food fanatic. When I moved to Denver, I met some people who were vegetarians who led me to a health food store. It was a completely new world for me. I grew up eating homemade white bread. I never had store-bought bread at home except for rye bread on some occasions to accompany German or Polish food that my mom cooked. I recalled eating all raw vegetables straight from the garden that my mom planted since I was little. She always preached at me never to use pesticides or artificial fertilizers. There was a big pile of stinky compost in the middle of the garden throughout the year. We always took turns dumping the pail of compost from the house. So that's how I grew up with an "organic" garden. Lately, many people say it is important to buy and eat organic food. It is like it is new to them, even though I shared it with people for a long time. They thought I was an extremist because I always read the food labels. Actually, I grew up that way, not realizing that I was different. I remember when I was 12, my dad wanted to treat our whole family to McDonald's. It was a rare occasion.

I am glad we didn't make a habit of that. That was back in the 1960s. I thank my mom for all the years of cooking especially from scratch. She also taught me how to do the gardening, sewing, making handmade things, crafting, cooking, and being creative. She never bought prepared food except for a few things like chips. Hats off to her. I owe all that to her. Today I have my own business preparing health foods all because of the way Mom helped shape who I am today. Bon appétit.

Chapter 6

Real Life Begins

After graduation, I went to my parents' home in Pennsylvania where hillbillies dwelled in beautiful country right in the middle of the "mini Swiss Alps." My whole family was there; four brothers and one sister were reunited. Janette, Michael, Nelson, Paul and I drove up the mountains. We took the inner tubes and ignorantly walked through the dense forest where rattlesnakes were in abundance. We had flip flops or bare feet and dared to jump into an unknown adventure. We didn't know that Pine Creek was really low all the way. We practically walked in the creek rather than floating on the tubes because our inner tubes were scraping the rocks in the shallow water. It took hours before we arrived at the final destination: home. Dad drove up and found us in the middle of our way home. Mom was worried sick. We got a ride home and faced mom yelling at us as grown children with an 8-year-old brother. Sigh... They had bought a new home and moved there just right before my graduation. They had no idea what to expect. I had no regrets because that adventure was a great experience.

It seemed like my parents moved every time I graduated from school: Clarke School for the deaf, Girard High School then Paier

Art School. Finally, my parents settled down in the country in Jersey Shore, Pennsylvania. They are still alive and have been in the same house since 1979.

Two weeks after my graduation, I felt it was time to begin my own journey. An unknown and exciting adventure awaited me in my blue Maverick. Approaching my dad with hesitation, I let him know that I was ready to leave. My dad didn't want to let me go as it was hard for him to comprehend me with no job or a place to live. I assured him that it was going to be fine. He offered me money. I didn't accept because in the past we had disputes over money. So I had a little cash on me. I wanted to have faith in the Lord who took care of me. I recalled the time He took care of me when I hitchhiked to Ohio. I wanted that feeling of feeling alive and trusting the Lord to lead the way. I always prayed for His protection and He showed me the way. When I said good bye to everyone, I was driving away from a familiar to an unfamiliar life. I drove ten hours every day for four days. Sometimes I read a book while I was driving as I was bored looking at the road for so long. The hearing people could listen to the radio or music. I didn't have that. Once, there were two men who were a little older than me who were being friendly to me as we passed by each other on Freeway 80. I was wary and extra careful because I was alone and didn't know what their motives were. I felt that I wasn't supposed to be friendly to them for my own sake. I bumped into them at a gas station. They approached me and tried to get acquainted with me. I had to remain silent and ignored them. I felt my heart racing from nerves. I kept praying and asking the Lord to look out for me. I stopped and slept in the rest area on the way to Denver, Colorado.

The day came that I arrived in Denver, I asked around where the YWCA shelter was that my sister Janette mentioned to me.

When approaching the receptionist, I asked her if there was a room available. There weren't any. I asked the Lord to jump into the situation. The lady said that there was a boarding house for ladies right in the heart of Denver. There was a beautiful mansion that reminded me of where I grew up in Clarke School. I knocked on the door asking if there was room for me. She said that a lady just moved out, and I came just in time. However, I only lived there one week because it was reserved for another person. Two meals a day were included in the rent. Wow, what a great blessing. I had a roommate named Kim who was free spirited and easy going. Later she told me she was Buddhist, the same kind that my sister was. Meanwhile, I called Kate, my old classmate from Clarke School, to let her know that I had moved to Denver. We graduated in the same class at Clarke School. I hadn't seen her for eight years since graduation. We got together. I mentioned that I was looking for a job and a permanent place to live. She told me that she knew a friend who would get me a job as a geographic map painter so I waited for the job opportunity to come up. Back at the mansion, Kim and I discussed where to rent and we looked for a place.

Meanwhile, I was looking for a job as I had only a few dollars left. I went to Manpower because they offered temporary jobs right away. The first job I was offered was dishwasher for the night shift (from 11 P.M. until 6 A.M.), and I got paid the next day. I met a guy named Ronnie there who was handsome, charismatic and fun. He was new to Denver too since he came from the Deep South. We became fast friends. While working for Manpower, there were different available jobs. I needed to save money to rent a room for the next house, so I went to the blood bank and they paid me $25.00. It wasn't much but it helped me get by. Anyway, I went to visit my friend Ronnie right in the heart of Denver a few blocks from where I stayed. How naive I still was about city life. I was not aware that it was a high-crime area. So I went to Ronnie's apartment complex, and I rang the doorbell. There was no answer and then a guy going in opened the door ahead of me and invited me to come in. I saw his roving eyes. I felt the Holy Spirit speak with warning, "Don't go in!" I was taken aback and I realized that I was not supposed to be in there, so I left quickly. I felt that I was being protected and was glad that I listened and obeyed; otherwise, I could have gotten myself into serious trouble.

My roommate Kim found a house where a redneck guy Rick was renting the rooms. I asked Kim to make an agreement not to get intimately involved with that guy. She agreed. We moved in, and I had the whole basement to myself.

So by the end of the week, I was called to come for an interview for a job as a map painter and I got it. It was a very friendly environment as it was a small company. Thanks to Kate who led me to that job. The Lord used people to make some connections, and He was always faithful. It was not my dream job since I was looking for a job as a graphic designer. I realized it was a challenge in a competitive world. Having no means of communication devices made it even more difficult. I had several interviews and one of the employers said that he liked my portfolio but the problem was how to contact and communicate with the client. The main reason they didn't want to hire me was that they didn't want to make extra efforts in communicating with the clients for me. If I had turned the clock forward to today, there are fabulous means of communication like the video phone. It was like I had gone to art school for four years for nothing. I got really discouraged. So I went on to map painting.

During my stay in the house, there was a severe thunderstorm. It was so bad that it shook the whole house. I ran down to the basement where my bedroom was. I sat on the floor cramped in the corner shielding myself from the lightning. This fear had been instilled in me since I was about 14. I had a traumatic experience while I was carrying a heavy metal chain to fetch our family dog that got loose. Thunder and lightning were so close that I dropped the chain and went quickly inside the house. That flashback put me in the same state of fear. I was fearful of lightning until I was set free from the spirit of fear much later.

I was uncomfortable with my housing situation because Kim broke our agreement about sleeping with that guy she hardly knew. I lived there for a month. One day Rick was yelling at me for whatever reason. I was calm and refused to give in to his demands. He got angry then he punched the wall. I knew it was time to move out right away. I refused to tolerate that kind of behavior, so I moved on. I found a place to live from a newspaper ad. My roommate was an Asian model in her 30s, and the location was north of downtown Denver in a rundown neighborhood which was affordable for me.

I continued working as a map painter until I found a government job as a paste-up artist for the Revenue Department. I remembered that it was my turn to have a job interview after so many rejections. I cautioned the interviewers, "It is going to be the last interview. I am done with art." I had a tiny glistening light left in me. I had a good interview as we had a lot of dialogue.

There were some other people competing for that job. They hired me right on the spot for a part-time job. I was caught off guard and gladly accepted the job. The Lord cared about me...even though it wasn't the ideal job I wanted.

A great communication breakthrough was a portable teletype for communicating with others. My friend Diane told me about it, and Kate knew someone who was selling a TTY. I went to buy it and took it to my home and work. My hearing friends and co-workers were excited about it. It was the beginning of my freedom and independence. It was a great feeling of newfound liberation.

One incident occurred when I was living north of Denver where the part of town was run down and the crime was high. I went to the laundromat because I had no washer or dryer at the house where I lived. I left my clothes in the washer and had to go on quick errands. When I returned, I found two empty washers. I approached the guy who worked there and I asked what happened to my clothes. That guy shook his head with a tough luck attitude look. I demanded to get them back. He was on the verge of losing his temper, so I had to leave there empty-handed with great disbelief. I didn't have many clothes to begin with. It was hard to let it go, it wasn't fair since I was actually poor, struggling to survive. Life seemed unfair, but the lesson was not to avenge, accuse or get back, just trust the Lord for His provision.

Eventually, I found a stray, black lab mix puppy in the back alley. I loved dogs as I grew up with the family dog called Rex, a German shepherd. So I decided to name that puppy Rex after the family dog. I tried to train it; however, my housemate complained that it howled at night because it didn't want to be alone in the basement. So it slept with me. It was getting spoiled and it seemed to be untrainable. So I had to give it up. It was another thing to let go of without holding resentment.

Diane kept calling me through TTY and always inviting me

to join in the deaf activities. I remembered the first time I got to Denver, Kate invited me to go to a deaf picnic. I had all the bitter flashbacks of the incident where I was being mocked as an oralist in Hartford, Connecticut. I told Kate that I refused to go. I was deeply scarred by that experience. She kept gently encouraging me to try again, trying to convince me that these people were not like who I had previously experienced. It took me a while to reconsider and give it a shot. I joined her, and we went up to the beautiful Rockies where the deaf picnic was held. I was really scared, although I had an invisible shield and sword ready to fight. To my surprise, I found them to be very nice, and some had oral training with signing skills. I met Diane there. She couldn't speak but was raised using ASL. She was very patient lip reading me as I had no idea how to sign ASL. I bumped into her again through a deaf gathering at the Rainforest restaurant downtown. She kept asking me where I lived. I thought, "Okay." I was using her to meet other people. I thought she was dumb and low verbal. One day she came to my place unannounced. I looked down on her with a bad and prideful attitude and told her I was busy. However, she kept trying to connect with me. I couldn't stand her and wanted to get rid of her. She was very persistent and that drove me crazy. So I thought to myself, since there was nothing better to do, I liked swimming at her apartment complex that had an outdoor swimming pool. I still resisted her in my heart as friends. Towards Christmas, I didn't book a flight back home because I wasn't able to afford it. I got a TTY call from Diane asking me if I had plans for Christmas. I sighed, "Oh no, not her again!" I tried hard to keep her distant, but she kept showing up in my life. I thought about spending a few days with her for Christmas since there was nothing better to do. It was my first Christmas and New Year away from my family.

I Can Only Hear God

I accepted her invitation with a see "whatever happens" attitude.

I went to a Christmas party with another group of friends before going over to stay with Diane. It was around 11 p.m. when I arrived at Diane's house in the foothills of The Rockies. I tried to go in, but she had locked the door for the night. "Oh great," I thought to myself out loud. It was a one-hour drive from my place. It was a good thing that I brought my homemade blue jeans quilt that my mom made from all of my old jeans that she saved. I also had my pillow and a suitcase of my winter clothes. Since there were snow flurries out, I decided to sleep in my car with hot air blowing on me until I was warm. I was in my quilt wrapped like a cocoon. When I was waking up in the early morning, the snow was covering my good ole Maverick. I went to the house and found that the door was unlocked. Diane was delighted to see me and thought I slept in the neighborhood. "Nope," I said reminding her that the surroundings were completely unfamiliar to me. She couldn't believe that I survived through the wintry night. As she welcomed me, the Christmas spirit was so obvious and I enjoyed it.

One day, she asked me for my opinion about the essay she wrote for her graduate school application. Whew, with a prideful, smart attitude, I was thinking that her English was at second-grade level. Knowing that I went to a very advanced, academic, private deaf oral school, hearing

Diane and me

college, hearing art school and communicated with hearing people who advanced my English, I was expecting to give out a lot of corrections. Literally, I wanted to roll up my sleeves and shine my knuckles on my chest. When I read her graduate school application essay, my jaw dropped with disbelief. I asked Diane three times if she wrote it all by herself. She looked at me puzzled, and her reply was a clear yes with her concern about her English errors. At last, I literally wrote down asking if she actually wrote the essay by herself because I wasn't sure if she lip read me right since I labeled her a manualist who knew nothing. She said, "YES," as a final straw. Her essay had perfect English and better vocabulary than I used. I was devastated. Then I heard the Lord's voice, "Veronica! Humble yourself and tear down the wall of communication barriers." It was a clear rebuke. I had to humble myself with great humility. Waking up to reality, I had to learn sign language from the deaf who did not have the gift of speaking. Immediately, I started to learn signing. I never regretted it and the world opened even more. Diane became one of my closest friends. She taught me so much about life. She especially helped to transform me from a country blah-clothed gal to a radiantly, colorfully clothed one. She was my maid of honor at my wedding. I thanked the Lord for her coming into my life especially since she helped me become a better servant.

Since my housemate wanted me to move out, her hearing coworker Diane and I looked for a place to live. There was a nice house right on the compound where they worked. I had been going to deaf Catholic Mass and I befriended a priest who knew ASL. I was hungry for the Lord's Word and he gave me a deaf Bible. I was thrilled because I had never owned one. I read the whole Bible about three times. I didn't understand most of it. I was so frustrated and wanted to learn more. It seemed every time I made a closer step to the Lord, the devil's schemes were against me.

I Can Only Hear God

My housemate Sue decided to have a beer party and invited both hearing and deaf people, although I was not up for that. I was planning to leave before the party started, but a guy named Bo showed up earlier than expected. Wearing a roughly worn, straw cowboy hat and sporting his rugged beard, macho Bo strutted by full of himself in his pointed, tipped cowboy boots. Shifting his shoulders, he started conversing with me. I had absolutely no interest in him while looking at his annoying swagger. Since Sue was busy preparing the party, she couldn't rescue me from him. Hesitantly, I talked with him. He asked me questions and had his way of getting my attention. He was hard of hearing and used ASL beautifully. He discovered that I was trying to start a pillow-making business on the side. He asked to trade reupholstering of his car seats for cocaine. I was shocked and blew him off. He had a way of dealing with me. I still refused and was not interested in drugs. He was amazing using seducing words saying that the cocaine was healthy. The devil got me hooked on the idea of the healthy stuff.

Sooner or later I found myself becoming fast friends with Bo. He was a Harley-Davidson member, and he introduced me to his Harley friends. I loved riding around on the motorcycle with him. With my being so naive, he actually introduced me to a completely new circle of friends who were drug dealers, users, even lords. I was so unaware. He took me everywhere that I would never have imagined. I wrote a long letter to my parents of my adventures in Denver and my future plans to travel the West Coast with Bo in his van. My dad responded quickly and pleaded with me not to hang out with that guy. Dad had a hunch that Bo was bad news and expressed his concern about my friendship with him. About a month later, Janette, my sister decided to fly to see me with urgency. I didn't realize that I got my family really concerned about my well-being. Although she stayed with me only for a week, she saw something in Bo and warned me about him. I just brushed it off. She kept saying he was dangerous.

My former classmate from Clarke, Kate, who had been a faithful friend, took me skiing up in the Rockies to Vail, Steamboat Springs, Aspen, and other ski resorts. I met another circle of deaf people from all walks of life. Vail was my favorite, as it was an hour to go down and it was more powdered snow and more fun to ski. Kate, who had skied all of her life, was a graceful skier whom I always admired, and I wanted to ski like her.

She found out about that guy Bo I was seeing and she flatly warned me about his reputation. I just shrugged it off. She explained that her girlfriend was married to him and got divorced because of his instability. How ignorant I was about the dangers. I was about to fall into a trap.

Later on, Kate met a guy and they were engaged. I was invited to her bridal shower, my first-time experience. I had no idea what to expect. I thought it was a normal party. How wrong I was. I wore blue jeans with a flannel shirt and brought a gift wrapped in a paper sack as it was a last-minute thing. When I showed up at her bridal shower, Kate came to me upset saying, "Veronica, do you understand that a bridal shower is supposed to be semi-formal so you are supposed to wear a dress? I am embarrassed." I just shrugged and didn't take it personally as I couldn't do much and knew nothing about a bridal shower. Her class was totally different than mine. Her lifestyle was sophisticated while I was simply a country lady who knew nothing about that glamorous lifestyle. I grew up getting second-hand clothes or we ordered clothes from a catalog. I grew up eating home-cooked food and never went out to eat at a restaurant except for special occasions at Friendly's or McDonald's as a family treat. Anyway, the women assembled in a circle in the living room, and there were only two of us who were deaf. I was sitting there and I realized that all the women in that room were all dressed up, and I felt out of place. I sat there dreading when Kate would see the brown bag wrapped gift. When it was time for the opening of gifts, Kate noticed the paper bag wrapped gift. Her disapproving expression showed; however, all the ladies burst out laughing and thought it was funny and creative. I had to laugh, too. Kate was still upset about the whole thing. Wow, I had so many things to learn about life outside of the box.

One weekend, Bo came to my place. He was telling me how great cocaine was. He kept at it. Finally, one day he snorted the coke in front of me. Out of curiosity, I tried it. It didn't affect me much as it was a short rush and short-lived. I mentioned it was a rip-off as it cost $200 for a teaspoon even though I risked myself snorting at work in the government building. He convinced me the more I used it, the better it would become. How deceiving he was to me. He shot the coke in his arm. "Ooh, I hate needles! I can't even stand flu shots or anything with needles!" I told myself. He convinced me it was nothing compared to that. I hesitated at first. I thought to myself that I would just try it once and for all. I yielded to him and let him shoot me once. Again, it was a rush and short-lived. Oh boy, I was so scared as my heart was racing fast. I felt I committed a big crime. I grew up in Clarke School. I heard stories of heroin addicts. I was assured that the cocaine was the opposite. It was a stimulant drug and non-addictive. Then the Holy Spirit spoke straight to my heart to stop right there and no more yielding to coke, period! I was surprised and told him immediately that I would not do it ever again. He snorted and made a disgusted face.

Sometime later, Bo came over and invited me to meet his mom and spend the weekend visiting. I went along and met his concerned mom who was nice and meek. I stayed overnight and woke up and saw Bo who looked so distraught. Out of suspicion, I asked him what was wrong. He finally admitted to me that he was shooting cocaine all night long. I was furious blasting at him and told him straight that he needed help for the addiction he had. Eventually, he agreed to go to Drug Rehabilitation.

I was commuting to two job locations, one in downtown three days a week and the other eastward two times a week. At my mapping job, it was declared that I was one of their best map painters. They were willing to give me longer hours even though it was only part-time. Sometimes I worked late at mapping for extra money. In Denver, if it snowed, it snowed hard and filled up the road fast. I loved driving on unplowed, powdered snow as it was very peaceful and beautiful. One afternoon, I was on my way home from work, and the blizzard was getting worse with almost zero visibility. My ole Maverick only had one snow tire and its heater didn't work, so I prayed for the Lord to bring me home safely because I saw many were stranded on both sides of the road, even nice, new and big cars. I kept driving and praying and I got home safely.

Later one winter morning, I didn't realize that there was ice under the thin blanket of snow close to my place. I was driving slowly towards the traffic light. There was a red light, and the car stopped in front of me. I gently put on the brakes, but my car was sliding down about 100 feet. All of a sudden the thought came up that I had no car insurance. (Back then it was not required by law to purchase it.) I cried out "Jesus!" as I was going to hit the back of the other car. All of a sudden, my car turned sideways just barely missing it by one inch. The car drove off untouched. Wow, I kept thanking the Lord. He heard my cry, and how amazing that he responded to my cry quickly.

In May 1979 in the morning, I was about to go to work. There was a thin film of ash on my ole Maverick. Without my knowledge, Mt. St. Helens erupted with pluming ash a few days before. There was a warning not to wipe the ash off but to use water to wash it off without scratching it. I was in awe when I saw that in the news as it was devastating. How little I knew that the Lord was to relocate me to Washington.

Although two people had warned me about Bo, I refused to believe that he was that bad. How deceived I was. I didn't see or hear from him for a long while. I had to move again because Diane was accepted by the University of Maryland and was leaving, and my co-worker had relocation plans.

Bo's friends invited me to stay with them in a house with five or six different people living there. There was a spare bedroom for me to rent. I had no choice, but to live there temporarily. Annie, who lived in that house, asked me to help cook for people in the house so my food bill was to be waived. How little I knew that my housemates were drug dealers. I was told not to go down in the basement no matter what. I accidentally went down there to call them for dinner. I saw big packs of marijuana and all kinds of drugs. How did I get myself into this mess? I felt a very evil presence in that house which I had never experienced before. They had parties every weekend drinking and doing drugs. I felt sucked into the darkness. Later on, I was told that one night I was sleeping when a narcotics agent came out and put the spotlight on the house. The other people quietly stayed low. I was surprised that they didn't come to our place and arrest us. I thought, "Whoa! What danger I was in."

One day at work, I heard a tiny voice saying to me, "Get out of Denver now." I just simply ignored it and went on. Later on, I heard it a little bit louder with the same message; again, I ignored it. Finally, for the third time, I felt I was being yelled at, "GET OUT OF DENVER NOW!" I literally jumped out of my work chair. "Whoa!," I said. "OK, OK, Lord! What about the job?" He said to give a two-week notice to my boss. I went to my boss and handed him my notice. He stood with shock and disbelief. His response to me was, "How will you survive? You will starve." I worked there for only six months, and everyone was surprised. I couldn't explain to them. My co-assistant gave me a warm farewell party at her stable family home. I knew that the Lord had better plans for me so I had to trust the Lord about where I was heading.

Since I thought Bo was recovering from rehab; he came to me saying that he needed the money badly for an emergency. I had no idea how he knew that I had a savings of $800.00. That was the most money I ever saved in my entire life. He begged for the money and made a promise to pay me back in a few days from working under the table at his friend's drywall business. I gave in and gave him all $800.00, all I had. I told him that I needed the money as I was leaving Colorado in a couple of weeks. I didn't hear from him and I kept asking his friend where he was. No one knew. When the word went out about a farewell party for me, Bo showed up with a bad attitude and threw a gift at me that he bought. I wondered what went wrong with him. The party lingered and I opened the bathroom door that had a problem with the lock.

I Can Only Hear God

There was Bo shooting cocaine into a fifteen-year-old girlfriend of mine. I was shocked with disbelief that he dared to do that. When he was out and sitting on my bed, I yelled at him and told him he was a hypocrite and a liar. I commanded him to never touch my innocent friend again. I knew that I was never to see my $800.00 again. I had to comfort my young friend and told her never to come back to this kind of circle of friends. I encouraged her to move on and have a good life without drugs. I had never been so furious in my life, and I was glad that I was leaving all that behind. Since I left Denver, I never looked back.

Chapter 7

Moving On

The next day in early September, one year and a half since graduating from art school, the good ole Maverick was packed. I left some stuff behind that I was to come back to get after settling down somewhere. I said to the Lord, "OK, here I am. You guide me." In my mind, I planned to travel to Utah, Idaho, Oregon, Washington, back to Oregon, California, Arizona, Nevada, back to Colorado to get the stuff then decide where to settle down. However, the Lord had different plans in mind. When I got to Utah, I camped out in the park and hiked up halfway and saw Robert Redford's home below. Recalling that night of camping out alone, the fear gripped my heart that anyone or animals would hurt me and I had no one to rescue me. I heard a soft voice assuring me that I was being watched over and taken care of. Then I drifted off to peaceful sleep.

Waking up in the beautiful sunny morning, I cooked myself breakfast. Before I left Denver, I had made a connection with a friend Henry who moved to Provo to attend college. We went out to eat in Provo and had a nice chat. Then I realized that from that moment, I had to go alone traveling through Utah, Idaho, Oregon, and Washington.

The snowstorm hit Deadman Pass in Oregon with no warning. There were many hauling trucks and 18-wheeler trucks passing me. The wet snow came down hard, and I had no snow tires on my car. It was scary as the trucks plowed the snow onto me that left me with zero visibility. There was no way to pull over except moving forward slowly. It seemed forever as it was about eight miles long going about 25 to 30 miles an hour. As I was going down to the valley of Oregon over the pass, it became clear. It was a strange phenomenon. I was so stressed out and became exhausted. I went along the Columbia River in Oregon then through Portland. I passed over the Lewis River going north on I-5 towards Seattle. I saw a lot of mud flow and tree debris from the eruption of the volcano. I have never forgotten the sight of it. The Lord is much bigger than that. I meditated on how massive the exploding fumes were that came out of Mt St. Helen's. The incredible massive destruction was very small to the Lord.

"Heaven is my throne, and the earth is my footstool."

(Isaiah 66:1)

Finally, I showed up at my close friend Leah's home in Marysville, Washington. She opened the door, scanning me with disbelief. Wearing a cowboy hat, cowboy boots and flannel vest with blue jeans, I was upbeat after a long travel alone. I was anxious to spill all the beans to her since I last saw her at Clarke School graduation in 1970, about 9 years prior. She was married to Steven and had two children, five and under one. I stayed with them for a month, feeling restless to move on but I was too broke to continue traveling the West Coast as planned.

Moving On

A great culture shock came to me when Leah and Steven took me to primitive Lummi Island. There was little electricity. I met the Bocock family and they were hippies who warmly welcomed me to their homes. I became fast friends with Betty and Glen even though they got tired of me talking about the Lord. I used to make them wheat pita bread, and the flour was all over the house. Their little children were running around and I played chasing them. I went back on my days off. I became friends with other people there, too. I always shared the love of Jesus with them. One of them named Ziga could not stand me at all. She was two-faced, always smiling and then turned around with her cynicism against me. She always avoided me as much as possible. She was very deep into New Age, Eastern religion and continued searching. She was very intelligent. Everyone on the island looked up to her.

I found a job from an ad for a live-in housekeeper for a Mormon family in a country setting. Moving in with the Mormon family gave me an eerie feeling. All seven children and the mom and dad greeted me and led me to a bedroom right above the living room. I had absolutely no privacy and I was given the rules.

I had an incredible multi-tasking job. I cleaned the whole house that was always in a mess, did the laundry, cooked and cleaned up the kitchen. There were teenagers leaving their litter and bad attitude behind and little children who were out of control with no discipline. I was expected to take care of the children and tend to their needs. I was also expected to cook meals for the family. They were asking for the impossible for a superwoman to do all that! I was also expected to meet with the wives to go bowling once a week. I felt so awkward with the Mormon ladies.

One time, I was asked to prepare a special occasion dinner

for the family and their guests, with two little children eating separately in the kitchen. I was expected to feed the screaming, crying children in the kitchen and be a perfect hostess serving all the glamorous food and desserts. I was totally stressed out. How could that be? I even helped the children do the homework. I hurt my right wrist because I overdid it. So I decided to fly home to visit my parents for two weeks and escaped that prison that I was caught in for two and a half months. Upon my return, I was at their doorstep and saw my things sitting out front. I rang the doorbell. There was a new live-in housekeeper who was tiny who said, "Your things are here because you have been fired from the job." I was surprised, shocked, and stunned. I had no clue that my boss wanted to fire me and didn't have the nerve to face me. I felt released. I needed to move on.

I found a studio apartment in Everett, Washington. I had to go to the Division of Vocational Rehabilitation asking for help because of my injured wrist that happened to my right hand. I was an artist and I was stuck and limited with the job search. DVR sent me financial help until I recovered. I went to see the doctor and he put a brace on my wrist. It took about three months to heal. However, the help was not much, just enough to pay the rent, food and a little for gas. One time, I was completely out of food and was broke. I had to scrape pennies crying out to the Lord, "If you want me to starve, I accept the deal." Somehow, I got the check in time to buy the groceries I needed. I began to read books about Jesus and how to walk with Him. I read the Bible in my free time while my wrist was healing. Deep in my heart, the Lord used the situation where I could rest while learning about Him.

One day, I was looking for a job in the newspaper ads. I heard the Lord's voice saying to me, "Veronica, I want you to stop looking for a job. Just trust me and I will guide you." I said ok. I met a lady named Liz; Leah had referred her to me. Liz told me to meet her at Everett Community College for ASL class. We made the meeting appointment at the college campus, but I planned not to go because I had no gas in the car. I felt the Lord impress on my heart, "Veronica, put your shoes on and take a bus to the college now!" Grunting, I was moaning and I was already late. So I had to run to catch the bus for the campus. I was running to the classroom out of breath. Liz greeted me in the classroom and motioned me to sit by her. It was like we became instant friends.

The intermediate ASL teacher announced that the ASL teacher for the beginners had not shown up so it was going to be cancelled. Instead, Liz raised her hand, saying that I could teach. I insisted that I only knew a little ASL. Before I had a chance to protest, the teacher said that I got the job."

Liz pushed me up and clapped her hands and said, "Go for it!" Me, teach ASL in college? I freaked out but remained silent. I had to lead my beginner's class to the room. I felt I was leading them to the slaughter. I thought it was a joke. Then I heard a small voice.

"This is a job for you."

"Wow, I need help from you, Lord," I prayed.

About thirty students filled the classroom with their eyes set on me waiting for my motion to start the class. The first thought that came was to teach them the ABCs finger spelling. Then I shared the difference between signers and oralists. I explained about the deaf culture which I was learning about and emmersing myself in. I was learning as I was teaching. It was a strange phenomenon. To my surprise, the class loved me and they were inspired! I got paid $15 an hour for two hours for eight weeks. The Lord knew that I needed that money.

One lady from the class named Cassandra invited me to her home for dinner. There was an excitement for her family of three children to meet me as a deaf person. After dinner, Cassandra sat down with me and asked me straight questions about compromising my faith. She showed me the Scriptures that shed some light about choosing the path of righteousness. I didn't fully understand why she was telling me this, but I kept it in the back of my mind.

I was back in my apartment meditating on all things that were happening to me. I felt the Lord wanting me to see the job counselor referred by the DVR. The appointment was set in Seattle. I got to share what I wanted for a job—artist. So the DVR lady had full confidence that I would find a job. She was to be in touch with me in a week or so. About a week or so later, I got a TTY call that there was a job interview not far from where I lived, so she made an appointment for an interview. I met the owner of the sporting shop that had silk screening on all kinds of sporting clothes like jackets, hats, and t-shirts. I was asked how much an hour I wanted to get paid. I was caught off guard, not knowing what to expect. I gave him the estimate. He hired me on the spot as an artist designing artwork for the sporting clothing and wanted me to work right after the weekend. Lord gave me favor, and I walked in obedience not to look for a job in the newspaper ads. I just let Him guide me, and it was effortless. What an amazing Lord I served.

I had been attending St. Patrick's Catholic Church in Seattle where the interpreted Mass was held, and the deaf church occurred once a month. There was a deaf potluck after the interpreted Mass that the priest named Father Dick signed. I usually went up there to take the reading from one of the gospels. I was working with

Moving On

Sister J. I met a guy there named Donald, at the deaf potluck after the Mass, who was hard-of-hearing. We seemed to hit it off and I invited him over to my studio apartment for lunch the following weekend. When he showed up, we talked all day. We felt thumping all afternoon, not able to figure out what it was. We kept chatting until it was time for him to go home. I still felt the thumping sound as I went to sleep.

Awakened by a bright light in the kitchen at about 1:00 A.M., I was half asleep asking myself, "I thought I turned it off before I went to bed." I didn't like to sleep with the lights on. Then I realized that something was up. I got out of bed and walked toward the kitchen. I saw a young, Indian-looking boy there stealing food. I yelled, "Hey, what are you doing?" He was grabbing the doorknob and unlocking the door. He was out in a quick flash like a bird. I saw him running down the stairs. I was in a daze trying to figure out how he got into my apartment. Then I noticed my closet door was open. I went inside of it and was shocked with disbelief to see a big hole in the wall that was torn down. I saw three teenagers high on drugs sitting on the floor in the vacant, chaotic apartment. The young man who saw me peeking in was groaning, "Oh no!" So I called the police through my TTY. The police came and contacted their parents. The vacant apartment was a disaster, and I noticed the stove and the wall were black with smoke, and gross garbage was everywhere. It was an unbelievable sight. For the whole time living there, I noticed the teens going up the fire steps to climb in the window, but I didn't know the apartment was vacant. I thanked the Lord the apartment complex was spared as it could have burned the four old apartments down. Then I knew where the thumping sound was coming from. They were tearing down the wall. The landlord immediately advised me to move out as it was not safe anymore. "Where could I go?" I thought. So I was thinking about going next door to a brick, two-story convent where the nuns lived and asking for a temporary place to stay. Bravely, I went up and rang the doorbell. At the door, there was a middleaged, tiny lady with a nice smile asking if I needed help. I explained the situation with the break-in in my apartment and that I had to evacuate that day. Sister Sylvia said she was more than happy to help me out, but she needed a reference from Sister J who was involved with the deaf ministry where I worked at the Catholic Church. So I contacted Sister J about the situation, and she was more than willing to help me out. I was instantly accepted to move in right away.

Sister Sylvia led me to a bedroom I could use as my own. I asked her the price for the rent. With all generosity, her response was, "Never mind. You need time to look for a place to live so make yourself at home." There was a chapel downstairs where I could spend quiet time and meditation. The priest came over every evening to give Communion. Three nuns were living there in the big place and shared their meals with me. They were adorable and loved God. I found out that Sister Sylvia was also the principal of the Catholic school in Everett. Wow, she led a busy lifestyle! I found the wonderful loving nuns were humans like us.

In the meantime, I was looking for a place to live and was working the two jobs that the Lord graciously gave me. Before I drifted off to sleep, I heard a voice saying that I ought to marry Donald. I thought in disbelief, "Hey, no way! He is not for me at all!" Thinking it was the Lord's voice, however, I felt the wrong vibes that I didn't understand. I said, "I don't want to marry him. He is so opposite from me, and he is no leader." I thought it was the Lord's voice, but it was from the enemy who deceived me. I had allowed myself to believe it was from the Lord, so I yielded to accept the idea since I was desperate to get married. I did not want to be an old maid. The devil knew the desperation I had for a husband. He got me hooked as bait to compromise. That was the first strike.

While I was staying there, I had been meeting Donald after church for fellowship. Having a discussion with him led to the decision to look for a house to rent to share with roommates. We found a big, four bedroom in Seattle. Bad move! Strike two for me. I had the whole basement to myself. It was a very nice house and we shared the kitchen. It wasn't too bad because most of the housemates were hardly at home. I was always cooking and experimenting with healthy recipes. One day, I had fallen to temptation by being intimate with Donald. That was strike three. Before I knew it, I was throwing up and felt nauseous. I had to go to the clinic to check if I was pregnant. The nurse came to me and congratulated me that I was positive. I groaned with disbelief. Strike three and I was out meaning that I welcomed the heavy burden. I was so proud that nothing would ever happen to me.

> *Be not deceived; God is not mocked; for whatever*
> *a man sows, that shall he also reap.*
>
> (Galatians 6:7)

I informed Donald of the unexpected news. His first response was, "Abortion is the only option." I barked back at him, "No, I will never consider it. I never even thought about it!" I felt distraught and disbelief with his reaction. He was not interested in marrying me or anything serious so I decided to end the relationship with him. He moved out. I didn't know what to do so I later confessed the bad news to Sister J. She encouraged me to seek counseling from the Catholic Community services.

Chapter 8

A Humbling Experience

I was humbled before the Lord and repented for my sins of stupidity, lack of faith in Him, and my fear of being an old maid. I remembered that lady Cassandra from ASL class at Everett Community College who warned me of compromising my faith. The Lord used her to warn me beforehand. I realized that the devil spoke to me as a counterfeit Lord's voice. How blind I was. I realized that the Lord would not do anything against my will or wish. He is not the kind of God who would twist my arm to do something against my wish.

I remembered that my brother Nelson, who visited me a couple months back before that incident, spoke to me about Jesus as our Savior and Baptizer of the Holy Spirit. So I was praying to Jesus to baptize me with the Holy Spirit. I kept at Him almost every day. One day, I was lying down on the deck asking the Lord for the baptism of the Holy Spirit. All of a sudden, I got water splashed all over me. It was a raven in the gutter splashing the water. "Great!" I thought to myself.

I continued working as an artist, and my contract was done with my ASL class. I still felt nauseous and at times threw up in the mornings. I finally went to see the doctor, and he confirmed I was two months pregnant. I didn't know what to do with work because I was always sick. My boss was merciful and let me work at home. One day, I felt so discouraged and felt the Lord had abandoned me. I was in the kitchen washing the dishes. Suddenly, there was a pure white dove sitting on the grass in some perfect rays of sunlight. I felt the dove was sent from the Lord promising me that I would be baptized in the Holy Spirit, the great Comforter. I was greatly encouraged on that day.

As I was talking with my counselor from Catholic Services, she encouraged me to write down the pros and cons of keeping and giving up the baby for adoption. I was praying when I heard a clear voice that said, "The baby belongs to Me." I knew it was His will for me to choose adoption for the baby. I had perfect peace. The counselor gave me a list of couples who wanted to adopt the baby. I had to go over the descriptions of them and decide who was most suitable for the baby. I felt led to pick one couple, and I had a peace about them even though I never met them in person.

My counselor found me a temporary home to share with a Catholic family who welcomed me to stay with them through the pregnancy. Everything was taken care of so I went with the flow. I was still hungry for the Lord's gift: the baptism of the Holy Spirit. However, I saw a poster somewhere that Transcendental Meditation was being offered for free. I fell into that temptation, a shortcut to being baptized in the Holy Spirit. However, I didn't know it was not scriptural. It was not aligned with the Word of the Lord. I went into the TM building, and a serious-looking Indian man welcomed me and offered me service. He gave me a secret word. He called it a seed that I needed to say over and over while meditating. I practiced with him for a bit. When I did that at home,

A Humbling Experience

I felt a war waging inside of me. I had a flashback to when I was chanting when I was involved in Buddhism. The more I meditated with the secret word, it got worse so I had to stop. I prayed and repented asking the Lord for forgiveness. I had no one who could disciple and teach me the Lord's way and His word. I did ask Sister J if Transcendental Meditation was OK and her response was, "Sure, no harm done." Oh boy, I was confused.

At the last trimester of my pregnancy, I flew to visit my parents to break the news. My parents wanted me to keep the baby. I said that I already made up my mind for the adoption. They couldn't understand. My sister came to me saying I was brave to go through the pregnancy and then adoption. She admired my strength.

When the time had come for me to go to the hospital, Sister J came to support me while I was going through labor. To my surprise, Donald dared to show up while I was in labor. It did throw me off guard as I was totally unprepared for his presence. After giving birth to a beautiful, olive-skinned son, Donald wanted to keep the baby. I was so confused because I had planned to give him up for adoption during the whole pregnancy, and then the unexpected came up. I was confused about Donald's motives. I wanted to keep the baby after seeing him. I have never forgotten his big eyes. I named him Anthony Lee.

I was in the hospital for three days. The nurse spoke to me, "You are ready to be discharged, so we will take the baby to the foster parents." The reality hit me so hard to let him go forever and I cried hard. Donald offered me a ride home. He wanted to discuss further plans. We talked for a few days deciding what to do. Finally, the Lord spoke to me clearly, "Veronica, this is MY baby! Give him to ME and do not marry Donald!" I cried and cried. When Donald came home from work, he said, "No, we cannot be married, and you go ahead with the adoption."

So it had been two weeks since I gave birth. The baby was in foster care waiting for my signature to release him for adoption. Since my stay with the Catholic family was over, that left me no choice but to stay at Donald and his roommate's home for a few days. During the last two nights before I left Donald's place, we were talking. Unexpectedly, I was ministering to him when he confessed his personal problems to me. For three hours straight, I actually felt like I had stepped out watching the Holy Spirit speaking to him through my own mouth. It was amazing and I learned a lot from the Holy Spirit. We decided to stop and take a break so we could eat dinner. While cutting up the chicken and vegetables, I felt oil running through my body starting from my head to feet. Then I collapsed on the floor and I felt electric zapping from my head to my toes back and forth. I thought that I was going to die. I lied down motionless and cried out to the Lord out of fear of dying. The Lord spoke to me in a gentle voice, "Don't be afraid, for I am with you." Peace overcame me. Donald called 911 asking for immediate help. He kneeled down by me begging, "Don't die on me. Please forgive me!" over and over again. When I tried to speak, I spoke garbled words that didn't make sense. A few minutes later, there were three huge, great-looking medics coming to my aid. I felt sheepish looking up at the giants and trying to speak to them to no avail. One of the men told me to be calm so he could take my blood pressure. I was still lying down unable to move. I felt like my mind was commanding my limbs to move, but to no avail. I just laid there limp and helpless. My blood pressure was normal. Two of the paramedics were trying to help me sit up on the floor to check my blood pressure again. It remained normal. Then they tried to lift my lifeless body up to sit on a chair. Still my blood pressure remained the same. With their built-up frustrations from lifting my lifeless body, they managed to hold me up standing up straight. My blood pressure stayed the same. They let go with frustration, "There is nothing wrong with you. Just go to bed and sleep!" So they carried me and dropped me on the bed and left. I went into a deep sleep, the most peaceful sleep that I ever experienced, I felt like I was being carried up in the clouds. Then I woke up after an hour. The Holy Spirit again took over ministering to Donald. He kept repenting for the sins that he had done against me and the Lord.

Since that awesome experience, I completely surrendered to Him that I would never again compromise my faith like I did when I got pregnant. I made a vow to Him that I would never let it happen again. I was on fire and had so much zeal to serve Almighty God and still do to this day. I learned that I would never help the Lord look for a man for my life. I just gave it all to Him trusting that He had a perfect plan in my life. I was content and didn't want to get married or date any guys. The next day I left Donald's home for my friend Liz's, the counselor from Everett Community College, who offered me her home for a couple months until I could find a job and a place to live. Her home was located in the deep woods in Snohomish right by the "Lost Lake." It was very quiet and the view of the lake was tranquil. It was one of the worst months of my entire life. I was grieving, and tears were always running down my face.

Before I left their house, Donald's roommate talked to me about Women's Aglow, and he encouraged me to attend one of the meetings. It happened to be close to Liz's home. I decided to go even though there was no interpreter. Many happy ladies greeted me. There was a speaker and I felt the Lord's love coming through her, and I kept crying through the whole meeting. The ladies tried to comfort me and showed me the love of Jesus. I have never forgotten that day that the Lord showed up even though I didn't understand a word that was spoken.

Finally, one day, Liz came to me, "Ok, now you stop right now and get the job that's being offered at the college campus." She told the college that I was taking the job as teacher of Beginner ASL for eight weeks despite my protest. I didn't want to go anywhere but wanted to go curl up in the room to continue grieving. The pain was unbearable. I had to cry out loud, even screaming. I knew Liz was right that I needed to move on. I cried out to the Lord to take away the intense pain I felt. A month passed, and I was invited to meet all the friends from Lummi Island at the Bamboo festival in Seattle. There were three deaf families living on the island along with a couple of hearing families who knew how to communicate through ASL. I shared the gospel with all of them and babysat their kids. They knew me well, and they were concerned about me having a baby. They bet that I would keep the baby since they thought I would be a great mother. They were anxious to meet me that day. I was overcome with perfect peace just a week before. When I met with them, I broke the news of giving up my baby up for adoption. They were shocked with disbelief. Ziga came to me and asked, "How did you get peace after giving up the baby?" I responded that the Lord was the one who gave me a perfect peace. I was in awe that the Lord used me to plant the seeds of faith into their lives.

Chapter 9

New Life

I was still teaching ASL at Everett Community College when I moved to a small house with a roommate. Eventually, I found a job as a youth advocate for troubled deaf teens. When I first started working, there was only one hearing staff member who knew sign language to communicate with the teens. The youth came from broken homes. Their irrational behaviors at times were threatening. They were informed that if the staff felt threatened, we had the right to call the police. We shared the 24-hour shift every other day.

One day, I was sleeping in the staff's bedroom, and I noticed a light on in the house around one o'clock in the morning. I went out to see what was going on. Fifteen year old Mike, who was tall, medium build with dark hair was very agitated and was ready to punch me. I commanded him to calm down and tried to assure him that I was there to help him and he was willing to listen. I prayed silently rebuking the schemes of the devil, and there was a great change in his countenance. Wow, he calmed down and poured his heart out to me. I prayed with him to have peace. So he went to bed for the night. "Whew, what a close call," I thought. I decided to pray for peace and protection in my work environment before I went to my job.

I contacted and informed the deaf community that Mike needed male role models, so the two deaf guys took over. I got transferred to another house where I worked with a deaf teen named Pam. She was so sweet and very angelic with no warning she could become abruptly violent. I worked with her having lengthy conversations. I prayed with her and I helped her to trust the Lord to help with her behavior. I was living with a roommate named Sue who happened to know signed English. We lived in a tiny house with a big yard bordering a Christmas tree plantation. It reminded me of a doll house. I had my own bedroom with two big windows with the sun seeping through. I love the sun and a bright room. Every morning I would go down on my knees speaking in tongues without knowing what it was. I thought I was speaking garbled words that gave me bubbling joy, and I felt great to start the day. My roommate Sue thought I was nuts since she heard me speaking every day. I didn't care what she thought of me. Otherwise we got along fine. I did that for nine months.

I went home to visit my parents for Christmas. My younger deaf brother and his friend from Bible college were there visiting too. I was sharing what had happened to me when the medic men came to my rescue, and I was still speaking garbled words that didn't make sense but I felt joy from doing that. He proclaimed, "You fell under the power of God and spoke in tongues. You got baptized in the Holy Spirit!" He suggested that he and his friend pray to confirm if I actually got baptized in the Holy Spirit. They laid hands on me and prayed. A booming voice came out of my mouth, singing in tongues at the top of my lungs at one o'clock in the morning for about thirty minutes to an hour. My parents were sleeping and never woke up. He and his friend were amazed and were praising God. Wow, I didn't know it was the wonderful, funny experience of the baptism of the Holy Spirit for the whole nine months. Even though I begged and kept bugging the Lord for that baptism of the Holy Spirit, I still didn't know that I already received it. Oh wow, the Lord was faithful to see me through.

It was time for me to buy a new or used car as my ole Maverick was sputtering and was about to give out. I decided to buy a car even though I didn't have any savings to put toward a down payment. I lived from paycheck to paycheck. So I went down to the Ford dealer. (Never again with Ford...Fix or repair daily is a true motto.) I went down to the hungry wolves competing to sell a car to me. The salesman led me to a big, used car that had many problems. He pressured me to trade my car and pay something. I don't remember how much. I bought that big car that was a piece of junk. I drove home with it with no peace in my heart. When I got home, it took me a long time to get it started. I drove it back to the Ford dealer the next day. I met the same dealer. I told him that the car had many problems. I burst into tears feeling hopeless. I didn't have any money to buy another car. I needed the car for work. I was so desperate and to my surprise, he said that he had a new car for me but it was a demo. So I signed up for the loan paying $149 a month for four years. It was all I could afford. It was a blessing to get a newer car. It was a Ford Escort that just came out as a new model. I knew that the Almighty God took care of me in a time of need. I had no credit or anything to prove that I was able to pay monthly. It was all God working out.

A few months later, I was struggling to keep up the car payment. I thought of selling the car, and I told the Lord I just couldn't do it. I asked around to see if anyone was interested in buying my car.

Just before the payment due date, the exact amount of cash came in the mail. Someone wrote a note saying, *"Trust the Lord with all your heart, and do not lean on your own understanding. In all your ways acknowledge Him, and He will make your path straight."* *(Proverbs 3:5-6)* Wow, it was an anonymous donation. From that time on, I was faithful to pay every month until it was all paid for. Again, the Lord knew my needs and touched a person's heart to meet my needs. What an awesome God I serve.

After Christmas, I went back to Seattle to work. I wanted to look for more work and found an ad to take care of an 11-year old deaf, blind boy. I contacted the agency for the part-time job. That precious boy had multiple handicaps like autism and mental challenges. His grandmother had been taking care of him. I went to his bare room that had only a mattress with sheets on the floor. I asked her why his room was like that. I learned that his name was Ronnie and he had impulsive, violent outbursts and tended to destroy anything around him. "Oh, no!" I thought asking myself why I was taking that job. I had always prayed with him before starting to work with him. I took him out to the playground and put him on the swing. He seemed to enjoy, it and he would go for an hour. I tried to interact with him and communicate in a tactile manner. He seemed limited. He was very peaceful with me and, at times, he got frustrated but never violent.

I relied on the Lord for every challenge I was up against and learned His ways and trusted Him for whatever I faced. It seemed that He wanted me to grow in faith in Him and mature in Him.

As the time drew near for me to start a new chapter of life, I contacted the deaf community to inform them that Ronnie needed help with special services. A couple of deaf ladies showed their interest and took over. Many years later after I had children, I always wondered about how Ronnie turned out. My friend told me that her brother-in-law was in a group home tending to Ronnie. With high hopes and excitement, I contacted the staff and wanted to give him a trampoline as we were moving to the Philippines as missionaries. I met with Ronnie, and he seemed that he didn't remember me since he was in his early 20s. Then about eight years later after our final leg return home from the Philippines, I happened to pick up the Seattle newspaper. Ronnie was in the newspaper. It was a lengthy article about him. He was working in a Safeway in Renton as some sort of helper/cleaner. I knew that the Lord was showing me how He used me to lead Ronnie to have a productive life even though he might not understand. I knew it was the power of prayer that led him out of his violent behavior and loneliness as he was stuck in his bedroom for the first twelve years of his life.

Diane, Leah, Leah's husband, and Betty.
Lummi Island, 1982.

Diane, who led me to have a breakthrough with Deaf Culture, came to visit me in the summer of 1982. Two months later, she moved to Seattle to join with me working with troubled deaf teens. She stayed with us in a tiny house on Stone Ave in Seattle. She slept in a spare room off living room. One winter night, we decided to buy a kerosene heater to warm up the house. The heat didn't work well and was too expensive. We put plastic over the bedroom windows. There was no heat in the bedroom. A few months later, my bedroom walls and windows were covered with horrible mildew. In Washington, it rained in the winter and very seldom snowed. So it was a pretty wet winter, and it was a bad idea to put up plastic and not use the heat. It was such a mess. So we decided to move to a bigger place for the three of us. We found a nice, well-lighted basement apartment in the mansion above us close to Greenlake. We had our own bedrooms. Mine was the master, meaning I paid a little more rent, but I liked the spacious bedroom and bathroom all to myself.

My friends from Lummi Island had been growing in the Lord. Betty from Lummi contacted me that her mom Tillie wanted to meet me. When I called her to make arrangements for me to go meet her at her home, I met a wonderful couple, Tillie and her husband Bill. Their daughter-in-law was there, too. She was hard of hearing. We had a Bible study and learned a lot especially since they came from a Catholic background. They understood where I was coming from. The sweet couple always encouraged me to speak out boldly especially speaking in tongues. I was very timid and private about it. They prayed over me and I had courage to be bold. Ever since, I changed from timidity to boldness. I had a lot of zeal to share the truth of the gospel. I went there once every week for about a year.

At that time, I was serving as a leader in the deaf Catholic Church as deaf parishioners met for monthly potluck meals after Mass. There was a priest who knew ASL and led the Mass. I did the readings of the gospels. I always ended up preaching after reading the Scriptures. Oops, I had fire inside of me that I could not hold back. I kept apologizing to the priest named Father Dick. Funny thing was that he was happy that I took his place sharing the Word of God. I even laid hands on the deaf. It seemed that they didn't understand what I was doing. It was like a spiritual blindness over them. I spoke to their lives. They knew that I was different from what I used to be. They couldn't deny that. They just didn't know what to do with that.

For two years, I became more active in the deaf Catholic Church and went to Cursillo (a Catholic retreat) in Sacramento, California. It was a neat experience gathering the deaf to share the Lord but it was not enough. I hungered for more. After the retreat, I heard about the Christian Faith Center in Seattle and I went there once a month. I was inspired and enjoyed learning the Word. I was excited to share with the deaf Catholic Bible study. They scowled. I talked with Sister J about it, and she said that it was not a good idea to go to two churches at the same time. I was struggling inside.

One weekend, Diane and Sue went out of town so I was alone. I went into a deep sleep. All of a sudden, I woke up with my heart beating really fast. I heard a familiar voice saying that if I move, I die. My heart was racing. I couldn't figure out what went wrong, but the voice kept at me, "Don't dare to move or you are going to die!" Wow, I tried to calm myself then I figured that I needed to call 911 to see if there was anything wrong with my heart.

When I got up from the bed, I felt a heavy presence of fear. The voice kept saying again and again, "You are going to DIE." I had to crawl away from all the heavy bombardment and it seemed forever to reach the TTY in the living room. It was a heavy battle that I had never experienced. I kept crawling and finally when I reached the TTY, I heard screaming," YOU ARE GOING TO DIE!" I dialed 911 and typed, "Help."

In a few minutes, I crawled to the door to unlock it. The medics came in. They somewhat knew where I lived. They checked my heart and said that I was fine, but they wanted to take me to the emergency room to make sure everything was okay. The doctor checked my heart and wanted to put on a heart monitor to make sure.

As soon as I was left all alone on the hospital bed in the emergency room, my heart raced once more and the same voice came back saying that I was going to die. I saw my heart rate went up on the monitor, and I cried out for a nurse or doctor. He came in and looked at the monitor. My heart stopped racing and was back to normal. He was huffing and grumbled, "There is absolutely nothing wrong with you!" It was a strange experience. I was lying down for an hour and everything was normal. I had the nurse call my friend Mary who went to Bible College with my deaf brother in Texas to come get me. Mary was kind to get up early around 6 A.M. and came to pick me up. She brought me back to my place. I shared what happened with her and that I didn't know what to do. She shared the scriptures about spiritual warfare.

Therefore, take up the full armor of God, so that you will be able to resist in the evil day, and having done everything, to stand firm. Stand firm therefore, having girded your loins with truth, and having put on the breastplate of righteousness and having shod your feet with preparation of the gospel of peace; in addition to all, taking up the shield of faith with which you will be able to extinguish all the flaming arrows of the evil one. And take the helmet of salvation,

_and the sword of the Spirit, which is the word of
God._

(Ephesians 6:10-18)

She prayed with me. She left for work. I went to sleep on the couch, and I had a beautiful dream that I was floating on clouds that surrounded me with such overwhelming peace. I saw the devil trying to punch through the clouds but couldn't touch me. I was laughing with joy that he couldn't touch me. It was a stepping stone for victory.

A few months later, I had a powerful dream that is still vivid to this day. There were many people like a crowd marching toward me. I saw them like demons coming after me. I had a battle with the spirit of fear. I was up against the wall with no place to escape. I was trapped as the demons were marching closer and closer. I rebuked them even though I was fearful. They were advancing towards me. Again I raised my voice rebuking them, still in fear. I was scared as they kept marching closer to me. All of a sudden, I felt the boldness rise up in me, and with all of my strength and the spirit of authority, I fearlessly rebuked, "In the name of Jesus, Lord rebuke you!" Then poof, they all disappeared! I woke up with a great sense of VICTORY. I knew that I had overcome the spirit of fear that no longer bothered me again since childhood. Praise the Lord!

Over the next few months, I became friends with a deaf, blind lady named Colleen who lived a mile from where I lived. She was a wonderful Christian and she did not care if I was Catholic. She knew that I had a personal relationship with Jesus. She used to go to Calvary Temple as it was a totally deaf church. Anyway, I used to have closed-captioned movies at our apartment with the deaf fellowship. Some deaf from Calvary Temple came to join us. I borrowed the movie projector from the library to use for that event. There was no VHS, cable, or Netflix. Some of them kept challenging me that I worshipped Mary, the mother of Jesus, because I was still going to Catholic Church. They accused me of worshipping idols. I just ignored them and kept emphasizing Jesus is the one I had a relationship with. I felt that they were hypocrites not knowing how to love. I told myself that I wouldn't go to that church.

Anyway, my deaf friend Chris whom I met at Cursillo came to visit us for a few days. I called other friends from our church to join us for breakfast before he returned to California. That morning I was cooking a big breakfast, and I got an unexpected phone TTY call from Colleen, my deaf, blind friend. She said that she went to the emergency room the night before because she put Vicks in a pot of water and she didn't realize that she put the burner on high instead of low. She covered it to warm it up and when she put her face over the uncovered pot, all the boiled Vicks exploded, splattered and burned her all over her face and her mouth. She was carried by ambulance to the emergency room, and her face was diagnosed with third degree burns. Her face was swollen and the doctor advised her to avoid water on her face and to use straws to drink any cold beverage. She came home after a short stay.

She asked me to come get her to go to the store that had a special sale. I thought it was strange but I told her that I already invited friends over for breakfast and would take her to the store after their visit. I felt the Holy Spirit nudging me to invite her over for breakfast. So I asked her if she wanted to come over to join us. I just ran out and drove and picked her up and brought her over. I made her a cold smoothie as she couldn't eat a hot breakfast.

Her face was swollen and stiff with red skin. Her eyes were almost shut, and her lips were parched. We were fellowshipping, chatting away and eating. I felt the Holy Spirit speaking to me in a small voice, "Pray for healing of Colleen's face." I just shrugged it off and chatted. Again, He spoke a little louder. Again, I felt that Colleen was not able to receive. I continued chatting then I heard a louder voice with great urgency to pray for her. I shrugged, feeling embarrassed and went ahead to see if Colleen was open to that. She said yes. I asked everyone if they were in agreement to pray for her face, and they nodded. I had no more excuses left. We went to the living room to pray. Colleen sat down on the chair and everyone was circling around her. I prayed, "Father in heaven in Jesus' name, take away the pain from Colleen's face and heal her face and mouth. Thank you, Lord. Amen." It was a brief prayer. We just thanked the Lord. Colleen got up and signed loudly, "No more pain, no more pain!" We stared at her and we saw a great transformation on her face.

The swelling went down before our very eyes. She was able to move her face and was able to smile again. We were in awe praising God. Then everyone went home. I took Colleen to the store and couldn't find any sale that she saw in the newspaper. The salespeople said that there were no such sales. We left the store in bewilderment and went back to her apartment. I felt the Holy Spirit telling me to tell Colleen to wash her face with water thought it was against the doctor's order. She hesitated and splashed water on her face. She felt great. All of sudden, her face was peeling right before my eyes. She rubbed the old skin off. I said goodbye and left.

Colleen returned to see the doctor in a few days, and he was shocked to see her face as healthy as baby skin. There were no signs of scarring. She proclaimed that Jesus healed her. He stared at her with amazement.

She had a testimony to share at her church. Wow, the Lord used us not as Catholics, but because of our faith in Jesus. What an awesome God.

Sister J asked me to help her prepare for the Catholic deaf Convention of the Western region that was to be held in May. I was more than happy to help as I was excited. We worked on it, and we were about two weeks away before the convention started. I felt impressed to visit a wonderful hearing friend Glenna who was an interpreter for her church. She lived on Magnolia Hill in Seattle near beautiful Discovery Park. After lunch and sweet fellowship, I decided to go for a walk before heading home. It was breezy as the park was near the Puget Sound. All of sudden, I heard my name Veronica being called. I knew it was the Lord's voice. He said, "I want you to leave the Catholic Church now!"

I asked him, "What about the deaf Catholic Convention that I was responsible to help prepare?" He said, "Yes." I didn't want to leave the Catholic Church, and He asked me why. Oh I thought, "Well, umm, the convention, the priest's vestments, the deaf ministry."

He said, "Ok, you choose to follow Me or the Church." I hesitated for a moment and said, "Of course, I want to follow You."

He said, "Ok, you leave the Church now!" That was the end of the conversation. I was dumbfounded. I was given a choice to obey Him or not. WOW! I had to scramble my thoughts and words on how to approach Sister J and all. I felt it was best to write a letter to her to tell her that I had to obey the Lord to leave the Church. I felt bad because I had to cut off just before the convention that I was involved in organizing. Oh, she was very upset and didn't understand what the Lord was doing in my life. I had to trust the Lord to take care of it.

> *Not everyone that said to me, Lord, Lord, shall enter into the kingdom of heaven; but he that does the will of my Father which is in heaven.*

> (Matthew 7:21)

I Can Only Hear God

Chapter 10

New Direction

Shortly after leaving the Catholic Church, my roommate Diane and I went to see the Gospel Drama. The leader Debby invited me to be part of Hands Extended traveling all over the USA. The Hands Extended is a drama group that involved eight to nine deaf and hearing people who performed through music, skits, mime, and preaching the gospel of Jesus Christ. It is a faith-based and independent group. I was taken aback and wasn't sure if I was good enough. I felt I didn't know the Word well enough to share it. On top of that, I just left the Catholic Church. Debby said to me, "It is something you need to pray about." Again, I was surprised by what she said.

As soon as I got home, I said to the Lord, "I am going to fast until I hear from you that you want me to go." I was given a week to inform Debby of my decision. There were three weeks left to join that drama group. Starting a fast with water, I was still working and when I got home, I read the Word and prayed. It continued for three days to no avail. So frustrated, I decided to break the fast and I sat down with soup and read the Bible. The Word literally jumped out of the page with the story about how the Lord called Abraham out of his home country to travel to the unknown.

Get out of your country, from your family and from your father's house, to a land that I will show you.

(Genesis 12:1.)

Then the voice of the Lord spoke to me, "You are going to do the same. Also get out of your comfort zone." Wow, it was simple, although it seemed to be asking a lot. I informed Debby that I was in. I gave two weeks' notice at work and my move-out notice to the apartment owner.

On a May spring day just before joining the drama group, I got ready for the seven-month trip, packing and putting things in my friend's storage. The last thing I needed to do was to withdraw money from the bank, so I went to the bank close by. After getting the cash, I walked to the car and found myself locked out. I realized that I left the keys in the car's ignition, and my jacket was there, too. It was chilly out as it was cloudy. I went back inside the bank. I asked a person there to call my roommates to bring my extra key, but no one was at home. I sat down on a chair waiting not knowing what to do, so I read the pocket Bible. I

Hands Extended Drama group (1982), I'm in the 3rd row back on right with my brother, Nelson, behind me.

prayed asking the Lord for help. I had fallen asleep for a bit and awoke fresh by the Lord's gentle voice, "Call AAA (American Automobile Association)." I was a member of that organization. I decided not to bother the people in the bank. I walked next door to a small health food store and asked the lady there if she could make a call to AAA. I felt a strange sensation when she said, "A guy is coming to help you in 20 minutes." So I went over to my car, freezing and looking up at the gray clouds. I prayed, "Lord, I am freezing, please help keep me warm." On the spur of the moment, I literally saw the clouds part a bit. The sun's rays were shining on me, and I felt warm.

Finally, the tow truck with the logo of AAA showed up. I noticed two guys in the truck. An unshaven guy wearing a red and black, checkered jacket was slumbering. The driver was dressed in a perfect white uniform. He had dirty blonde hair with deep, blue eyes and an angelic, smiling face. He was very courteous. He approached me, and said, "Good morning, ma'am," handing out the tablet for me to sign my name for the service I requested. I thought to myself no one on the West Coast had ever said that to me since the East Coast. It was very unlike West Coast mannerisms. He brought a long, thin flat metal stick with him for unlocking the car. He said to me, "I don't want to damage your new car. I will go to the other side. Please sign your name." As I was signing my name, I looked up. He opened the door on the other side and reached for the tablet on which I had just finished signing my name. He said, "Thank you very much, ma'am. Have a good day." He got in the truck and the other guy in red plaid was still sleeping. I was dumbfounded. I walked around the car and got in on the passenger's seat then moved to the driver's seat. I was in shock trying to figure out what was really happening. I heard the voice,

"Don't worship the angels as they are your servants. I am your God that you worship only." Wow, I thought to myself, "the Lord sent me the angel. Ok, ok don't worship him as he was helping me." I drove home full of excitement.

My roommate Diane was at home. I had to ramble off the awesome event of the day to her. She said that was an angel. I timed myself signing my name and it was seven seconds. I timed walking from driver's side to passenger's side. It was exactly seven seconds. There was no time for that guy to use the metal stick to pry it open. He just opened the door. I had to relive that event over and over. It was amazing love the Lord showed me. I was on cloud nine.

Another miracle happened before joining the group. It had been years of a bad habit of mine saying "s..t" out loud if I had small accidents or was frustrated. I said this nasty word at least 25 times a day. I tried several times to stop swearing, but nothing worked. How could I possibly be a good example to preach the gospel while on the road? What a great concern I had. So I said to the Lord, "Will you please remove that word from my mouth for good?" Two weeks after joining the group, I felt something missing for so long and I couldn't put my finger on it. Then the great realization hit me hard. The word that I swore for so long was gone forever. Wow, the Lord did it for me.

Ask anything in My Name, I (Jesus) will do it.

(John 14:14)

We started the orientation in Lummi Island for two weeks. I was talking with Debby who was the director of Hands Extended, our gospel drama group. I asked her who was joining us. When she mentioned the new deaf member's name, I exclaimed that he was my brother. Debby had no idea that we were related. He was traveling from Texas as he just graduated from Christ of Nation Bible College. I was excited and I was waiting for him to show up. He didn't know that he was on the team with me. When I saw him coming to the compound where we had orientation, I ran to him and hugged him. He was confused about what I was doing there, and he thought that I was visiting him from Seattle. Then he found out that I was in the group, too, and he was so surprised.

There were eight people in the group in total. All of them were hearing except two of us. We had to learn and practice the skits, drama, and songs that related to sharing the gospel of Jesus Christ. Only the hearing did the singing. It was a learning experience especially since I had just left the Catholic Church. I was surrounded by Christians. Every morning, we had devotions of quiet time and group sharing. All of them had to learn to use ASL. Debby was a great inspiration teaching everything including ASL. All of the hearing learned very fast but didn't understand the deaf culture yet. We were told that we were to travel by faith meaning that we didn't have any funding to support the travel expenses. All we had were a van and trailer that carried the musical equipment, our luggage and the schedule of our performances. We started a few in Washington and Oregon then headed eastbound to Montana, then south, onward east then up north then south.

We went to a town called Whitefish, Montana, a cute small town with a breathtaking country mountainside and a beautiful lake. There was a tiny church between stores and we were greeted by a pastor named Harold. He said that we could sleep on the church floor. Upstairs a coffeehouse connected with the church. It was an outreach ministry for people in need. We were there for a few days. We performed and ministered to the congregation. My brother, Nelson and I did a lot of skits and dramas and didn't share from the pulpit yet. I felt a connection with that Pastor Harold. I felt something about him that I couldn't put my finger on.

Six years later, I read Harold's first book, _The Complete Wineskin_, without realizing that I already met the author. Then a year later, we felt led to go to the Gone with Spirit conference in the next town from where we lived. There were a few speakers. I recognized one of the speakers who was very radically preaching and was an anointed prophet. We went home, and I tried to remember where I had seen him. I asked the Holy Spirit who he was. I was blow-drying my hair before going back to the conference when the light bulb went off. It was that pastor in Whitefish, Montana. On our way, with my husband and our two little children, we ran into Harold and his wife, Linda. I pointed at him saying, "You are the pastor from Whitefish, Montana! Do you remember me?" He said of course he did. We reunited. Harold and Linda and my husband Johnny and I have been friends since that day. It was no accident.

Meanwhile our theater troupe traveled all over the USA, from church to church, deaf college to deaf community center, to Attica Prison in New York. It was full of adventures. Sometimes we spent a few days entertaining ourselves when we got blessings. The biggest struggle I was dealing with was the hearing and deaf cultures in the drama group. I felt it was so unfair for the hearing to use the deaf language, ASL, to minister to the hearing church especially since the hearing drama group members were just learning ASL and the deaf culture. There were many clashes between the two different cultures: six hearing to two deaf.

> _As iron sharpens iron, so one man sharpens another._
>
> (Proverbs 27:17)

New Direction

Like iron sharpens iron, the group of eight of us shaped our characters with godly attitudes. We had arguments and tried to understand and resolve the situations. I always cried out to the Lord for His wisdom, direction, advice and all I needed. I read more of the Bible and began to understand the LORD's way, not the WORLD'S way. It was a great challenge.

The first three and a half months we performed in many hearing churches, and my brother, Nelson and I didn't get a chance to be on the pulpit to share the Word or testimony after the drama was done. It felt unfair. One time during the first month, I felt like quitting the group, and I actually was going to do it. I poured out my heart to the Lord. I felt reassured not to worry about it. While traveling, I was leaning on the window. All of a sudden, I saw graffiti on a new bridge saying, "DON'T WORRY ABOUT IT!" Whoa, actually they were louder words from the Lord.

While traveling through Texas, the van's transmission broke down on our way to the performance. It was a good thing that we were in town when it happened. Our group prayed and cried out to the Lord for finances for a new transmission. After the drama, we got an amazing offering that met the need to replace the transmission. What a BIG GOD we serve. It happened again and again; the Lord's provisions met our needs on the road. Many miracles happened. That's where my faith grew a lot.

One of the most rewarding experiences was spending one week at a deaf camp in Louisiana. It was my first time interacting with deaf Christians since I left the Catholic Church. We became counselors of that camp, encouraging the deaf youth. There were many activities including a Bible game. That was a completely new world for me. The Lord had been teaching me on the trip. I was sharing the trials I was going through with one of the leaders there outside of my group. I expressed that I wanted to leave the group at the end of the month when the trip paused for a break for a change over. I was being challenged, "Humble yourself and seek for God for His righteousness." Also I was encouraged to look into myself instead of pointing at others, because it is the Lord's problem to deal with others. It was hard for me to let go and let the Lord handle them.

When we arrived in New York at Hickory Hill Camp, it was beautiful. It was time for refreshment and changeover. Nelson decided to leave the group instead of finishing the final leg of the trip. Instead of leaving the group, I was going to confront the leaders of the group Debby and Leslie. When I was on my way to the building where they were preparing for a one-to-two week orientation, I was being filled with ambition to conquer the hearing culture and demand the deaf rights to stand on the pulpit. All of a sudden, the Holy Spirit came in front of me and spoke to me, "Hey what are you doing? Jesus died on the cross and never defended himself or demanded his rights since he never sinned!" I gasped," I am sorry. Please forgive my attitude." I repented. I lost all ambition and let it roll off my back and humbled myself. As I entered, there were Debby and Leslie wanting to talk with me. I thought that they were going to confront me about something. I just held my breath. I actually stopped breathing. Debby and Leslie were whispering to each other and had a joy of the Lord. Debby broke the news to me saying that they had talked about me getting involved more in speaking from the pulpit especially at the deaf churches on our East Coast schedule. I was dumbfounded. What if I missed what the Holy Spirit had spoken to me? I was even more humbled and felt worthless to accept the new challenge. However,

I replied gladly, "Sure, I would love to do that." I knew that it was a test of my humility and obedience. WOW, what a testimony. I knew that the Lord wanted me to continue the final leg of the trip, to continue to grow in HIM, and to be more like HIM.

During the orientation, I realized I needed to be baptized in the water. It meant to me that I wanted to die to self and follow Jesus as my Lord. I asked Chip who led most of the seminars to baptize me. He felt honored that I asked him. He announced the following night that I was to be baptized in the freezing swimming pool. On September 14, 1984, I got immersed and when I came out of the water, I yelled "Glory to the Lord, I am a new person! My old self is gone! I want to follow Jesus forever!" Everyone applauded and shared the joy of the Lord. A new beginning...

One of the most powerful and extraordinary performances was in Attica Prison in New York. Debby had to apply a few months ahead and even gave all the information about our group's records to be fully examined before offering us entry. One of the worst riots just broke out a few months before we went there. I was really scared, and it was a foreign experience for me. I prayed a lot alone and with the group.

The guards told us that there was a time frame to get out of the prison on time. When we entered the prison, we had to go through 11 gates with guards at each one. I was getting nervous as we were on our way to a small auditorium. There were a few inmates waiting for us. Oh, man. They were huge and tall. We got everything propped up on the stage. The few inmates and the prison chaplain joined us in the form of a circle and held our hands and prayed. There were a million "what ifs" racing through my mind because they were criminals who could attack us. I didn't realize that they were Christians and were devoted to serving Jesus. Then about fifty inmates showed up, and there was only one guard standing at one door in the back. I had to look up to Jesus for His protection while we performed skits and music. The message of salvation was offered, and almost all the inmates raised their hands meaning that they wanted to surrender their lives to Jesus. The guard called out that we had to leave right then. Actually, we had to run through 11 gates to get out on time. Wow, I felt the Lord's presence through all the performance. I relived it in my mind again and again. I was in awe that the Lord was all powerful. I was no longer afraid ever since that prison experience. Jehovah-nissi means "Our banner, a banner of love and protection", and the name Moses gave to the altar he built after defeating the Amalekites. (Exodus 17:15)

We went all over New England, Pennsylvania, New York, Virginia, Washington, D.C. (Gallaudet College), Georgia, and finally Florida. I was given many opportunities to share the gospel and testimonies from the stage and offered the salvation of JESUS. Many deaf responded. I had opportunities to pray with them and encourage them in faith. There was always a pastor to follow up with spiritual counseling and encouragement.

We stayed at my parents' house for eight days in the "mini-Swiss Alps" mountain area close to Jersey Shore, Pennsylvania. There were several places to perform nearby. My parents and my little brother Paul went to see our performances more than once. They enjoyed them very much. The seeds were planted in their hearts in which I had faith that they would come to know Jesus personally.

There was a scheduled performance at a Baptist Church in Williamsport close to my parents' home. However, their pastor had to cancel our performance due to a conflict of some kind. The deaf there were disappointed. But the Lord had better plans. We performed in a church about an hour from Williamsport, and the deaf from Williamsport followed us there. The next day, my little brother Paul and I, along with the other deaf Christians from Williamsport, went to the Lycoming Mall and ran into the same deaf people who saw us perform in the other town. They were selling something for the deaf Club there. Some of them who didn't know Jesus expressed how inspired they were. They invited the drama team to perform at the Williamsport deaf Club. I asked Debby if we could squeeze it into our schedule and it worked out. When it was time for us to go to the deaf Club, Debby asked me to do the sharing of salvation with the secular. The deaf at the club were excited to see us. They were drinking and smoking while watching us perform. I was nervous and didn't know how they would react. To my amazement, they took it well after I shared the beautiful words and good news explaining why Jesus died on the cross for them as well as for us. They listened attentively, and the room was quiet. Their hands were still, not moving. I felt the anointing on me and I knew it was His grace on me, and His words were coming through my mouth. It was an awesome experience. I trusted the Lord to work in their hearts.

It was a rewarding experience that our group stayed at my parents' especially since I had just left the Catholic Church. At first, my parents didn't like my group because they were Christians apart from Catholic and were not perfect but were expected to be perfect. Some of them didn't understand how to respect an owner's property because they grew up in a dysfunctional family. They had the heart to serve the Lord and tried to set a good example. I had to explain what needed to be done to make my parents comfortable.

Debby came up with the idea about how to be servants and show them the love of Jesus by cleaning the house, washing the windows inside and outside, cleaning more than one fridge, washing all the walls inside the house, cleaning up the yard that was about 1- 1/2 acres. My parents were very impressed and became comfortable and got to know each person of the group. Mom said, "Wow, they did a wonderful job and it was the nicest group I ever met. The group seemed smaller because I got to know everyone better." That is the way to show the love of Jesus. We need to be the light of the world as it is lost.

On the trip, I yielded to the Lord more and more as I was growing up in the Spirit and reading the Lord's Word (the Bible). My character started to change especially through the hardship of getting along with the group and meeting all kinds of people from all walks of life. My main struggle was that I was deaf and the hearing didn't understand my ways and how I felt or behaved. There was a definite clash between two different cultures. For instance, the hearing talked in the van and I didn't understand what they were saying, so I asked them what was being said. They didn't bother explaining, and I became hurt and upset. They thought that I had a bad attitude towards them. I had to explain to them about my feelings of rejection. That repeated the vicious cycle, and it made me angrier and more vulnerable. They were upset too because they didn't understand why I was upset. I had to learn to surrender to the Lord daily instead of becoming bitter and ending the relationships and crucifying my flesh by not letting things bother me. I had to learn to trust the Lord for any positive outcome. I grew close with each of them especially one lady name Gay. She used to throw pillows, dolls, or anything at me to wake me up from snoring. Gay was a light sleeper. I got so mad at her for waking me up all night. We were always upset with each other. We had to work through our relationship. I became fond of her and we became good friends. We laughed about it and moved on.

As the group separated just before Christmas, I felt the Lord speaking to me about there not being Hands Extended after our separation. Two couples in our group fell in love and got married eventually. There were so many fond memories of how the Lord knitted our hearts together for a lifetime. There was a special bonding, and I learned that the Lord blessed us for trying to understand the different cultures, and we respected, accepted and loved each other despite our differences.

I was hospitalized twice during the seven-month trip. The first time I could not breathe due to my cat allergy. My lungs were inflamed so they had to treat me for a day in Maine. A couple weeks later, I was reaching for something in the van, and it felt like a knife was stabbing me in the back. I had excruciating lower back pain, and I could not walk. I was sent to the hospital in Rhode Island. I had to stay in bed for two days. My group came to visit me and cheered me up. I knew Ryan back in the college days and he came to see me. I had an opportunity to share the gospel with him, but the seeds had been planted in him. I was released with orders to stay flat in bed for a couple weeks. I couldn't afford two hospital bills and lifted them up in prayer questioning the Lord why bad things happened to me when I had an opportunity to share with the deaf churches. Why was I being restrained? Was I being punished? That ran through my mind over and over.

I stayed at a lady's home for two days before the deaf pastor Milton decided to drive me to meet my parents at my deaf brother Michael's wedding (about a seven-hour drive). With the Lord's help that day, my back seemed manageable while the wedding and the reception were going on. I prayed and claimed healing. I was brought home and laid down for a week. I was able to rest and read the Word and meditated on what the Lord was trying to teach me. I had been memorizing JAMES 1 for the past few weeks. It was talking about enduring the trials that shaped my character, attitude, and becoming a better person for His glory.

> *Consider it all joy, my brethren, when you encounter various trials, knowing that the testing of your faith produces endurance. And let endurance have its perfect result, so that you may be perfect and complete, lacking in nothing.*
>
> (James 1:2-4)

I was able to return to Hands Extended after two weeks of rest, and I was asked to share after performing. The service was anointed and my back was almost back to normal. I had to trust the Lord and not try to understand why I missed two weeks of the deaf ministry. I knew that I had to experience and understand James 1:2-3 because for some time Debby wanted us to memorize the whole chapter of James 1. I kept putting it off and she kept at me emphasizing how important the chapter was. After going through the ordeal of the allergy and back pain, I understood. The greatest blessing was that I was filled with the overflowing joy of the Lord, and both hospital bills were paid for.

As Christmas was drawing near, we were performing in Florida. I felt that Hands Extended was about to end. Debby released us to go home for Christmas for two weeks. She said that she would contact us for further notice about Hands Extended plans. After Christmas, it was announced that the plan for Hands Extended was dissolved. So I took the train from Pennsylvania to Seattle, Washington, after New Year's Day of 1985.

I Can Only Hear God

Chapter 11

Seeking the Lord's Will for My Life

A lady I met on the train westward said that she would mail me a Bible. I had been reading the deaf version Bible, and I wanted to change to a more accurate translation. Since I was on the Hands Extended trip, someone suggested I read the King James Version. I prayed about which translation would be best for me to read. When I got back to Seattle, I got a package from that lady on the train and it was the New American Standard Version. I started reading it and felt it was the right one for me. Since then I have received three bibles as gifts in the same translation in a twenty-year span. Lord knows what I need that fits me as an individual. Although when I study, I do like to browse several translations to get a better understanding of the Word, like the facets of a diamond.

Susan from Lummi Island moved to Seattle and lived in a one bedroom apartment and had been going to Christian Faith Center. She changed her name from Ziga to Susan since she became a new follower of Jesus Christ. She invited me to stay with her since I had come back to Seattle from our seven-month drama trip. I wanted to go to Calvary Temple deaf Church (Assembly of God) to get involved in the leadership, but the Lord said flatly NO. I felt led to go to CFC with Susan, and she interpreted the whole service every Sunday and Wednesday. It was just me and her. I decided to focus on the Lord's will in my life and grew deep in the Word. I lost almost all friends in the deaf community because when I shared the Good News with them, they didn't want any part of it. I was sad and disappointed, but I moved on to be alone with the Lord and focus on my growth in HIM. Eventually, I gained new friends of believers.

After seven months going there, I felt the Lord speaking to me to go to a Bible school's two to three year program. I did ask Him about the interpreter situation. The Lord spoke to me to go ahead to apply for the fall of 1985. So I took a leap of faith and applied. I was turned down because the program required an interpreter to go through the Bible school for two years before she could interpret for anyone. I consulted the Lord for His advice. He said to wait. The elder Ron called me and made an appointment to meet with him. So I went to see Ron, and he said that he could write down the special request for me to enroll in the Bible school. We wrote a long list to submit to the president of the Bible school. After submitting the supplication, the president flatly said no. We tried again with a different supplication. An astounding "NO" rang for the third time. Then I turned to the Lord, and He said that I would go to school and not to worry but to trust Him. Even though there were only a few days before school started, Pastor Casey heard what was going on. He overruled the president's third NO. Then I was in the Bible school in a blink of an eye. Debi was my interpreter. Bless her heart. While taking classes, I learned to depend on the Holy Spirit to do the assignments.

One day, we had class on the book of John. The president of the Bible school Mr. Frederick was teaching that class. He shared how I had faith in the Lord and endured in believing in the Lord to be enrolled in the Bible school despite it seeming impossible. He was impressed how the Lord put me in the program even after three NOs. He was making a point about how important it is to put faith in the Lord not in man. The Lord spoke through that teacher to show me that just by obeying and being faithful to Him, He brings blessings.

I joined a singles' ministry for the fun of meeting people. I met Sheryl, Dave, and Ben and became good friends with them. We hung out a lot. Sheryl said that she envied me because I was so transparent. She said that she had been struggling with being plastic and was afraid to be transparent maybe because of peer pressure and social standing. I didn't understand that until much later. It is very essential to be transparent about who we are in Christ. Nothing is hidden. We all do have struggles, defeats as well as victories and must overcome the obstacles in our lives. Yes, there is always the risk of rejection. We need each other to support each other, pray for and encourage each other.

Around the fourth month of Bible school, my spirit became more restless, and I couldn't concentrate on anything even though I tried to ignore the nagging. I tried to press down whatever was nagging me. The Spirit of the Lord spoke and reminded me to do His will when He called me to do it. I refused to believe what He asked me to do until I was convinced. I was afraid that it was going to cost me a lot. Finally, I went down on my knees and asked for

His forgiveness for ignoring what He wanted to say. I surrendered my will to Him and I sensed a great manifestation occurring. I couldn't figure out our big God and didn't understand what He was trying to do. It was a good thing to know that He knew what He was doing. I had to CHOOSE to step out in faith, to accept the challenge for what He was about to tell me.

He called me out of Christian Faith Center to go to another church called Faith Hope Love Church. I said, "Lord, you have to be kidding me! Why did you send me to CFC in the first place?" I felt that I needed to trust the Lord, no more figuring it out or reasoning with Him. His thoughts and ways were much higher than my limited ways and thoughts. So I chose His best. I felt like a dam that was pressured and was ready to burst open inside of me. I had to step out in faith.

I didn't want CFC to think that I was being rebellious so the Lord used one of the elders David. He was chosen to speak with me as he heard that I was leaving for another church. He said to me, "Make sure that you have Scriptures that the Lord gives you regarding leaving CFC for Faith Hope Love Church. Don't be afraid to come back. I release you to go to Faith Hope Love Church where I used to go. Lord bless you!" I felt the burden leave me.

The following Sunday, I was driving to FHL Church, and as I was getting closer, I was tempted to turn around and go back home. However, the spirit of God wooed me to arrive at the final destination. I was upset and I crossed my arms sitting out front pouting and having a pity party. "Lord," I said, "there is no interpreter!" Ben was interpreting orally. After the service, there was a humble lady named Saundra who came to me and signed ENGLISH to me. "the Lord told me that I am supposed to interpret for you." This was a JOKE, I whispered to myself. She couldn't even sign! "Oh, Lord, why are you doing this to me?" He said to pray for her every time before the service. I was determined to pray twice a week on Sunday and Wednesday.

I was still going to Bible school while I was attending FHL church. During the end of the first quarter towards the beginning of January, I was torn between staying and leaving the Bible school. I argued with the Lord who was dealing with me about leaving the Bible school at the end of the quarter. I pleaded to the Lord, "Why did you send me to Bible school in the first place? Now you want me to leave after the president's three no's? I am embarrassed to leave the Bible school looking like a loser!" the Lord asked me, "Do you want to do My Will or go your own way?" I had to swallow my pride, and I decided to choose His Will regardless. I didn't understand His perfect plan. I consulted President Ray about what the Lord had told me. He said that he didn't believe that because he believed that the Lord had big plans for me to oversee the deaf ministry at Christian Faith Center. I felt so bad. I struggled and I knew deep in my heart what I needed to do. I wrote Ray a letter thanking him for allowing me to be part of the Bible school and apologized for the confusion plainly telling him I had to obey the Lord. It was the second time I had to leave in the middle of great, important events of my life and I was tested. The Lord was training me to simply be an obedient follower, regardless of people's opinions.

Since Susan moved to the apartment upstairs to take care of an elderly, bedridden lady, I had to look for a roommate. The Lord wanted me to ask Alice, who was hard of hearing and whom I barely knew. We both felt that we were not compatible. I was not interested. Again, I felt impressed that it was His will for me to invite her to be my roommate. I went ahead asking her against my wishes. She didn't know if she wanted to room with me. I was relieved and went on looking for a roommate, and again I felt impressed that she was supposed to be the one. Then she called and decided to move in. AHHH. I asked the Lord for the purpose in that. I didn't know right away but after living with her for a year, it brought me to the light and entrusted great growth in me in reaching out, encouraging, being humble, being ready to listen instead of my rambling talking, and growing to be more understanding and sensitive to others. That's what the Lord wanted. He wanted to build character in me, even though the situation was annoying.

Friends from Faith Hope Love Church.

Eventually, Diane moved into our studio apartment with us. Diane and I slept in the sunroom without a heater, but there were always beautiful sunsets if there were no clouds. We prayed together and had a Bible study and some other deaf joined us. Diane and Alice grew up in the Lord who blessed me.

One day, I was praying fervently, and I saw a vision to set up a place like a coffeehouse to bring the deaf to the light of the gospel of Jesus Christ. I saw multitudes of the deaf coming into the Kingdom of God. I put that down in case it came to pass. Nothing happened with my efforts and I let it go. I put it on the shelf until the Lord resurrected it back to life if it was His will.

At FHL church, I was pulled in immediately to teach ASL and about 30 showed up. Three out of this class became excellent interpreters in a very short time. It was definitely a great GRACE of God pouring out to the three of them.

Saundra became a professional interpreter for the deaf after she went to college for two years in an interpreting training program. I was in awe how the Lord could transform them through His Grace.

The deaf ministry was born at the church. Pastor had announced that he saw my faithfulness and wanted to place me as an overseer of the deaf ministry. That is what the Lord was teaching and training me to do.

I developed a friendship with Ben as the time went by. We did a lot of things together and he was learning sign language. Sometimes he helped interpret at the church along with the other interpreters, Saundra, Connie and Sarah. All of them were wonderful and God-sent. Ben and I started the singles ministry at FHL, and we recruited singles. We had great fun and we became close. (As a matter of fact, we had a reunion with Ben and the rest of the singles along with their spouses and children a couple years ago.) Anyway, Ben was the leader of the Singles while I was the coordinator for activities and retreats. We had mime skits at the church and performed at Salmon Days in downtown Issaquah. I thought that my relationship with Ben was leading to another level as I got emotionally involved even though I was cautious.

I asked Ben if he wanted to meet my family for a summer vacation. He said that he had business in Washington, D.C. so we worked it out. He drove an airport rental car to my parents' place. He had never been on the East Coast before. It was a good experience to travel through Maryland and Pennsylvania. My parents greeted him, and I reminded them that we were just good friends and nothing more.

Family Reunion, 1986.

Mom was still upset about me leaving the Catholic Church two years back. She wanted me to talk with her priest. I said it was fine with me, and I wanted her to have peace of mind. Mom called the priest and made an appointment for Ben and me with the priest. We prayed before we went to see him at his church office. We greeted him, Father Bill, a friendly person, but he seemed nervous. Ben interpreted for me. When he asked me questions about my faith in God, I told him the story about the Lord calling me out of the Catholic Church to serve Him. He gave me a choice to follow the Church or only the Lord. I chose Him who could save or destroy my soul. Father Bill said, "Right, right, I understand. Yes, it is important what you need to do." I was able to share testimonies how the Lord blessed me. He said that he would talk with my mom to tell her that I was doing fine and that I was not crazy. We shook hands with smiles and went to my parents' home. Mom told me that Father Bill just called and said that I was good and that she need not worry. She seemed relieved and happy. The Lord was faithful to see me through and worked things out.

Two years back, I felt the Lord speaking to me that I would get married even though I protested against it. I was happy being single and I gave up the idea of being married and having children after I gave up the baby and I hit my 30s. During the month of November 1986, I fasted all day to seek the Lord about my relationship with Ben as I wanted the Lord's perfect plan in my life. While protesting against getting married, I wrote down a two-page list of what I expected in my future husband and gave it to the Lord. I said to the Lord, "If you could pass this list, then I am okay to get married. However, I still don't want to get married." That's why I had to seek the Lord that day. I felt impressed "You will meet a husband on June 1, 1987." Then I ended my fast for that day thinking that the Lord meant Ben. However, it wasn't Ben. He kept saying that he liked me as a good friend. I had to keep my emotions nailed down trusting the Lord that He would work it out. Meanwhile, we decided to have a singles' retreat up in the mountains in Cle Elum for a weekend in May 1987.

For the first year, I was full of fire in my bones that I couldn't hold back and chose to speak out in prophecy in front of the congregation every Sunday and Wednesday. I couldn't understand what was happening to me. I felt foolish but the only thing encouraging me to keep going was that people kept coming to me confirming again and again that my words were accurate and spoke to people's lives. The Lord spoke to me that I was fulfilling the call as a prophetess.

> But if I say, 'I will not mention His word or speak anymore in his name,' His word is in my heart like a fire, a fire shut up in my bones. I am weary of holding it in; indeed I cannot.
>
> (Jeremiah 20:9)

A year later, I felt a great burden to set up 24-hour prayer although I didn't know there was a couple who were intercessors and leaders of a prayer group. I went ahead asking Pastor for permission to have 24-hour prayer. I didn't hear from him for so long and I felt a nagging in my spirit to keep asking the Pastor. So I asked the children's pastor to ask Pastor for an answer yes or no to go ahead with the 24-hour prayer. Finally, Pastor gave me a heads up. It was announced in church inviting anyone to join the prayer group. I was the one to stay put for the whole time, praying in the Spirit, reading the Word, and taking short naps while others were there. A lot of people came in at different times. I have never forgotten that Sunday morning when heaven broke loose! There were miracles and healings. One thing that grieved me was that the pastor didn't give the Lord the glory but kept it for himself. Shortly after, the church split and eventually was dissolved.

On my 32nd birthday, April 10, 1986, Sarah, a friend and interpreter, called me to say she wanted to take me to Women's Aglow in a North Bend hotel convention room that morning. Cindy Jacob was the speaker, and I didn't know who she was. Sarah interpreted the whole message. Bless her heart. Then Cindy said that she felt led to anoint with oil anyone who wanted to come forward. All the ladies went up front leaving me behind. I tried to hold on and not be disappointed when I saw the small glass tube jar that had oil in it was running out. Sarah said to go ahead to the front to be laid hands on for prayer, and it was not too late. Cindy asked the Lord to refill that oil and, actually, right in front of my eyes, the oil was being filled up. She poured oil on my forehead and I was slain in the Spirit. I was overcome with the Lord's presence and He ministered to me. Cindy said that it was the beginning of a new ministry for me. I knew that the Lord chose to give me double blessings and a double portion of anointing for His purpose and glory.

Chapter 12

Surprises From the Lord

About eight months after I joined Faith Hope Love Church, Ken informed me that his good friend John was coming back from South America after almost a year. For the past year, he had been telling me about John. When I saw John's picture, I thought to myself that I didn't like his moustache and that he needed to shave it off. Shhh, don't mention that.

I saw John for the first time when he was standing on the pulpit preaching hot. I thought to myself, "Wow, I finally see a zealous brother who loves the Lord!" I wanted him to preach at the singles' ministry that I coordinated. I contacted Ben, the leader of the singles' ministry, and asked him to invite John to share his powerful testimony about his stay in South America. We were glad to have him speaking to the group, and we were able to ask him questions about his experiences. I wanted to know more about his work in the mission field. He had contracted hepatitis, lost weight and almost died. I felt an urgency to invite him and Ken for dinner at my apartment that I shared with two deaf ladies, Diane and Alice. I had an opportunity to ask John more details of his close-call experiences with hepatitis while he was in South

America. He shared that he had to walk and took different buses with no ambulance. He had to walk because of the mudslide; the bus couldn't get through but he needed to go to the hospital. He continued walking despite having no strength and was very weak and was tempted to lie down and let go. However, he kept going until he finally got to the hospital with yellow eyes and yellow body. The doctor took him immediately and gave him a big shot of antibiotic and made him rest. He was told that if he hadn't come in then he would have died.

When I asked John when he got sick, he said March 28th. I checked my journal and saw that I had prayed for five hours that day and asked the Lord who I was praying for. I realized that I was interceding for John on the same day he was walking in death of hepatitis. I thanked the Lord for that revelation. It must be someone important--my future husband! Wow.

Johnny and I got to know each other for a short time over two months. He was off again to Barbados for long-term mission work. He asked me to see him off at the airport. I was visiting Ben and had dinner and almost forgot about seeing Johnny off at the airport. I got there almost too late, and Johnny kept asking where I was and said that he had to board the plane in ten minutes. His family and a couple of friends were there. I wondered why he would be interested in me while other people were there for him. As soon he was in the line to board, there was an announcement that the plane was to be delayed, and everyone had to get off the plane. It went on for two hours. That was the turning point. We really built our relationship. He kept asking me to teach him sign language (not my favorite thing to do) the whole time. Yeah, two hours. He was happy to learn the alphabet and some signs and went on the plane. Of course, we exchanged our snail mail addresses. He wrote me a letter saying that he ended up meeting a hard-of-hearing guy at Abundant Life Church and learned more sign language from him. God had humor and made Johnny's life interesting getting ready for me.

In November 1986, Ben invited me over to friends for Thanksgiving dinner. We were chatting and Betty, the elderly lady who was leading the prayer group with her husband Bob at FHL church, asked me if I wanted prayer for healing for my hearing. Five of them were praying for me. After that, I felt a great pain in my ears. I mean a really sharp pain in both ears. So they continued praying for me. Before I knew what happened next, I was on the floor squirming. I was being cast out from all kinds of demons of occults I was involved with in the past. It went on for two hours, although I felt like it was five minutes. I recalled the demons making sarcastic comments when Betty said "Blood of Jesus Christ" over me. I was set free, indeed. I felt like I was flushed out as clean and white as snow.

> *Purge me with hyssop, and I shall be clean; wash*
> *me, and I shall be whiter than snow.*

> (Psalms 51:7)

I was praising the Lord for He delivered me from all the demons that I invited a long time before. I was singing for three days. Then I felt something more in me that I couldn't put a finger on. I called Betty to tell her that there was something going on in me. She said to come right over to see her. When I sat down with her, she asked me simply, "What is the first thing that flashes in your mind right now?" Reluctantly, I saw the vision of my dad slapping my face and pushing me down the stairs. I thought I forgave him a long time ago. However, she asked me if I forgave him. I said, "Yes, I did a long time ago, but I had resentment against him." She said that part was my being unforgiving because I resented him in my heart. She encouraged me to invite Jesus to the picture of my dad slapping me, then forgive him and accept the way he was. She reminded me that he didn't know what he was doing and to let him go. My flesh screamed," NO," but I said, "It wasn't fair," out loud. She said that she understood and asked me if I wanted to forgive him. I accepted it and I visualized Jesus standing there with Dad who did that to me, and I spoke out loud, "Help me, Jesus, to forgive Dad. I accept the way he was for he didn't know what he was doing. I let him go." It was a simple prayer, but I felt the heavy weight lifted up from me. My tears were running freely. It was a lot of pain to face and go through. I felt chained from both of my wrists, chained to two balls that had been broken free from me. That was how I felt the heaviness that weighed me down for so long. I was so angry toward all men, always frustrated and very emotional. It all went down the drain. IT WAS GONE. I became a new person. Deliverance and forgiveness made me a whole new person. WOW. I praised the Lord with all of my heart, and I was filled with the overflowing joy of the Lord.

I had a job working in the art department at Boeing in Aerospace for about eight months. The contract was over so I consulted the Lord about what I should do next. He said to set up my own business cleaning houses, businesses and churches. Oh no, it was the last thing in the world I wanted to retire doing. I had a really bad experience when I worked part-time for a small cleaning company. They placed me in one of the homes that gave me chills to think about. Two huge, very friendly, St. Bernard dogs lived there. Many offensive smelly droppings which were the size of cow manure, about twelve to sixteen inches wide, were all over the wood floor and on the rug in the beautiful living room. No kidding. Seriously, the owners dared to do that. Who was supposed to clean up that mess every week? ME! The company chose me to clean their house. I don't know how I did it. Naturally, I gagged over and over all the way through this horrible ordeal. Finally, I told my boss I quit after four times hoping the owners would use their common sense. The company may have thought I was the dumbest one who could do it. Maybe they thought deafness had to do with intelligence. No. I used my brain to quit. Anyway, the Lord said to me to start a business cleaning houses, so I hesitated. I obeyed the Lord and did it. The business prospered by word-of-mouth spreading from North Seattle down to Renton and from Magnolia Hill, Seattle to Issaquah. I hired two deaf ladies to help me keep up with the demands. I relocated to Renton since it was in the middle of the radius for my business. I had my business going for two years.

Two months later, after Johnny left for Barbados, I had a dream. I saw Ben then I turned. Right there was Johnny. I said to him, "What are you doing back here? You were supposed to be in Barbados for mission work." He never responded, then I saw Ben's face pleading for my attention. That was the end of the dream. I woke up. It felt so real.

I received Johnny's beautiful card with a picture of lilacs, my favorite flowers, and my favorite crystal glass. He wrote a nice, short message. I was annoyed that Ben didn't give me the actual stuff like Johnny did, not realizing the Holy Spirit led Johnny to catch my attention. Just around Christmas time, Diane ran to me in the foyer of the church exclaiming, "Johnny is here!" I said, "What is he doing back here? I thought he was going to stay there for a long time!" I went to see if it was true that Johnny was back. There he was. I said, "What are you doing back here? You were supposed to be in Barbados for mission work." He never responded. Then all of sudden I remembered the very dream that just happened. I asked the Lord what that was supposed to mean.

Johnny was thinking of leaving Faith Hope Love Church for another church a short while after his return from Barbados. I begged him to stay and get involved in the Singles Ministry. I said that we needed him because he had so much zeal for the Lord and had a lot of wisdom and knowledge of the Word. He said that he would pray about it. Then he decided to stay. We became good friends and were very active in Singles Ministry. We had fun and shared many things like spiritual stuff and our interests. He shared one time about a burden he had for natives for the gospel's sake in another country. So I shared with him about watching the movie The Emerald Forest based on a true story that changed my life forever. I never wanted to be a missionary; even my deaf brother saw in me that I was to be a missionary before I got pregnant out of wedlock. I refused to acknowledge it. I didn't believe that I was to go out of the country even though I was born in Scotland. Anyway, that movie changed my heart crying out that natives needed to hear the gospel of Jesus. That was a missionary heart that I didn't realize. I was sharing that with Johnny as we shared very much in common in our visions. We were so compatible.

In the middle of May 1987, we asked Johnny to be a speaker for the singles' retreat, and Ben also spoke. The Lord showed up, and that weekend was surely blessed. However, I was confused about my relationship with Ben. Before the day the retreat ended, I went for a long walk conversing with the Lord especially about Ben. I was tempted to continue walking and to never look back. I was determined not to go back, then the thoughts of "what ifs" ran through my mind. What if I encountered a bear on the way, or I had no place to stay? I would be cold and hungry. So I decided to go back to face reality. I was determined to cut off Ben even in friendship. When I went back to the retreat, Johnny came to me asking me where I was. He wanted a ride home. I was concerned about Johnny liking me. So I asked him if we could go out to eat dinner the next time because I had something to say. He was like, "Yeah, sure," and his eyes lit up. I groaned silently.

Johnny was like a brother to me, and I enjoyed his companionship. Whenever I worked at the church, he showed up to say hi. Sometimes Ken, Johnny and I would hang out during my breaks. The singles always hung out in Ken's home that was across the street from the church. One day, Johnny found out that I was 32 years old, and he was shocked and refused to believe me. I showed him my driver's license and still he wouldn't believe it. There I go with the baby face. He refused to accept the fact that I was 7 ½ years older than him. "Now you know!" I grunted silently to myself. At that time, he was 25.

We shared a lot as we had things in common. He shared his vision of preaching the gospel to the tribes after reading the book called Bruchko. I shared mine too after watching the movie called Emerald Forest, and it was an eye-opener for me to see the need to reach out to the natives with the gospel. Johnny looked through my small library and found a lot of pamphlets and books that he had been reading, too. What a coincidence. No, sorry, it was actually of the Lord.

In March of 1987, I came home after long hours of cleaning three to four big houses daily and I was so exhausted. I pulled out veggies to make a quick stir-fry. At that time, I was a vegetarian for two years. I sat down wearily at the table alone and said grace. Then suddenly I heard the Lord saying, "I have a GIFT for you," with excitement. I was so tired and not in a good mood to catch the excitement.

"Okay, how will I know it's from YOU?"

"You will know by the Holy Spirit who will quicken your spirit," said the Lord.

"Oh, okay," I responded lifelessly.

The next morning, I started looking for the GIFT. Days, then weeks passed. I told myself to forget it.

I talked to my dear friend Ken. He was always there for me even though he was busy at church since he wore many hats doing different jobs. I expressed my concern about Johnny's liking me and how to talk with Johnny about our relationship. I asked him the best approach using proper English instead of putting him on the spot. You know, deaf tend to be blunt but hearing don't do that. So I was trying to be sensitive to the situation. So I told him that I wanted to make clear where Johnny and I stood in our relationship as just FRIENDS. I practiced, "Johnny, I wonder if you wonder if I wonder where we stand in our relationship." Ken helped correct my English. Actually, I had to memorize it. I was nervous to approach Johnny.

That day I was cleaning the church on a Saturday and the front door was locked. I felt the Holy Spirit nudging me that someone was at the door knocking while I was washing the floor in the kitchen. I got up and went to see if anyone was there. There was Johnny. What a surprise. He said he prayed that I would come to the door. From that time, he knew where I was working at the church every Saturday. When the time came for us to go out for dinner, we chatted away. I waited for the moment to talk to him like I practiced with Ken. "I wonder if you wonder if I wonder where we stand in our relationship."

He responded simply, "Oh, I don't know yet."

I was dumbfounded, then I heard a really quiet voice speaking, "This is the man you will marry."

I said, "HUSH! He could hear you. No way!"

Johnny began telling me how his old pastor prayed with him recently and prophesied, "A woman will steal your heart."

I asked if it happened yet. He said not yet.

Then the Holy Spirit said, "It will be you!"

I was surprised and was struggling with the Lord. Oh boy, I didn't know that He had a sense of humor and was having fun with me. I tried every moment to block the thought that we were in a relationship. We were enjoying our good friendship, nothing more.

Troy, Ken, Ben and I always hung out memorizing the scriptures, quoting and sharing them long before Johnny came back from South America. One day those precious guys came over to my apartment to hang out. Johnny showed up with his briefcase full of his tools. I forgot that he was planning to come to fix my TTY. The way Johnny poised his soul made those guys leave hastily. "Oh boy, he doesn't own me!" I thought to myself. I pleaded with them to stay, and they said that they had to go. Now I was alone with him. He was very preoccupied trying to fix the TTY. I saw him removing the tabs. I saw the dust, and removing the dust solved the problem. We had a chance to engage in conversation. He noticed that I had pamphlets from David Wilkerson and Keith

Green. He exclaimed that he had always liked them.

I had a really traumatic experience with my right eye. In the middle of the night, while I was sleeping, I awoke with a wet, runny right eye. I mean really wet, so I got up and went to the bathroom. I was freaking out that my eye was bleeding. It was a strange phenomenal thing happening to me. I thought that I was losing my sight. I went to see a natural doctor because I didn't want any knife touching me. He tried everything in his power to help me with homeopathy remedies. It occurred three more times. Finally, one morning it happened again. I didn't know what to do but I called Ken at church with the relay service through TTY. He said not to worry. He was sending a prince riding on a horse to come to my rescue. I said, "Ken!" He called Johnny and asked him to come see me through that terrible crisis. When Johnny showed up in a disgusted mood, he was blunt with me to never mind the natural doctor or my standing on the Word believing in the Lord's healing. What he meant was that believing in the Lord's healing made the Lord use the doctors, too. He announced that he was to take me to the doctor who would cut the thing out of my eye. I was freaking out. He assured me not to worry and he would be there to support me.

When we went to the clinic, Johnny talked with the doctor very closely and negotiated the price for minor surgery. Johnny said that I was in and to get ready for the eye surgery to remove the alien stuff from my eye. I think it was called subconjunctival hemorrhage maybe from combining working with the household chemicals and wearing contact lenses. When I was getting ready for the assembly line for the surgery, I was number ten or so. They gave me anesthesia to help me stay calm but awake. I was praying to sleep because I didn't want to see the scalpel touching my eye.

By the time it was my turn, most of the anesthesia had worn off. I was watching the doctor performing a quick surgery. I was forced to watch the whole thing that I had fretted about all along. When it was over, I was relieved and never had the problem ever again. I was impressed that Johnny took charge of my life and took care of me. I didn't expect any of that. I was thankful for a real friend. Wink, wink.

Johnny asked me if I had time to go for a walk in the park in Renton. We had a long conversation. He asked a lot of questions about my deafness and my life. It was on a more personal level. When it was time to go home, we arrived at the parking lot of my apartment complex. We saw a baby duckling running around. We had no idea where it came from with no mother in sight. We tried to catch it. Johnny caught it and brought it to our apartment. I had no container but then I remembered that I had a small box of tampons so I ran to get it and empty all the tampons. I handed the tampon box to Johnny to put the duckling in it. He was kind of frozen. I didn't realize that it was very awkward for him. With much gladness, we found a tiny home for the little bird. We sat on the couch watching the duckling poking out of the box. It was so cute and we wondered how the baby got to the parking lot, a long way from the lake. The mystery remains to today although I believe the angel of the Lord put it there for our time of bonding. I later visited Johnny occasionally at his parents' house to see how the duckling was growing up in the chicken coop in the backyard. During that time, a deeper bonding developed.

A couple days after the pastor announced that I was overseer of the deaf Ministry, I got a letter from Johnny that he put on the door at my one-bedroom apartment in Renton on June 1st, 1987. I read his letter full of brotherly encouragement saying how he was proud of me. Then the Holy Spirit said, "This is your husband."

I said, "No!" Johnny was supposed to come over to my place for dinner that evening. Then I remembered last November when I was fasting and praying for a relationship, I got word from the Lord saying on June 1st I would know who my husband would be. I was freaking out and blocked the whole thought. When Johnny showed up at my place for dinner, I thanked him for his nice letter. I was making an appetizer and he stopped me. He said never mind about the dinner. He said to me, "Shh, this is a secret that I am taking you out to the Space Needle to eat." I was taken aback not expecting it. I said to myself, "No one has ever taken me out to the Space Needle to eat in a restaurant for the whole time I lived here for seven years." I always wondered who would take me there. It was so unexpected and a surprise.

On the way to the Space Needle, we went to a souvenir shop. He was toying and joking around, showing the real side of him. As we went on the elevator going up the space needle about 500 feet high, Johnny was testing me by saying, "Oh, I am scared." I got a hold of his arm and made him comfortable. As we entered the restaurant, it was a new world to me as I had never gone to fancy restaurants because I couldn't afford them. We sat down and he said to order anything I liked. I ordered salmon that I hadn't gotten a chance to taste since I moved to Seattle seven years before. He jokingly put a spoon on the windowsill as we were on the rotating wheel that revolved around for about an hour. When we came back where the spoon was, we knew it was an hour so we went another hour. That night was magical; actually, the anointing and the presence of the Lord was so real to both of us. We felt the great transformation from good friends to lovebirds that evening.

Surprises From the Lord

That night we knew that it was the Lord's will for us to be husband and wife. On our way to my apartment, Johnny was singing a song. I instantly fell in love with him. There was no holding back or fighting against the Holy Spirit who had wooed me for so long. Remembering the dream I had that Johnny came home from Barbados, I asked him what brought him home. He was telling me that he was at the beach one day. He was lingering at the beach when he remembered that he had to catch the bus. He ran to the bus stop but he missed the bus. He had to wait for a long time for another bus. The Lord spoke to him that there was something much more important than the bus. He wanted him to go back to the States or he would miss it. After his return, he saw me and I inquired why he returned. He didn't know how to answer me yet. As time went on, he realized that I was the one he could have missed. He was glad that He obeyed the Lord to come back home for that surprise from the Lord in which I would be his wife.

Engagement picture

Chapter 13

Wedding Bells!

The next morning, I was dazzled and in awe to see what the Lord had been doing in our lives. I realized that the Lord opened both of our eyes to see His plans in our lives. I felt like Cinderella. Sorry, no glass slipper. Oh, it was exciting. Immediately I ordered a TTY to give to Johnny for our communication's sake. I felt that talking through the relay took forever and was not personal. I surprised him when I came over to his parents' house and gave him the TTY. He was caught off guard. Then later he explained that it was a commitment to do that as he reluctantly accepted. We called each other every day. I had a flasher to let me know that the phone was ringing. At the end of June, we happened to talk about the meaning of our names. I told him mine meant the true image of Jesus. He shared his name meant GIFT. I was astounded. Yes, I had a WITNESS in my spirit that JOHN was a GIFT to me from the Lord. Wow. I didn't tell him right away until he formally asked me to marry him. I didn't want to scare him away. Wink, wink.

I visited Johnny at his new business shop after I got off from work. We prayed and asked the Lord where He wanted us to go to church. We decided to leave Faith Hope Love Church. There was a tiny church called New Life Christian Fellowship with about 75 people attending right in the heart of Issaquah. I felt comfortable there and it was easy to get to know everyone. One of the interpreters from Faith Hope Love Church followed us there so I had an interpreter. Pastor's wife, Joy, who was a fast learner, helped interpret and two others followed learning to interpret. Johnny, his mom, and Becky shared the interpreting.

One Sunday on July 12, Johnny wanted to take me out to visit friends Ron and Val at a campground past Steven Pass. I had waited for Johnny to ask me to marry him for over a month. I asked him while driving on Highway 90 just after North Bend eastward, "What's keeping you?"

He read between the lines that I was waiting for him to formally ask me to marry him. He said, "Well, I wanted to ask you over a candlelight dinner overlooking Lake Washington but how about here?"

I said it was such a beautiful view of the Cascades Mountain and I replied, "SURE, Why not?!" He pulled over to the side of

Johnny asked me to marry him on July 12th, 1987.

the freeway and asked me to marry him. I heartily said YES! Then we got out of the car, and he kissed me. I had a self-timer camera and took a picture of us as an ENGAGED couple.

Wedding Bells!

We went to the campground where Ron and Val were camping out. They were the first people to hear the news of our engagement. Johnny had wanted to ask me out to pop the question but it didn't work out. Later that evening, he took me out to the Fog Horn Restaurant on the Kirkland waterfront after visiting friends at the campground in the mountains. So he asked me to marry him again on that romantic sunset evening. "Of course I do!" I responded with overflowing joy of the Lord.

We were overjoyed to announce our engagement. We prayed about who was to marry us so Johnny asked Pastor Frank, his first former pastor, Steve Lightle, his spiritual father, and our pastor Rick McIlvaine. It turned out to be our pastor and he requested we go to marriage counseling for three months, two hours each time. He said that he was not 100% sure if he would marry us but would let us know maybe halfway through. He wanted to make sure that our marriage was of the Lord. Johnny asked my parents if he could have my hand in marriage, and they welcomed him to be part of the family.

Recalling the list I wrote down for what I wanted in a husband, I pulled it out from my Bible cover pocket. I read it and I realized that Johnny was more than I asked for. The Lord had more hidden jewels about Johnny. Wow. He is a Big God I serve.

Our pastor requested we ask the Lord apart from each other for at least three scriptures that quickened our spirit to confirm that we were meant for each other for life. He challenged us and made us look at ourselves and the reality. Everything went smoothly; about six weeks later he informed us that he accepted us to be married, and he was more than happy to wed us. He said that God was interested in our marriage. What he told us was prophetic.

My bridal girls at bridal shower

Then we had three months for the wedding preparations. We sent out 250 invitations and needed to select a wedding party. I asked the Lord who to pick for the maid of honor and bridesmaids. It was hard because I was close to many people. I felt impressed to ask Diane because she touched my life in a special way. I would never have understood or learned ASL and the deaf culture if it weren't for her. Secondly, I felt impressed to ask Val, my precious sister in the Lord. She was always there for me building bridges between deaf and hearing. She seemed to understand whenever I had issues, and we encouraged each other in faith. Her youngest daughter, Kelly, was the flower girl. I struggled over who was next. I wanted to have a large wedding party but the budget didn't allow it. I kept thinking on the second bridesmaid. The soft voice spoke to me to choose Alice who lived with me for a short while. Oh boy, I looked back and realized I was a mean taskmaster, but I learned to give grace and mercy. I became more compassionate to reach out and encourage. She really was changing and was growing in the Lord. I thought that I wanted to bless her to be my bridesmaid. We became good friends. I realized that one of my gifts was to pull the hurting or low esteem individuals and build them up knowing who they are in Christ.

Bride and groom!

Looking for a bridal dress was pretty short and easy. We went to JC Penney's and found a beautiful dress that suited my personality. It fit me nicely. However, I had a piece of lace to be sewn like a cross, over my heart to be more modest. I asked a friend from church to be the emcee, and I arranged for decor and flowers for the church, the bridesmaids and myself. The flowers were prophetic for me because they were orchids and roses and it was only later I realized we were going to be missionaries for eight years in the Philippines. The Philippines' flower icon is an orchid. I asked for volunteers to prepare finger foods and punch bowl drinks. I was expecting around 150 people as RSVPs were counted. Betty, Bob and Steve were intercessors for our wedding. The anointing and presence of the Lord was amazing. Many unbelievers came to us and they felt it was different and peaceful like they hadn't encountered before. We were to be married on October 24, 1987, in Foursquare Church in New Castle. (The church building is no longer there, It was transferred to another location about 3 miles away.) Over 200 people were overflowing and some were standing. However, the presence of the Lord made the difference. There were three interpreters for the deaf. My personal interpreter Susan stood right by Pastor Rick. We had been close since we were roommates, and she interpreted for me at CFC. Also, she was a faithful, precious friend. The other two interpreters were Connie and Sarah who were amazing ladies and precious friends. Larry, a friend of Johnny's, volunteered to take pictures but no video because the battery was dead and he forgot to recharge it. Praise God, there were other friends taking pictures, too. Johnny's mom made the cake that was beautiful and everything was all set.

The night before the wedding, I had a bridal sleepover with the wedding party. Diane, Val, Kelly, Alice, Susan and I slept over at Alice and Diane's apartment having fun. Val made me practice the song for the night after the wedding with feather scarf swinging. We had a lot of laughs. We prayed for the Lord's favor, blessing, peace and grace for the next day's event. I was filled with excitement and peace.

Johnny and I came in agreement not to kiss for one week to save up for the wedding bells to be rung. Val was the one who helped with the hair and makeup for all the ladies. Everyone was so pretty. Mom was there helping me put on my wedding dress. She gave me some kind words to calm me. Betty, Bob and Steve were praying all morning before the wedding for the Lord's grace and favor and, most of all, His presence. I was excited but nervous, and the day finally came. I had not seen Johnny the day before the wedding. The wedding started late about 3:00 P.M. as it was supposed to start at 2:00 P.M., but more people kept pouring in. My family all came except for Janette who lived in Hawaii. Johnny's whole family and some relatives came. Many friends came. About one-third of the congregation was deaf. There was excitement in the air. When

Wedding Day with my parents

my dad escorted me down the aisle to the front where Johnny was, my eyes were fixed on Johnny. I noticed the tears that he was holding back. Dad kissed me as he gave my hand to Johnny. We exchanged our vows in our own words and Johnny signed me a song. Finally, we exchanged our custom-made rings and we were announced as Mr. and Mrs. Dunnington. We kissed for a long time - about 45 seconds! Everyone started clapping and cheering us on. Pastor Rick tried to give Johnny a hint to stop. Everyone thought it was funny. At last, we lit up the candle as one and had communion.

Pastor Rick called some men forward: Johnny's best man, Ken; the groomsmen, Steve and Matt; my brothers, Mike and Nelson; Steve from our church; one elder, David, and the associate pastor, Rob from FHL; and the pastor, Steve of Foursquare Church to lay hands on us and pray. They all prayed and gave words of prophecy. The most powerful word of Prophecy was that the Lord would send Johnny and me to the world to evangelize the lost and bring the lost souls to the Lord. (It came to pass.) This went on for 15 minutes or so. Then finally we walked out as a married couple. I had never dreamt that it would happen because when I gave up the baby out of wedlock, I thought it was the end. The Lord was faithful to see me through and saw me fitting in His blueprint.

There was a reception, just finger food and cake. After the photo shoot, the food ran out before we knew it. We threw the bouquet and Johnny used my garter as a sling-shot. We smashed cake into each others faces. Then we had a Jewish dance along with three people from our church playing guitar. It was wonderfully fun because most of our friends, both deaf and hearing, got involved dancing. After dancing, we were famished and were ready to go to the hotel on our first night. Our best man surprised us with a Lincoln Town car as he was our chauffeur. Some pitched in to surprise us. Bless them. Ken drove us to the Hyatt Hotel in Seattle that Johnny booked for two days before taking off to Barbados for our three-week honeymoon. Johnny carried me to the hotel. The Lord blessed our union.

The next day we went to the airport to see my parents off. Mom said that God did indeed answer my prayer for a specific husband I asked for. After I gave up the baby for adoption, I told Mom that I would not sell myself short with a husband. I specifically told her that I would marry a Man of God who loves the Lord with all of his heart and would not smoke or drink. I got what I asked for. All Glory to Him. He is faithful to see me through.

Wedding Bells!

Wedding party

Romance begins!

I Can Only Hear God

Chapter 14

Honeymoon, World Changer

The flight to Miami, Florida, was exciting because we were romantically in love. The poor man who sat next to us thought we were crazy. We had a few hours layover; we took a taxi to a famous beach in Miami. It was a warm, sunny day as we walked on the beach hand in hand. Feeling breezy and being in love was a blessing. Then we caught the plane to Barbados. We were expecting to stay at Johnny's friend's house for two weeks, then stay in a hotel for one week, but it fell through when we got there. We didn't have enough money left over after renting one of the summer cottage rooms for three weeks. The owner, George, a grumpy elderly man who always was shirtless, led us to our room. It was like a primitive room with a foam king-sized bed on a wood board, dripping sink and a toilet with a shower and plastic shower curtain. I got excited that this was preparing us for our future mission work. Johnny was surprised with my uplifting positive attitude. We asked George if we could use the kitchen for three weeks because we didn't expect to stay in a rented place for three weeks.

We could save money by buying food and cooking. George grumbled and said, "Ok, since the chef just left for his vacation for three weeks, but when he gets back, you have to get out of the kitchen." Another condition he said was not to use the oven. We were able to use the refrigerator and stove. Wow, what perfect timing. We thanked the Lord. We were really poor so we were buying the food, and I made homemade flat bread cooked in a pan every day. Johnny doesn't want to think about eating it again. We had Muesli, pancakes, fruits and vegetables and peanut butter and jam but no meat. We rationed the food daily as we waited for money to be sent to us from the States.

Honeymoon!

We went to Abundant Life Church the first Sunday we were on the island. Johnny's hard-of-hearing friend invited us to join the deaf church because they were expecting a deaf guest speaker from the States. So we waited in the steamy, small room with a few other deaf. I was so surprised Chip Green showed up as the guest speaker. When he saw me, he said, "Oh my word, oh my word, Veronica!" We hugged and he asked me what I was doing in Barbados. I told him that it was our honeymoon and got an unexpected invitation to this deaf church. He was the one who water baptized me in New York when I was with the Hands Extended drama group. Wow, the world was getting smaller.

We took the bus to town, church and Johnny's friend's parents' huge beautiful mansion that blew me away. I didn't feel connected with that Christian family because of the social standing. It was hard to understand people like that.

We decided to hitchhike around the island as we were flat broke. A couple picked us up. They were smoking weed and offered some to us. We said, "No thanks." They were friendly and drove halfway up the island. We got a ride around another half. We were able to meet the locals who had goats roaming around. When we arrived in the town called Bridgetown, we hitched one more time back to our pad. A guy picked us up and he asked us if we wanted a free hamburger for a 90-minute timeshare presentation. We were salivating for meat. We accepted it and went to the hotel and listened to the whole hour and a half while our stomachs were growling with hunger pangs. I had to stop my vegetarian diet for two years so I could start eating meat and poultry again. We couldn't wait for the hamburger and we dreamt of big, juicy beef with tomatoes and lettuce stacking up with catsup and mayo. When it was time for lunch, all we got were small, dry, scrawny hamburgers with nothing on them. The burgers were three inches wide, and we had devoured them and that was it. We were still hungry but rejoiced anyway.

Johnny caught fish for our dinner

Our pad was located on one of the most beautiful beaches of the island. Johnny and I went snorkeling, saw many fish and speared fish for our dinner and other meals. We played cards (rummy) a lot. I always won, and he never played that game ever again with me after our honeymoon. He found out that I had been a rummy champ a long time before I met him. George was always there; he kept telling us not to talk about God. We had no idea what made him say that. Maybe he knew by what he saw in us. We spent a lot of time relaxing on the beach or in our pad.

Two ladies worked there. I noticed one of them named Pat was medium height and heavyset but strong. She looked miserable and had no joy. I felt pity for her. About a few days after our arrival, Pat came to us, saying, "I know you both are Christians and you remind me of a missionary couple who came here who witnessed to me. They led me to the Lord Jesus Christ as my Savior." She shared her life story that she was adopted by the owner George and his wife. She was bitter against her real parents who gave her away. Johnny and I ministered to her, and she had a choice to forgive them and let them go. We prayed with her. She was a changed woman. She was overflowing with the joy of the Lord and it was

Debbie, Me and Pat

contagious. Debbie, Pat's adopted sister who was born again and had been faithful going to Abundant Life Church, was greatly encouraged. Both of them wanted to talk with us for days. It was the Lord's perfect will for us to stay in that pad instead of Johnny's friend's house.

One Sunday, we were on our way to church and afterward, we were walking around before heading home. We saw young men working down an open pit in the road. Johnny said, "Hi there." All of them came up and said that Johnny looked like a television evangelist. Johnny started sharing the gospel with them. All of them except one were interested. One guy asked Johnny a lot of questions and Johnny asked him if he wanted to ask Jesus to come into his life and have a personal relationship with Him. He said YES and we prayed with him. He was so excited. Johnny gave his new Bible to him and encouraged him to attend Abundant Life Church the next Sunday. We saw him there and made him comfortable and met some people at church. Wow, it was awesome.

We met a couple from England named Stella and Ken who invited us over for lunch after the church service. We didn't expect to see the FEAST. There were more than 15 courses of mouthwatering food. Our eyes were bigger than our stomachs. We ate and ate until we were stuffed. We were not hungry for two days. They called us to stop by to see them. They gave us delicious, cooked blue fish to take to our pad. Wow. The Lord was taking care of us and our needs. He knew what we needed. Also, another day they took us out for hamburgers and ice cream. There was always timely provision for food. We never starved. The Lord used the English couple to reach out to us in time of need.

Finally, money arrived a few days before our return to the States. We used the money to go out to a nice restaurant. I felt like Cinderella again and we had a candlelight dinner with a tropical breeze. The food was phenomenal after eating the poor's man food for two and a half weeks. It was a blessing and a final touch before we returned.

When we were ready to leave our comfortable pad, the chef returned. We greeted each other and told him that we used the kitchen and it was all cleaned out. Wow, how timely it was. It was the Lord working everything out for His glory. He amazes me all the time.

About two years later, we got a letter from George letting us know that Pat passed away from breast cancer. Johnny immediately called George and he answered. He expressed how thankful he was for us because Pat's life was changed by our willingness to minister to her and love her. He couldn't thank us enough, and his life was touched because of that even though he didn't want anything to do with God. His life was changed, too. Wow, the Lord actually led us to become missionaries right on our honeymoon to change the world. It is never too early or too late. Praise Him Most High.

Our honeymoon pad

Chapter 15

Marriage Begins

Upon our return from our wonderful blissful honeymoon, we were back to reality in our new home across the street from New Life Christian Fellowship Church and Pastor Rick and Joy's home. There was half a room full of wedding gifts that were not yet unwrapped. We invited some friends and Johnny's parents to witness the opening of the gifts. Everyone blessed us. We were overwhelmed and overflowing with the joy of the Lord.

Johnny returned to work at his own business repairing VCRs, TVs, radio, and electronics. I went back full force with my business cleaning houses and business places. We set our routine, going to work, eating breakfast and dinner together, praying together and reading the Word.

One Saturday morning, I wanted to make Johnny a special breakfast with a new recipe for healthy pancakes. So I served him with wonderful love. Johnny said they tasted terrible. My heart sank to the floor. I made another recipe for healthy pancakes. I served them with gladness and hopefulness. Again, he said they tasted terrible. Feeling hopeless, I reached out and tasted them from his plate, and I screamed, "Soy sauce!" He looked at me like

I was a maniac. I explained that there were two soy sauce glass containers, and one of them was maple syrup and the other one was soy sauce. Both had the same color. With encouragement, I said to Johnny, "You took the wrong container. That has soy sauce instead of maple syrup!" He looked at me feeling like an idiot. Then we had a wonderful breakfast with maple syrup. We still remember that day like yesterday.

Every Sunday we came home after church, and we ate lunch. Shortly after, Johnny laid down on the bed. I asked him, "What are you doing on the bed? Let's do something."

He replied, "No, I want to relax."

I said that I could not relax, and he encouraged me to try to relax. I didn't want to be alone doing stuff as it was our weekend off. So I decided to lie down to relax right beside him. It was new to me and I kept chatting away. He said that I could rest my mouth, too. Oh boy, now what? It took me a few years to learn new ways to relax. Our relationship balanced each other out as he was mellow and I was so active.

I felt the need to teach Bible study to the deaf. My friend called and wanted to have a Bible study at her house and said that her friends wanted to come. I told Johnny about it, and he wasn't too happy as I didn't realize how important it was to focus on my husband during the first year of marriage. I went ahead of the Lord and went to my friend's house where the deaf ladies met. When I started to pray, there was a deaf lady there who was Lutheran who spoke out, "I don't believe praying with you because I don't know what your doctrine is!" I was caught off guard not expecting a clash. I told her what I believed in and we ended up arguing. I tried to stop and she refused and wanted to prove that she was right. I wanted to go along sharing the Word. There were new believers sitting there watching us, and I tried to put a stop to it and was feeling bad. So I told my friend that it was best to stop and I would explain to her later. I left upset and I realized that it was not the Lord's timing for me. I knew that I had to focus on my marriage instead of meeting others' needs. It was my big lesson. I had to learn to be patient even though I had a restless spirit to get into ministry. How ignorant I was. My husband was in front of me, and he needed me the most.

About 2:00 A.M., I woke up needing to go to the bathroom. I went to the bathroom in the dark, and I felt a blob coming out of me. I flushed it then I realized that it was a miscarriage. I was six weeks pregnant as it was a honeymoon baby. I woke Johnny up and told him the sad news. I knew it was okay and the baby was with the Lord. I had to see the doctor to verify it, and he said that I did not need the RhoGAM shot because the baby was not mature enough to cause the problem. (I am Rh-negative.) We didn't expect it as it came as a surprise.

In April 1988, I was declared pregnant by Dr. Kato at the Valley Medical Center. He was a born-again Christian. He was very gentle and sweet yet serious. I was still cleaning houses and came home exhausted. It was becoming more difficult to keep up the energy to clean three to four houses a day. Johnny and I prayed for the Lord's wisdom about what to do. I was the breadwinner as Johnny's new business was less than a year old. We felt impressed that I quit my business and trust the Lord's provision. The scripture came to us, *"Don't you see that children are GOD's best gift? The fruit of the womb, his generous legacy. Like a warrior's fistful of arrows are the children of a vigorous youth. Oh, how blessed are you parents, with your quivers full of children! Your* enemies don't stand a chance against you; you'll sweep them right off your doorstep." (Psalms127:3-5 MSG) We came to a decision that I stop my business on May 15, 1988, and passed on the business to Diane. The Lord blessed Johnny's business four times more the next month. Wow, He was always faithful.

Motherhood came to reality. I thought that I would never have children again after giving my baby up for adoption. We didn't have health insurance. I found out that the state was able to help us out. Everything was paid for. Dr. Kato was a good doctor monitoring everything.

In the fall of 1987, Johnny and I decided to go to Bible school at our church once a week for nine months. We had systematic Bible study throughout the year. It was a rewarding learning and growing time in the Lord. As the baby was growing in my womb, we sought the names for the baby, and Johnny recommended the name Tiffany ("Appearance of God"). We thought it was a girl. However, we looked for names for a boy just in case. Johnny liked the name Reuben meaning, "Behold son." I felt it was a boy. I was thrilled when the baby was active kicking in the womb. When I was listening in the Bible School, the baby was always kicking. I believed the baby enjoyed hearing, too. Johnny started reading the Book of John daily to him as the baby was growing inside of me.

Johnny and I took Lamaze class and learned to breathe to stay calm through the pain of laboring. Johnny wanted to witness the birth and also support me. We got excited as the time drew close. We did a lot of reading about what to expect and prepare for when the baby came. I preferred breastfeeding as it was a much healthier choice for the baby. Also, I didn't want any drugs administered to me while giving birth to avoid any complications or ill-effects on the baby. I bought the lighting system for a baby cry alert so I could see the light flashing when Johnny wasn't around. I was all set.

However, three weeks before the baby was due to be born, my blood pressure was really high, and the doctor's order was to lie down on the bed until the baby was born. I said, "No way!" He said if I objected to his order, he would put me in the hospital. I said, "No, I prefer to stay home and will lie down until the baby comes along." I didn't know what to do because Johnny had to work and couldn't take care of me all day. Some of my friends knew about it and said that they would bring me lunch. There were no schedules or appointments. I just prayed daily and trusted the Lord in whoever came over with lunch and company. Johnny was so good to me. He cooked breakfast and dinner and brought them to me in bed and did the house chores. We ate together on our bed. I was supposed to lie down flat strictly. You know it was difficult for a hyperactive person like me to stand still. Different people came over for lunch each day for three weeks, and they kept me company for a bit.

The Lord was so good to me. I read and prayed. During that time there were no cell phones, no video phones, or computers even the I-Pad. I had nothing but books, paper, pen and Bible. The TV was too big and heavy to be carried to the bedroom. Imagine that. In the final third week, I was nesting so I painted the front panel of the drawers for the baby dresser. I sat up painting the sheep and heart on top of a baby purple background. I violated the rule by sitting up instead of lying down flat even hearing the voice of the doctor's warning in my mind. I did that for two days before the baby was born.

That day Johnny took me to the doctor for a check-up, and I had an ultrasound. Johnny found out which gender the baby was. He said, "Sunny son!"

"Oh, we are going to have a boy! His name is going to be Reuben, right?" I asked.

"Yes!" said Johnny with excitement. twelve hours later at two in the morning, I woke up because my water broke and it was all over the bed. I rushed to the bathroom and I realized that the baby was coming. I woke Johnny and exclaimed, "The water broke. I need to go to the hospital now!" He stood up fast out of bed like lightning and made a phone call. It was a go-ahead for us to go to the hospital at Valley Medical Center in Renton. When I got there, I was told that my blood pressure was really high. I was given IV to cause the contractions since the bag of water broke, and I didn't have any contractions starting yet. Slowly, I had contractions and I was not dilating.

About 9:00 A.M., Dr. Kato expressed his concern that if my blood pressure kept going up, it would cause seizures. He had to look at my feet to check for the signs of seizures. He gave me medication in an IV to keep the blood pressure down, but it didn't help. Johnny and I prayed for all to go smoothly. I had a private conversation with the Lord and I asked, "Lord, I want to have this baby by noon so I can have lunch. I am hungry! Thank you!" I had a wonderful labor nurse who was a Godsend. We communicated well and she was easy to lip read. The blood pressure was pretty high but was stabilized. Dr. Kato warned me if there was no dilating by noon, he was to perform a C-section.

Still, I wasn't dilating at all. Dr. Kato said that the baby wasn't moving down to the crown and it was still too high. I cried out to the Lord for a miracle. At about 11:30 A.M., the nurse checked to see if I was dilating--not a bit. So she said I needed to turn over on my side. After ten minutes, I told the nurse I felt like pushing. She checked to see if I was dilating; I was at number ten. I was dilated to 10 centimeters in ten minutes. I had to go to the birthing room immediately. Dr. Kato was having a lunch break upstairs, and he was called down immediately. I turned to lie on my back. I wanted to push. The nurse said to hold until Dr. Kato showed up. "Hey, where is he?" I yelled. Finally, he showed up on time. He caught the baby in his arms like a football. He wasn't properly covered as he didn't have time. Reuben cried out loud and was wide awake and alert. He looked right at me. I said," Reuben, welcome here!" He was perfectly healthy and he was red. It struck noon, and it was lunch time. WHOA, what an amazing God we serve. He was faithful to see me through. Dr. Kato was baffled, but he knew that it was the Lord's doing.

I had to stay in the hospital about four days for the blood pressure to come down. I was very exhausted because of high blood pressure. It had to do with hormone changes that affected the fluctuation of blood pressure. No visitors were allowed for the first three days because I couldn't handle stress very well-- just Johnny. His parents came for a short visit.

When I finished reading the Book of Joshua, I was praying for the middle name for Reuben. It came as Joshua. So I asked Johnny what he thought about it. He agreed. It meant salvation. His name was Reuben Joshua Dunnington. Wow, what a sunny son. I thanked the Lord for our healthy, hearing son. It was like a dream come true.

The nurse who taught me how to nurse Reuben was a Filipino

from Mindanao. She was there for me and she was very patient. She was so sweet. How little did we know that four years later we were to be missionaries to the Philippines! The first two days, I was having a tough time nursing Reuben. I was learning, and he was developing his sucking. After that, it went well. I didn't have high blood pressure again after I walked out of the hospital.

Johnny brought us home, and we saw the banner and balloons, "It's a BOY! Praise the Lord! Welcome home, Veronica and Reuben Joshua!" on the front porch. It warmed my heart and I saw His blessings coming and coming. That very night, I put Reuben on my lap while lying on the bed. Johnny finished the last few verses in the Book of John to read to Reuben. When Johnny mentioned Jesus from the scripture, Reuben smiled broadly. It happened again each time for the third time. Wow, I knew that Reuben listened to his dad reading the Book of John for the whole time of my pregnancy. The Word of the Lord gives life.

Chapter 16

New Life Begins

It was a challenge waking up all night for the first few weeks. Johnny would tap my shoulder and point his finger toward the crib when Reuben woke up crying. I breast fed Reuben often and he seemed to be hungry every two hours. I remembered the nurse told me that it was normal in the first month because of growing spurts. On the tenth day, Reuben kept waking up all night crying for milk or a change of diapers. Finally, when he was up crying, I picked him up and looked at him, "Hey, you go to sleep now!" with my upset and firm tone. He went right to sleep for the rest of the night. It was the last time I "yelled" at him. I realized Reuben was sensitive and understood what I meant. I was surprised and realized that I was lacking in patience which the Lord showed me.

My friends hosted a baby shower for Reuben when he was a month old. I was so happy to have a son, and I lifted him high to show everyone, even before The Lion King movie. It was a miracle that all went well when giving birth and I had longed to have a child after the adoption, another miracle indeed.

Johnny and I wanted to dedicate Reuben to the Lord. So we invited Johnny's parents to be part of it. Reuben got a beautiful outfit from his grandparents; however, he was screaming and crying throughout the dedication because he was hot. In prayer, we asked the Lord to give us wisdom to raise him in a Godly way.

Train up a child in the way he should go, even when he is old he will not depart from it.

(Proverbs 22:6 NASB)

Reuben our first born

I still continued going to Bible school with Johnny, and I took Reuben with me. He seemed content every time I went there. One day, Rick prophesied, "I see the Lord is calling Reuben to be a prophet!" Reuben was content listening to the Lord's Word for six months plus the pregnancy term.

I used the flasher when Johnny wasn't around. When I put Reuben down for a nap, I turned it on. Almost every day, he cried out loud. I had to tend to him figuring out what he wanted. He didn't want to go to sleep as he was always hungry. He was getting older. I felt that he wanted more security than milk, so I just let him cry himself to sleep. The flasher drove me crazy. I unplugged it for a few minutes then plugged it back in. If the flasher continued, I just unplugged it until he quieted down. Then I plugged it in and if the flasher wasn't flashing, I quietly checked on him in the room. He was sound asleep. Whew, I needed that break to catch up with the chores around the house and prepare dinner for Johnny.

One time when Reuben was three months old, he was

screaming in pain. I figured it was one of his colic attacks. He often got them. I tried to relieve the pain by moving his legs, rocking him and leaning his stomach on my arms. It got worse and he kept on screaming, I prayed and Johnny prayed. It seemed hopeless. He continued screaming for about two hours straight. Rick came over, hearing his screams across the street where he lived. He asked what was wrong, and he said that people down the street could hear Reuben thinking it was child abuse. Yeah, right. Rick prayed with us for the pain to stop. Eventually, it did. I had to avoid gassy veggies. I was emotionally worn out and cried out to the Lord for His grace.

For the first four months, friends and family were delighted to meet Reuben and wanted to hold him. He often spit up. One time, our friend came over with her fancy clothes and she wanted to hold him. He spit up a whole meal of milk, and it was all over her pretty blouse. How embarrassing. It was part of motherhood that I had to deal with. It was a blessing, and I learned to let go that it wasn't always pleasant.

In April 1988, after many prayers, Johnny went to the Philippines with a team from our church. Reuben was four months old, and I had perfect peace for Johnny to go for two weeks. I was excited for him and had the other wives join me for prayers for the team while they were overseas. One Sunday, I noticed that I only had $10.00 left and I felt impressed to give all to the offering at the church service. I trusted the Lord and the same day about 1:00 P.M., Rick came over and handed me over $100.00 and said, "the Lord bless you." I stood there in awe and thanked the Lord. I used the money to buy food. How timely.

At the age of six months, Reuben learned to sign milk. When

he wanted milk, there he went. I breast fed him until he weaned at nine and a half months old. I guess my milk wasn't that great or he was eager to eat. When he was seven months old, he wanted to eat everything even two bowls of oatmeal for breakfast and a bowlful of spaghetti. He swallowed the whole thing. It was a scary time. He seemed to be hungry all the time. One morning he wanted more oatmeal (adult oatmeal). I hesitated but gave it to him, and he ate the whole second bowl of it. He wanted more. I said that he had more than enough. He signed more and more. His belly popped out and it was twice as big. I talked with Johnny about the problem Reuben was having. That same evening we had Rick and Joy along with two of their kids over for dinner. I made sure that Reuben was full from dinner before they came. When we were ready to eat, Reuben was screaming wanting more food. Johnny and I were dumbfounded not knowing what to say or do. Rick felt that Reuben had a spirit of lust for food or a gluttonous spirit. We agreed. After putting Reuben down for bedtime, we had a long talk, and Rick asked who might have had the same problem in the past. I said I had a problem with eating so we decided to pray to ask the Lord to deliver me from that spirit of lust and gluttony for food. We then prayed for Reuben. All of sudden, Reuben was screaming out of his sleep and Johnny fetched him and brought him to us in the living room where we were talking. We prayed for Reuben to be set free from that spirit, and he went back to sleep with no problem. The very next morning, Johnny and I looked at Reuben very closely waiting for him to eat a big bowl of oatmeal. He just pushed the oatmeal away. We were stunned knowing that he was set free indeed. He never again ate a second bowl of oatmeal. He ate only half of his first bowl of oatmeal. He now had a normal appetite for a seven-month-old. Whew. Praise Him. He is our deliverer. An awesome God we serve.

Amazing things happened with our fish aquarium. It was filled with all kinds of fish like bubble eye and guppy. Reuben loved it, and there was a shelf beneath the aquarium holding fish food and other supplies. He was standing there touching the stuff. I told him not to touch it. He looked at me and Johnny with an innocent look on his face while his arm searched for stuff trying to touch it. It was like, "I am not touching things. My arm is."

I again said, "No."

Reuben said, "Yes!" with his hand sign. We were surprised and off guard. We tried to hide our laughs as it was so funny. I said, "No," again and picked him up. He knew what we were talking about, and he chose not to obey.

Wow, he was smarter than I thought. He learned at least 20 signs from that age of six months like milk, cracker, no, yes, mom, dad, more, please, and thank you. He also learned to read my signs whenever I communicated with him.

In May of 1988, Johnny and I graduated from the Bible school and celebrated. I felt that I had grown in a year. I learned to show the love of Jesus with my actions and I learned to be more tactful. I couldn't be so blunt with my words. What I learned the most was to put our gifts to practice, stay humble and be teachable. I thanked Rick and many other speakers who came to take their time to teach.

Chapter 17

Surprise!

Leah asked Johnny and me to house sit their house in Bellingham, Washington, for a month in June 1988. One evening I was steaming broccoli, my favorite vegetable. I gagged and went out of the house as I couldn't stand the smell. I suspected something was going on so I went out to buy a pregnancy test kit. It came out positive and I broke the news to Johnny. We knew it was a girl because the Lord already gave him the name of Tiffany when Reuben was conceived. Tiffany means the appearance of God. So we shared the news with our friends at Lummi Island that was close to Bellingham. We were excited and Reuben was trying to catch the excitement that he would have a sister/brother soon.

Shortly after, we decided to break away for a short vacation to eastern Washington routing from Bellingham. We camped out on our way and we stopped at Sun Lakes then headed to visit Johnny's Grandma Eula and his Aunt Ina. They enjoyed Reuben and our company.

In the fall of 1988, we flew to my parents' house as they had not met Reuben yet. Reuben was anxious to meet his other grandparents. It was sad that we lived so far from them. It was always a cherished time with them. I was five months pregnant at the time. Boy, I was really big. I was full of energy compared to how I felt with Reuben. I used to take three-hour naps every day but with Tiffany, I never took a nap once. However, I was much bigger with Tiffany than with Reuben. The very last trimester I didn't sleep well as I kept tossing over so I went to sleep on a beanbag chair. I would go back and forth to bed trying to get comfortable.

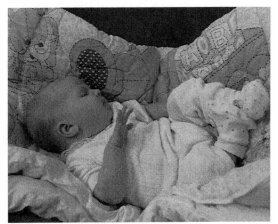

Tiffany our second born

I was redirected to Overlake Hospital. Again, the Lord provided everything for the doctor and hospital bills. When I was referred to my new doctor, Dr. Gary Rogers, I was cautious which doctor to pick. I had inquired of his belief or practice with abortions and his answer was no. I felt peace about it and went ahead and accepted him as my doctor. It didn't make sense for a doctor to take away life and add new life if I chose that kind of doctor. I had my own conviction against abortion.

During my pregnancy with Tiffany, I didn't have any problems like high blood pressure which I was thankful for. I recalled having contractions around 9:00 A.M. and went to church anyway as they were about ten minutes apart. After lunch, we called the hospital and they said to wait it out. About 5:00 P.M., the contractions were getting closer and I was admitted to Overlake. I walked around using my breathing method and around 7 P.M. I laid down as it was intense. I really wanted to bite Johnny and he took turns with Regina, a friend from church when he wanted a break. I was dilating but the bag of water didn't break yet. The doctor said if I wanted to have the baby right away, he could help break the water. Right after he broke the bag, I felt the contractions coming on strong a minute apart. It was so painful that I wanted to scream. That's why I felt like biting. It was a good thing that I didn't bite anyone and in about 30 minutes Tiffany came. She came too fast and her head and face really hit my pelvic bone and it bruised her face. Otherwise, she was healthy. Tiffany Veronica Dunnington was born Jan. 28, 1990, at 10 P.M. She was big at 9 pounds and 10 ounces. Another blessing from the Lord.

Before Tiffany was born, Johnny and I had been looking for a bigger place to live, like a two-bedroom home, and we had searched for a long time for it. One day we found an ad that there was a two-bedroom duplex up the hill from where we lived. We met the landlord at the house, and she showed us around. When she first led us to the house, I cried and knew it was home for us. It was a very nice, comfortable and newer home than where we lived. We were due to move in a few days after Tiffany was born. Our friends from church helped us move, and the ladies made me sit down and did all the unpacking and organized everything. Wow, I was not used to being pampered in this way. Bless them.

I had a different kind of problem with Tiffany. All she wanted was sleep. I had to tickle her feet or rub her neck to wake her so I could feed her. The milk was so full and it really hurt and it was a struggle waking her up. She fell asleep while sucking, and I kept waking her up. "Come on, Tiffany, you need milk to grow." She slept through the night, so opposite from Reuben. It was a blessing to be able to sleep through the night. That went on for three months before she finally was awake more than she slept. She started signing "milk" at the age of eight months and she learned the rest of the signs like Reuben learned.

Reuben liked the new addition to our family; however, I had to teach him to share everything with her. It was a challenge to change two diapers at the same time. When they were 13 months apart and both crying and screaming while I changed their diapers, I told them to stop crying and pointed my signing "no." I prayed for energy to keep up with them as they were a handful.

A miracle happened one day. I took my wedding ring off as I was kneading bread. I lost track of where I put it. I looked everywhere and even Johnny helped me look for it. Nothing. I kept looking in every corner, dresser, shelf, every area of the duplex. No avail. I lost it. No, I told myself. I cried out to the Lord as it was a special, custom-made wedding ring that Johnny had engraved, "I love you, Sweetheart. Johnny 1987." It had been almost a month since I lost the ring. One day, while I was making the bed, there was my ring. I had washed the sheets every week and made the bed daily. I knew the angel of the Lord brought it back to me. I was jumping with overflowing joy. I couldn't wait to break the wonderful news to Johnny when he came home from work. When I told him the amazing news, he was overjoyed. Wow, God did care for our little things. It helped build my faith, for with God, nothing is impossible.

Jesus looked at them and said, 'For people this is impossible, but for God all things are possible.'

(Matthew 19:26 NCV)

Chapter 18

Raising Children in the Ways of the Lord

I read Dr. Dobson's book about how to discipline the strong-willed children with tough love. One day, I had a battle with Reuben when he was one and a half years old. He pressed to test my authority. I put him down for a nap on our bed because I didn't want him and Tiffany to play so I kept them separated. He got out of the room to the living room. I told Reuben to go back to lie down for a nap. He shook his head saying no. I had to discipline him by spanking him with a wooden spoon. He cried and went to lie down and a few minutes later, he came out of the room again like nothing had happened. I told him to go back to the bedroom. He simply ignored me trotting away. I had to lead him back to the room and the cycle kept repeating. Oh boy, he was strongwilled. It went on for an hour. I told myself not to give in until he surrendered. He knew I meant business. I asked the Lord for His grace and wisdom and shared with Johnny. He was well pleased. Sometimes I cried because it was so hard to be consistent. Johnny took over when he came home from work and helped lighten my burden. We shared the responsibility to discipline them.

Whenever I took them out grocery shopping, they were ready to misbehave while sitting together in the cart. I pulled the wooden spoon out of my purse to show to them as a warning. They stood up behaving right away. It was so cute watching their eyes looking at me as I had a serious face.

Foolishness is bound up in the heart of a child;
the rod of discipline will remove it far from him.

(Proverbs 22:15 NASB)

I always enjoyed cooking healthy food for Reuben and Tiffany. I recall a cute episode with them. I sat down with them eating lunch. I made sure that they ate well with both of their eyes looking at each other and looking at me to check that I was watching them finish eating. They knew that they couldn't get away with skipping food. I avoided giving them candies so I gave them fruits to satisfy their sweet tooth. Sometimes I gave them healthy cookies or sweets.

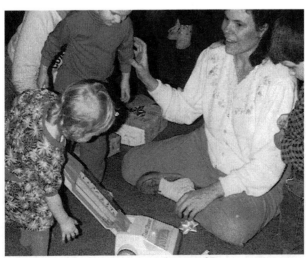

Reuben, Tiffany, and I

Tiffany didn't cry throughout her childhood, the opposite of Reuben. He was always screaming and shrieking loudly and had been dealt with a lot. Tiffany was quiet and was sly. One time I was wondering where Tiffany went as it was quiet. I knew she was in trouble. I looked for her and she was in the bathroom eating the toothpaste. I said, "Oh no. It is not food." I asked her, "Do you like it?" Her eyes were looking right at mine and she nodded yes humbly.

Whenever I was upset with them, I signed to them fast with no voice. They understood and stood quietly.

Johnny and I had so much fun with them, laughing and playing with them. We took them to parks for hiking and camping. Of course, we carried them in baby bags or Reuben on his dad's shoulders. We also took them to restaurants. We always received nice comments on how well-behaved they were. They learned to communicate what they needed or asked for permission.

We taught them the importance of showing respect to their parents as well as others. It was so important to train and discipline the children because they felt secure and loved.

> *My dear child, don't shrug off God's discipline,*
> *but don't be crushed by it either. It's the child He*
> *loves that He disciplines; the child He embraces,*
> *He also corrects.*

(Hebrew 12:6 The Message)

Ever since Reuben was two and Tiffany was one, Johnny sat down with them reading the children's Bible with them every night before their bedtime. If he wasn't able to do that, I took over. We faithfully read to them until they were ready to read on their own. Also, we prayed with them after reading the bible. I recalled one early evening Johnny had his side-job customer coming over to our home to pick up her VCR that had been repaired. While she was sitting and waiting, Reuben took his children's Bible and plopped it on her lap and boldly said to her, "Read the Bible!" She was pretty taken aback. It was funny to watch how innocent our child could be.

One Sunday, our family came home from church and had lunch. Johnny and I felt sleepy and Reuben wanted to color. I set him on his high chair and gave him all the crayons and a few coloring books to keep him busy for a bit. Johnny and I were lying in the bean bag getting cozy, and Tiffany was sleeping in the car seat beside us. We could see Reuben coloring. Once we closed our eyes, we were off to dream world. When we woke up, we were frantically worried that we left Reuben alone for so long. We went to Reuben to see how he was doing. He colored very detailed and finished by the time we woke up as it was two hours later. Wow, I felt guilty but he was totally consumed with the coloring world. I knew the angels of the Lord surrounded us with perfect peace.

When Reuben was three, he wanted to learn everything that he

Our family day

put his hands on. I bought preschool books, and he wanted to go through the lessons all at once. I was very frustrated because he didn't know when to stop. I told him that he needed a break, and we worked on a little bit every day. He was like a sponge wanting to learn about everything.

It was a challenge to sit down with him and work with him. I preferred to do something else like cooking, baking, or crafting but it was only short-lived because the babies grow up so fast. I didn't want to miss that. I had to crucify my desires and invest in my children's lives so their lives would be rich. They even helped me make bread, and they made their own dough and put it in the oven. They enjoyed their creations. Raising my children was my joy. We had so much fun watching them learn to sign, talk, walk, and make silly mistakes.

Reuben had a playmate from next door named Daniel. He was two years older and pretty unruly because he had a rough life growing up with his mom and her boyfriend. He had a babysitter taking care of him while his mom went to work. Reuben was always playing as David throwing the rocks at Goliath and waved a stick as a sword. He constantly talked about the Bible characters with Daniel. I always had my eyes on them, since I could not hear them so I had to keep on checking on them. One day, I saw Daniel kicking Reuben's privates and hurting him. Out of my instinct, I went out and spanked Daniel. He went home crying. I thought to myself, "Oh no, I don't want to get in trouble with the law." Then I prayed for ten minutes pleading for the Lord's grace and favor. Daniel's mom Debbie came over knocking at our door as I expected. She made an accusation that I beat up her son. I explained that he was pretty rough on Reuben. I was trying to discipline him but I apologized to her. She forgave me. We had a peace with each other. A few months later, Debbie came to me and thanked me for being a good example to her and to her son. She decided to follow God, and Daniel encouraged her to do so as well. They wanted to go to church. I was amazed and I knew that Reuben planted a lot of seeds in Daniel. Also, he set an example by loving him. She mentioned that she decided to break up with her boyfriend and move back to Alaska where she was from. That was awesome and I knew the Lord worked in mysterious ways.

> *You are the God Who does wonders; You have demonstrated Your power among the peoples.*

(Psalm 77:14 AMP)

Chapter 19

Finding the Lord's Calling

During the first year of our marriage, Johnny and I had a burning desire to go on a mission field. There was an opportunity for mission work in India, so we lifted it up in prayer. It turned out that it was not the Lord's will for us to go. About three years later in April 1989, Johnny joined the mission team from our church to go to the Philippines for two weeks. Our church had been supporting the Pastor of Faith Tabernacle in Cebu City for a few years. So they went to Cebu City and the Pastor sent them over to Bohol for a week.

Jody was the main speaker for a revival, but one day his voice went out. So Johnny took over and preached to the town of Valencia and about 90 came forward and got saved. The church was born there. Pastor Bong wanted Johnny to come back to Bohol to finish the work that he started. Johnny felt that was where the Lord was calling us to do mission work. When Johnny came back here and shared the testimony, we lifted it up to the Lord and waited for His timing to move to Bohol, Philippines.

In July of 1992, Johnny felt unrest in his spirit and shared with me. We prayed and it came that the Lord wanted Johnny to stop working and sell everything we had. We wanted to see my parents before we moved to the Philippines. We didn't know when we were to see them again. We had peace letting everything go except some things. We asked Reuben and Tiffany if they wanted to let go of their toys through a garage sale. They said that they were okay with that. They were darling and we were the ones who needed to be teachable like children. Everything was sold in two days. Then we stayed at Johnny's parents' for a couple of days to get ready for our long trip. We didn't know how long we were supposed to be traveling. We wanted to follow the voice of the Lord who led the way.

Before we were ready to drive to Pennsylvania where my parents live, we heard there was a Christian family camp where Harold Eberle was the main speaker in McCall, Idaho. We camped out there for a few days with Rick and Joy and their two kids, Anna and John. During the first meeting, when we went in listening to Harold, Johnny interpreted for me in the back of the congregation. Then he called our names to come up in front.

Reuben and Tiffany on tour around the country

We didn't know why. He also called men of faith to come forward to form a prayer canopy over us. All of a sudden, a lady came out of the blue to interpret for me out front.

Timothy Sherman prophesied over us saying that it was not just the sending of a missionary, but this was the developing of an apostolic man to the nation. We were amazed that the Lord would take foolish ones like us and raise us up to be mighty in Him and cause us to have His grace and ability. He would open our eyes to see and ears to hear. There was networking and work going on in the United States in which people would come over and help build churches, bring money and materials and provide necessities. We would not be going to lack any good. We were stunned and we were in awe when that man didn't know who we were and said many things about us that were right on. We didn't even know Timothy; however, we knew that the Lord was speaking through him to confirm to us that we were walking the path the Lord had prepared for us.

After the camp meeting was over, we continued traveling up to Glacier National Park in Montana then down near Missoula where the hot springs pool and cabins were. It was blissful soaking in the hot tub and warm pool. The night sky was absolutely amazing. We saw millions of stars as we sat in the country throwing pine cones into a small bonfire. It was incredibly beautiful. I saw the Lord's creation through that. We were there for two nights and continued to Bozeman to see my cousin Greg who lived there. We called and learned that Greg was out of town working, but we met his wife and went out for ice cream.

We found a run-down motel, so we stayed there for a couple of days. We went fishing nearby and caught many trout to cook for dinner. I bought some veggies and food and cooked outside of the room as we had camping equipment. We only had the cash from the garage sale and one paycheck to live on. We just trusted the Lord on the way.

We went to see Mount Rushmore. Finally, we arrived in Minnesota to see friends there and we stayed for a couple of days. We continued traveling eastward to visit my brother Jim and his family for a week. I loved hanging out with him as he was a great storyteller. For a long time, I had been praying for him to meet Jesus, even though I thought he was to be the last one to get born again. To make the story short, back in 1986, Ben went with me to visit my parents at a family reunion. During the day, we were having a family meeting to discuss our parents' will and desire not to be sent to a nursing home in the near future if anything happened to them. After that, Jim came to me and said, "Hey, you always talk about Jesus, Jesus, Jesus. What if I talk about golf, golf, golf?" mocking me. I just laughed because he was so funny.

Sometime after Tiffany was born, he called me at home through the voice-relay service wanting to apologize to me for how he treated me, and he was delighted to share that he now had a personal relationship with Jesus. I was blown away. The Lord was always faithful hearing our prayers.

> *They said to him, 'Believe in the Lord Jesus and you will be saved—you and all the people in your house.'*

> (Acts 16:31 NCV)

We were visiting Jim and Shelley's church, and Jim introduced us to the pastor and his wife. Johnny had interpreted the whole service. After the service, the pastor and his wife wanted to see us in their office. His wife gave me a beautiful gold nugget with a diamond and ruby ring, saying, "Father in heaven wants me to give this to you." I was speechless and didn't want to receive it because I felt unworthy. I was reminded through the Holy Spirit what the lady quoted from scripture to me at the family camp meeting. *Enlarge the place of your tent, and let the curtains of your habitations be stretched out; do not hold back; lengthen your cords and strengthen your stakes.* (Isaiah 54:2 ESV) I realized that if I didn't start stretching myself, I would not be able to receive anything from the Lord. I had to accept whatever He had for me. The ring has been a great reminder ever since.

While traveling eastward towards my parents', we reached Ohio. We were hungry and tired and decided to stop at a church that we had never heard of to attend Wednesday service. The pastor happened to be there and we got acquainted. There was no service that night so the pastor took us out and treated us to dinner and paid the motel bill for one night. Wow, it was the Lord's favor and He took care of us.

We were overjoyed knowing that the Lord was just amazing, and we all were jumping on the bed in the motel. The next day we drove all the way to visit my parents. We had a long visit with them as they had never met Tiffany.

Little did we know, God had much greater plans for us. We immediately found ourselves as arrows being shot forth from the hands of a mighty warrior, the Lord God, to bring deliverance to God's people and destruction to the camp of the enemy.

While in Maine, a deaf guy had been seeking the baptism of the Holy Spirit for five years and after being delivered from the occult and having a few scriptures explained to him, Jesus gloriously baptized him and he began a new language. We all joined in and praised God until 1:00 A.M. It was indeed an unspeakable joy.

In Virginia, a deaf lady who was just saved, was delivered from a spirit of necromancy (communicating with the dead) and then was beautifully baptized in the Holy Spirit.

At one point on our way home westward, going through Iowa, in the middle of a cornfield we had a tire "blowout" and after we prayed, the Lord led us less than ten miles to a little town where we were able to buy two new tires. This left us with only two dollars and still 1,800 miles to home. But God again showed Himself strong and carried us in His arms to Iowa where our friends lived. The Lord touched the hearts of some people who gave us enough money to make it home.

As we were on the road for three and a half months involved in people's lives and building the House of the Lord, we saw each day how God had gone before us and prepared the way providing for our daily needs. We always had a place to stay, whether in our tent, a hotel room or in someone's home. This trip helped to build our faith and prepare us for the Philippines.

Johnny with the little ones at Mt. Rushmore Park

Chapter 20

Preparation for Missionary Work

After a long journey across America, we stayed in Johnny's parent's house in a small basement apartment for a few months. Johnny met Fritz who invited us to go on a boat from Seattle to the Philippines. He had been fixing up the boat which took him and the team a year to finish. Fritz asked Johnny if he could volunteer to be involved in the food ministry of gleaning the food and things from about ten grocery stores once every week. It was unbelievable how much produce, meat, fruits and vegetables, bread and dairy products were thrown out. So we looked through it and got what we needed. Johnny took the rest to our unemployed church members, food banks, unemployed or disabled or those serving the Lord in full-time ministry. It was a great blessing.

God provided many refreshing times during our preparations to go. We had family time in Whidbey Island seeking God's will for us. Then the Lord spoke to me, *"Cease striving and know that I am God."* Isaiah 42:10. I saw that He was in complete control and that He wanted me to let Him be God. I had learned to rest and trust in Him, trusting and relying completely on Him. Listening to a brother in Christ who was visiting from the Philippines and sharing his powerful testimony, I felt my heart burning with fire. God encouraged us in so many ways since we serve Him in every way. We were especially encouraged when we received a prophecy at the last conference. "There is delay, but you will go." Then there was something about living conditions and fresh air. We sought the Lord, and it came to us that we were to live in Mabton, a small town about 45 minutes east of Yakima in Washington. We stayed at Johnny's deceased grandparents' house until August 1993. We were asked to help sell that home. So we lived there from March until August. It was indeed a breath of fresh air and a place in which we got many great visitations from the Lord. We attended at least three conferences where the Lord confirmed again and again that we were at the center of His will for us and that it was His timing for us to go.

While staying in Mabton, the Lord provided film-showing equipment for the Philippines. However, the Lord opened the doors to have a three-day crusade in Central Park in a small town with a population that was 90% Mexican, and 85% spoke no English. We showed the film of Jesus and shared the Gospel. We felt as though we were in a foreign field. God certainly prepared us for our future ministry for Him overseas. It was a direct result of our decision and commitment in July 1992 to leave all and serve Him.

We built relationships with our neighbor Vince and his girlfriend Gail in their late 50s. They always invited us over for Mexican food as their family gathered. They were there ready to help us and wanted us to be part of their lives. They had a little farm where Reuben and Tiffany loved hanging out with the goats, chickens, rabbits and cats. At the same time, we wanted to reach out to them, too. One day they talked about how they kept putting off getting married. Johnny offered his service to wed them. They got so excited and Johnny shared the gospel with them. They were more than happy to hear that God loved them. Johnny called Rick to help out with the marriage license. A couple of months later, Johnny and Rick together performed Vince and Gail's wedding outside under a tree with a few witnesses of family and friends as well as neighbors. It was a simple wedding with an authentic Mexican cookout. I never forgot how precious they were.

I always had a desire to reach out to the lost. One day I got acquainted with our neighbor Vince's daughter who was in her early 20s. She was telling me how she lost her precious wedding ring. I asked if it was okay if I prayed with her to ask the Lord to bring back the lost ring. She said, "Yes!" About a week or so later, she came to me exclaiming that the Lord answered her prayer.

Just a few months before the departure, the board members of INCOR felt it was not safe for our children to go on a boat that went all the way to the Philippines. So it left us no choice but to fly. We lifted it up to the Lord because we needed the money for the flight tickets. He met our needs so we booked a month before the departure for the Philippines. We packed the boat with 39 boxes of our household and personal items. We had seen what God did in our lives during the last four years as He had been preparing us for the mission field. The Holy Spirit has built line upon line, a little here and a little there in every area of our lives.

I Can Only Hear God

Chapter 21

The Philippines, Finally!

On Sept. 1, 1993, our first flight out of America to the Philippines through Korea was full of excitement. We only had $500.00 in our pockets with no support yet. We wanted to obey the Lord to go even though we didn't have the budget. We went out in faith trusting the Lord like we did when traveling around in America. The people from the Baptist Church picked us up at the airport. Fritz contacted us about us staying at the Baptist mission house for a week. We tried to make a connection with the church to make arrangements to pick up the boxes that were shipped on the boat Fritz navigated from the States.

We developed a network in Manila. I got really sick from infected tonsils caused by the bad pollution in that city. I got medical attention, and it took a few days to recover. It was scary because I never had it before.

I was learning the Filipino culture, gestures and different foods especially dried fish. Even though they spoke English, I couldn't understand them because their accent affected my lip reading. I was so looking forward to arriving at our final destination of Bohol. Pastor Bong from Bohol brought us to Bohol. We rode in a slow boat that had bunk beds everywhere that held at least 200 people.

It took four hours. By the time we got there, Johnny told me to stay on the boat with Reuben and Tiffany because Pastor Bong was showing him a few houses that he could pick from for us to live. Once they left, all the Filipinos came on the boat and surrounded us. I was scared inside. I thought, "What do they want? Our 12 suitcases or do they want to kidnap my children?" They were watching us and staring at us. I thought it was really strange. Reuben and Tiffany said to me, "Mommy, why are they looking at us?" I told them I had no idea. I tried to get their minds off of them. A young Filipino guy came to me asking me questions like what I was doing here. I had to look out for my children the whole time. I was agitated and upset with Johnny for leaving us on the boat. I wanted to get off the boat and get away from those staring people.

Two hours later, Johnny finally showed up and I told him that I didn't like the way he left us alone for so long. He just smiled. The guys helped us carry 12 bags out of the boat and put them on a wooden cart like Jesus' time. The Filipino guy with shabby clothes who needed dental work smiled and pulled the cart back, and its wooden wheel ran over my big toe. I screamed with pain and he pushed back the cart. I jumped around holding my pained foot. Johnny said, "Welcome to Bohol."

GRRR, I thought to myself, "I want to go home to America!" I was looking for a taxi or some kind of fancy transportation, but I saw a tricycle instead. I thought to myself, "This must be some kind of a joke!" I said to Johnny, "Remember that we have 12 suitcases that won't fit on that small thing." Johnny said not to worry. The suitcases were placed on top of a small canopy over the motorcycle and in the back in a slot. Everything was tied around with a plastic rope. There were five adults and two children fitting onto the

Our first transportation in Bohol, Philippines

small tricycle. I thought it was insane. Inside, I was furious.

As we were riding towards the house, right in the heart of Tagbilaran City, we stopped at the house. The very first thing I saw was a huge, six-inch spider hanging on the wall of the house. I was freaking out and thought to myself that I refused to live in the house where that big spider dwelled. As we went upstairs to the deck, I saw a family moving their furniture. I asked Johnny what they were doing. Johnny said that they wanted to move downstairs so we could live upstairs. It was becoming too much, actually a reality of culture shock. As it was getting dark and I was hungry and tired, I unexpectedly burst into tears. I cried out to the Lord, "I expect a miracle tonight!" Johnny comforted me and asked me what was wrong. I said that I didn't want to live there because there was no backyard for the kids to play. I didn't want the kids to play in the street since it was in the city. Johnny said it was okay and we should leave the suitcases behind so we could continue looking at two other homes. We went to see the second place that was an apartment. No way. I was ready to give up. We went back to riding in the cramped tricycle to another place; however, Johnny saw something and told the driver to stop and turn around. I asked him what was going on. He said to hold on as he climbed out of the tricycle and went through the gate. I was waiting with the kids, wondering. Johnny came out with a big smile. I thought that was strange. He said come on out and get inside of the building. There I saw a line of deaf children signing, "Hi." I cried that time with joy. I met the teachers for the deaf and older deaf teenagers. Pastor Bong brought Johnny to meet the director of the deaf foundation (IDEA: International deaf Education Association) at the Garden Cafe restaurant.

Johnny came back to get us to take us to the Garden Cafe to meet Dennis and eat dinner there. I was famished and ate heartily. Dennis invited us to stay with him and his family until we could find a place to live. He had two sons almost the same ages as Reuben and Tiffany. Dennis knew ASL but used Filipino sign language. It was a challenging week and it was like a breath of fresh air to be able to communicate. Dennis explained that in their culture people were full of curiosity and liked to stare because we were white, just like white monkeys. Oh, that explained it. In three days with the Lord's grace, we found a nice 3 bedroom/2 bath, furnished house with marble floors. The only furniture that was lacking was a bed. It only cost $60.00 a month to rent. The landlord and family lived on the compound, and they owned a small store. We only had $200.00 left in our pockets.

A month later, I found out the situation we were in when we were eating our last lunch. I asked Johnny if he had money left because I didn't have any more food left in the kitchen. He said, "No." I could go without food for a while but I didn't want our children to starve. So we held hands and prayed, "Thank you for everything. Although we don't have any food left to eat, we believe and trust You that You will bring food for our next meal."

Johnny left for a pastors' gathering after lunch. Then he came home around 3:00 P.M. and told me that he met some nice pastors. About 4:00 P.M., there was a knock at the door. Johnny asked me to get it. A Filipino couple with two bags full of food from the market said, "Welcome to Bohol. Lord bless you!" I was surprised and not expecting it. Wow, all thanks to HIM, a miracle indeed. It happened again and again in different ways.

Every single day for six months, I cried going through very difficult times having to deal with the frustration of communication, culture shock, isolation, and making adjustments. We had no washing machine or any other modern conveniences. I had to wash all the clothes, and my hands became raw and bled. I set up a routine for settling down in this third world country where I had no understanding of their foreign language or its culture. I was finding my home a safe haven since every time I went out, I met a challenge.

One time the tricycle driver said that I had to pay him 30 pesos when it only cost five pesos. He was trying to take advantage of me because I was an American. When I went grocery shopping, I realized that I had to get in line aggressively and stay close to people before paying the cashier. Otherwise, all the people would cut in front of me because I had given so much space in between. It took forever to go shopping. I decided to make the most of my time by wising up. I went food shopping at the grocery store early in the morning. The open-air market was my favorite place to shop. The market vendors knew I was deaf, and they were kind to me and always gave me a favor.

The only obstacle was that of communication because their English was their second language and my speech and lip reading were hard to understand. I felt isolated at times, but I was asked to teach signing class and Bible study class to the deaf. The friendship I had with Pastor Bong's wife made the difference. God spoke to me to press on and stretch myself which allowed Him to build Godly character in me. God's thoughts and ways were much higher than mine. The letters from friends and family encouraged us so much.

Our first monkey pet Chimpy

Like cold water to a weary soul, so is good news from a distant land.

(Proverbs 25:25 NASB)

Chapter 22

The Beginning of the Ministry

The very first seminar for pastors' leadership was held at our house for two days and one overnight. We were so caught up preparing for that event that we spent our last cent to provide the food for about 50 people who came. We had a cookout in the back yard. Fifty people were sleeping in all of the rooms of the house like sardines. Many of them refused to go to the bathroom or take a bath because they felt unworthy so they did so outside. I told them to use the bathroom but they didn't budge. I was so upset then I realized that I was dealing with culture shock. Some of them from the mountains didn't understand the modern conveniences, and they felt unworthy to be in a white man's house because of social standing.

After the seminar was over, I realized that we actually forgot that Reuben's fifth birthday was coming up in a few days. We didn't have any money to buy him a birthday gift. Johnny and I prayed for the Lord's wisdom and provision. I felt bad that we had forgotten about Reuben's birthday. When his day came, I told Johnny that I was to meet him in the Bohol Quality department store where he planned to look for Reuben's gifts even though we had not one cent. As I went to the Post Office to pick up the mail as usual, I saw a letter from Harold. I opened it to see what he wanted to say. There I found 900 pesos which were equivalent to almost $40. He said that he had been on another island for the ministry and thought about us in Bohol, so he sent us cash that he didn't need when he returned to the States. Whoa, I got excited and couldn't wait to see Johnny with that surprise a miracle indeed. When I approached Johnny, he looked sad and I waved the letter from Harold at him. He saw my smiling face, and that got him curious. When he opened it, he said, "Praise the Lord, for He never failed us as He was always faithful!" We got all the gifts that Johnny picked in faith. Also, I bought tiny gifts and surprises for a treasure hunt that I created. It grew into the Dunnington's tradition for Reuben's and Tiffany's birthdays annually.

How little our children knew about the situation we went through. They had faith in us that we were to take good care of them. It was exactly the same way our Father in heaven was taking care of us if we had faith in Him.

> *So I tell you, don't worry about the food or drink you need to live, or about the clothes you need for your body. Life is more than food, and the body is more than clothes. Look at the birds in the air. They don't plant or harvest or store food in barns, but your heavenly Father feeds them. And you know that you are worth much more than the birds. You cannot add any time to your life by worrying about it. And why do you worry about clothes? Look at how the lilies in the field grow. They don't work or make clothes for themselves.*

> (Matthew 6:25-28 NCV)

The Beginning of the Ministry

Johnny was asked to preach up in the mountains of Bohol a few days before Christmas. The pastor took Johnny with him on a bus and went all the way to the very top of the mountain. Typhoon #2 was starting to hit and I knew that Johnny needed prayer to come home safely. I was worried but had to give up my concerns to Him to intercede for his safety. Also, it was almost Christmas time, and Reuben and Tiffany needed him to celebrate with them especially since this was our very first Christmas in a new place in an unfamiliar country. The storm worsened and I kept praying for his safe return. He came home safely. He shared that the delay for him to come home was because it rained so hard and it was flooding, and the public transportation was halted. It was the Lord's grace and protection that the pastor brought Johnny from the mountain then across the bridge that was wiped out two hours later. So instead of coming home, Johnny stayed overnight at another pastor's home until the typhoon passed. My lesson was to trust God in what was beyond my control.

In January 1994, we were told that there was trouble getting our 39 boxes cleared through customs. Johnny and I interceded to get them through and claimed the promise of God that those boxes would come through without being stolen or compromised. In two weeks, we were contacted that we had to go up for visa clearance and clearance for the boxes, too. We all had to go to Manila and meet Alvin and his assistant Manning who helped us a lot for the first couple of years. It was miserable because it was so hot, muggy, and dirty from the pollution in the big city. Our way to immigration was excruciating because of bumper-to-bumper traffic and a heavy outpouring of rain. Unexpectedly, the unbelievable flashflood was filling up the low streets. Manning kept driving through flooded areas, and there was no way of backing out. The water went up almost to the car windows. We prayed as the car was still running and going for about five minutes and came out of the low street. I couldn't believe it, and I knew it was the Lord's hand on the car and us. Then we arrived at the Immigration Department. There was a long line to get a visa, and it was not done until three days later. We were told that they were to ship the boxes to Cebu and we were to get them. I remembered Don Moen's song that went like this, "God will make a way when there seems to be no way. He works in ways we cannot see. He will make a way for me. He will be my guide and hold me closely to His side with love and strength for each new day. He will make a way."

We finally got those 39 boxes intact and nothing was taken or lost. Since receiving all our ministry equipment and things, we began having film-showing crusades and preaching through Bohol. We helped Johnny set up the film-showing crusade. The crusade alone attracted crowds up to 500. We had a great family working together winning souls for the kingdom of God. It was amazing how the families welcomed us to stay in their homes, and we built relationships with them. They would kill the last chicken to feed us or give us their last grain of rice, if necessary. Speaking of relationships, it was a great blessing to share our lives with them. I felt very humbled by those experiences that taught me that living in a poor, third-world country had reshaped our values and outlook on life. Things that seemed to be important to us in the States no longer were.

I became friends with two sisters Emy and Fe who wanted to get involved with deaf education as they graduated and couldn't find jobs as teachers. Dennis hired them eventually. One weekend Emy and Fe invited us to meet their family on the next resort island that had a bridge connecting to the city. We took a tricycle to the bus stop for the resort island named Panglao. We brought our small duffle bag with our snorkeling stuff and my 35mm camera and put it in the back slot pocket. As soon we got off, the tricycle left with our bag. I cried out to the Lord. I had to tell Johnny what happened. He was unusually calm and prayed. Fe said the last resort was to go to the radio station to make an announcement because the tricycle didn't come back. So Fe, Emy and I went to the radio station and they explained that we were missing the blue bag with detailed stuff inside. They said for us to wait and asked us to come into the room. I saw the blue bag on the floor. I declared, "That's my bag!" The people there were happy and said that the tricycle driver dropped it off just minutes before we showed up. We gave the Lord our heartfelt thanksgiving.

Our first experience with young coconut water with Fe, far left holding baby

I Can Only Hear God

Chapter 23

Another Angle of Culture Shock

When we first moved to Bohol, one of the pastors referred someone to help us with the daily chores including washing clothes. We had her for only one week. I had to let her go. I realized after that the conflict we had, our communication was poor. She knew basic English. She asked me to buy her slippers. I thought to myself, "How dare she do that!" I thought she meant American slippers. Later, I realized she meant flip-flops. Another time she asked me to buy her bread. Again, I thought, "How dare she!" I learned she meant all kinds of rolls that were common locally. I thought it didn't go well. There were two different cultures in my house. I had to do my daily chores until we were able to afford to hire a helper.

Emy offered herself to help us in exchange for perfecting her English. We were glad to accept her as a volunteer helper. She already graduated from college but couldn't find a job. She was educated compared to the first helper we had. It made it a lot easier for me. I will never forget seeing the surprised expression on her face when we washed clothes together. Actually, there was a huge pile of clothes four feet high, like towels and sheets. I wanted to get the job done ASAP, just like the American fast-lane lifestyle. I was washing clothes by hand really fast and wrung them speedily. She opened her mouth with great disbelief like I was superwoman. She was content washing clothes even though it would take forever. I was dismayed by her slowness so I sped it up. Then I realized that the world was not going to end. At times, I couldn't stand her slow-motion washing dishes. I just freaked out. Everything was so slow everywhere. I had to learn to adapt to the slowness of life there since I was hyper like a tornado. I had to mellow out over eight years there and it is like God says, *"Be still and know that I am God. I will be praised in all the nations; I will be praised throughout the earth."*(Psalms 46:10 NCV)

After Christmas, Dennis asked me to teach ASL in the popular Garden Cafe where the deaf employees waited tables, cooked, baked and prepared food for the customers. I enjoyed that class because it helped me to learn about their culture. It was good practice for them to learn to communicate with me. So I asked them why they did that or what they called that. It was very refreshing.

Our first trip of Jesus film showing to one of many small islands close to Bohol

Tiffany and Reuben with rice threshing workers

Going up into the mountains reminded me of the time of Jesus. It was primitive with no farm equipment, no fancy transportation, no comfortable furniture, and no running water or electricity. When it rained, we had to walk in downpours of rain on the muddy trails or ground while thick mud built up on our shoes or thongs.

Ladies washing clothes

Later I learned it was best to walk barefoot. Then I would not have muddy shoes. We transported the film-showing equipment by bus, water buffalo or by hand. We ate fish and rice three times a day and slept on the bamboo or wood floor with mats on it. Walking to rivers, springs or where the water source was, we took baths with clothes on. Their way of life was a very simple but hard lifestyle.

Pounding rice

The typical daily life of many Filipinos.

My first impression from that culture was it was so different from ours. When we took a bus up the mountains, I sat up front by the window. The bus there was totally different: no glass windows, just wood or plastic windows to pull up. Everything in the bus was homemade and hand welded out of proportion. One time I

Another Angle of Culture Shock

Our transportation up the mountains for Jesus film showing.

was sitting with my arm leaning over the window. There was a fiesta going on so many people were desperate for a ride. Many people scrambled climbing up to the top of the bus. One Filipino guy climbed over me and left muddy footprints on my arm. How furious I was. I tried to cool off and tried to shake off the shock and upsetting attitude. I realized that most of the people were not educated, especially in the mountains. I had to let it go and had to be a good example. What I was doing was for the Lord's love to spread. It was a challenge for me to adapt to the culture.

One time all four of us got sick while we were up in the mountains doing the film-showings in different locations. We had pressed on walking one and a half miles up the mountains, wading through the rivers, and setting up the film-showing equipment to share the good news. That night I was miserably sick lying down on the bamboo floor having no comfort. I prayed and asked the Lord for His supernatural strength, comfort and healing. Actually, I fell into a deep sleep and didn't awake until morning and woke up refreshed indeed. Was it all worth it? I faced the temptation to quit and run back home to the city as a refuge, but the Lord always gave us the strength to press on. Seeing all people from all walks of life and from young to old keep coming to see the film-showing and surrendering their lives to the Lord Jesus was very powerful, touching and moving. Joy had filled my heart.

I cried out to the Lord for a miracle of provision for a new washing machine. Not many people owned one back then; only the upper class could afford one. For eight long months, I endured the hand washing then one day Dennis told us that his friend from America wanted to buy me a washing machine. I leaped with joy because the Lord answered my prayer since our move to Bohol. I thanked the Lord for the gentleman who was moved by love and compassion to give that to me.

Peeping Toms were very common in that culture which was very annoying to me. When I was doing aerobics while watching the videotape every morning about 5:00 A.M., I felt eyes were watching me. I looked at the dark windows and noticed the shadow of a person. I ran to see who it was. It was my landlord. "What is he doing?" I asked myself with a disgusting attitude towards him. I had to let it go. Then the other time I was doing the same exercise in the early morning, I felt the eyes behind my back. I turned around, and it was my neighbor's teenage son standing on something above the high wall of cement to look over. I said, "Hey, you go away!"

He was caught off guard and said, "No."

I kept telling him to go and he kept turning his head saying no. Finally, I waved to him and said, "Get out!" He got my message and finally went down the wall. I was shocked. How dare the men do that. I learned it was part of the culture that was so opposite of American culture. I felt my privacy was being threatened. I realized that I was shocked, and I prayed to the Lord for the solution. I had to accept the fact that I couldn't change the culture, but we decided to move to a new location where we had more room in the country and more privacy. We had land with a two-story house that was just being built as we were the first people living there. It was a breath of fresh air indeed.

I Can Only Hear God

Chapter 24

A Stepping Stone of Deaf Ministry

In October 1994, I started Bible study class in Tagbilaran City for the high school and elementary level deaf students for three hours a week. It was pioneer work since they had no exposure to the knowledge of the Bible. Dennis asked me to go to Jagna once a week to have a Bible class there also. I took about a two-hour bus ride and stayed overnight in the unfinished deaf dorm. It was definitely outside of my comfort zone since I had to sleep on concrete under a mosquito net and eat mostly rice with a few vegetables or fish. Fe was dorm mother before becoming a teacher for the deaf there. She wanted to sleep with me. She put her legs over me. I said to myself, "Whatever it takes for them to get to know you, Jesus, through my action." I was like the light that attracts the moths.

The teachers and children wanted to be around me. I taught them the different characters of the Bible. They thought Jesus was every character of the Bible and I had to explain to them it wasn't true. I said that the people in the Bible are like us who have a choice to follow the Lord's example. They had a lot of questions and it was hard to deal with the students from ages 5 up to 35. There were about 45 deaf students, and it was a challenge to teach different ages. They were fascinated with the pictures from books. They had an eye-opener to understand who the Lord is and what the Bible characters were about.

Deaf bible study in Jagna, Bohol 1994.

One of the teachers there said to me in tears that she was deeply moved as she watched me teaching the deaf the Bible stories they had never heard before, like the story of Adam and Eve. She also saw the sacrifices I made coming to Jagna once a week. I didn't think that I was doing enough as I was only reaching one-third of the deaf in Bohol. The Lord was faithful to show forth the fruit of my labors as almost all of the deaf had received Jesus into their lives and were eager to learn more of the Bible.

I requested visual aids like pictographs of the characters of the Bible, and some were donated. The deaf had a better understanding by seeing the actual pictures in action. This was effective and I challenged some deaf to come up with stories with pictographs. I used them for any age. It was interesting timing that the Lord sent us to Bohol because IDEA (International deaf Education Association that helps educate the deaf and train them vocationally) started ten years before we came, and most of the deaf were educated and were able to understand God. It was amazing how the Lord ordained that plan. I was forever in awe of Him.

After a few months in Jagna Bible study, four deaf teens wanted Jesus while I was teaching. I told them to wait until the class was over. After the class, they came to me begging for Jesus to be part of their lives. I had to be sensitive because I didn't want to ruffle feathers since the majority of the people were devoted Catholics. So I gave in and led four of them to a private room. There was no privacy at all because the dorm was unfinished, and all the deaf came up to the second floor peering down. I just explained at length what it would cost them to ask Jesus to be a part of their lives and forsake the worldly stuff. They said they understood and still persisted. I prayed with them and they were overjoyed repenting their sins and receiving Jesus as their Savior.

Deaf getting water baptized.

At the same time, I was teaching Bible study with deaf teens in the deaf dorm in the city. There were a few men who were already Christians from another island's deaf school. We had good feedback and more deaf joined to listen about God. Then I started a deaf church in Dao Diamond's vacant building that was going to be remodeled but it was condemned because of termites. Johnny and I were teaching there with about 20 deaf attending. One deaf lady named Alma wanted to be water baptized. She was the first deaf person that I baptized in water with Johnny. The word got around like wildfire. Even the word arrived at the Mayor's office in the city. When Dennis went there to ask for financial help for IDEA, the mayor said no because he accused Dennis of betraying the Catholic's way about water baptism. The mayor said, "I heard that that deaf American lady was baptizing the deaf high school students in the water."

Dennis said that he had nothing to do with that. Dennis told me that. I said, "Okay, I take the blame. I am just like Paul causing all the trouble." It was good that the word got all around Bohol because Jesus was being advertised.

> *We have found this man to be a troublemaker,*
> *stirring up his people everywhere in the world.*
> *He is a leader of the Nazarene group.*

> (Acts 24:5 NCV)

Dennis told me I had to stop teaching the deaf Bible classes in two towns I was working in because he feared the teachers would talk with the parents who would then pull their children out of the education program. He said the teachers felt threatened by me. The truth was that I was to share Jesus with them, and more and more deaf responded by receiving Jesus Christ in their lives. As a result, they had their own convictions to follow Jesus, not the Catholic Church. So I surrendered the whole situation to the Lord and trusted Him to work everything out.

One Sunday, none of the twenty deaf students that had been coming to church showed up. Later, I heard their teachers had threatened to recommend removing them from school to their parents.

Sharing the story of Jesus

I experienced many trials, hardships and testing. I learned the responsibilities that came with pastoring and teaching, facing oppositions, sharing the truth in love without fear, and gently bringing back the sheep when they got lost. On top of all that, I had to remember to show the love of Jesus so people would be drawn to Him.

> *Therefore, my beloved brothers, be steadfast, immovable, always abounding in the work of the Lord, knowing that in the Lord your labor is not in vain.*

(1 Corinthians 15:58 ESV)

This scripture encouraged me because I was thinking about giving up the deaf ministry and thinking maybe I was just wasting my time with it.

During a one-year absence, there were eight committed deaf Christians coming to our home for Bible study for a while before they were dispersed for work to different locations. It gave me joy watching them grow and remain faithful to the Lord even in the heat of persecutions from their teachers, peers, and family. A few deaf had received beatings from their parents for attending the Christian church. Catholicism was a way of life so they didn't know the difference between their culture and religion. I continued visiting the deaf on an ongoing basis at their workplace and their dorm to show them the love of Jesus and encouraging them in the Lord. I kept praying for the deaf for the whole year and trusted in the Lord for whatever outcome was to be.

Sharing the gospel with 200 deaf from Bohol during the deaf Feista

The Women's fellowship/prayer meeting was born in my home in the fall of 1996. Evan, who was a teacher for the deaf, was born again and was my right-hand gal for the whole eight years there. She and I hit it off really well, and she was always there for me. She invited and introduced her lady friends who wanted to be part of prayer. We believed in the unity that the Lord brings the deaf to know Jesus and grow in faith in Him. I had many opportunities to teach them and had sharing time with them which was very precious. We met every week for five years. By the grace of God, I was able to develop friendships.

A Stepping Stone of Deaf Ministry

*The Subenao tribe celebrating the feast of python
and welcoming us as their first white missionaries*

The Aeta Tribe in Bohol with the new tribal hall

*Johnny holding 9 foot python. One of our visits
of several Subenao tribe villages.*

Johnny helping skin the snake

Chapter 25

Healthy Distractions

We went to the States for a couple of months, and we had to move out of the house and put our stuff in IDEA storage. Upon our return, we rented our tree house. Actually it was pretty primitive; however, it was Reuben and Tiffany's favorite home in the country setting close to a cemetery. It was the worst house I ever lived in. When it rained very hard for more than two days, the kitchen got flooded by raw sewage under the house. There were rats running around especially in the kitchen, and fire ants took over the food if we were not careful putting the food away. One time I made two loaves of banana bread and I was cooling them off on the rack, and the next thing the bread was half gone. We lived there for three years because we couldn't find a nice home with affordable rent. That was a testing for me.

Johnny met a guy named Jun at the beach, and he was involved in the Subenao tribe that we had shared our vision with before we got married. Jun mentioned that there was a three-day tribal conference coming up on the island of Mindanao, south of our island. The Lord opened the door for the first time for us to preach to tribal people. We got really excited to go to Mindanao, the biggest island of the Philippines. How little I knew that the Lord would open many doors for me to minister along with Johnny. I thought to myself, "Well, since I'm deaf, I will just support Johnny and his work minding my own business." I was wrong. We saw God's hand on our lives in such a powerful way.

We went up the mountains of Mindanao to preach the Gospel to the tribal people who had never seen white people before. Just

Our trekking to the village for Jesus film showing in Mindanao

20 years previous in 1976, there were still headhunters offering their victims' fingers and heads to the gods of the forest. We had to walk across and down steep mountains, hills and valleys, even across the streams and on a bamboo bridge over a gorge. Two years back, that area was infested with NPA rebels. People did carry our bags for us which was a big help. We looked like we were in a Tarzan movie in which the white man would go to the jungle, and the natives would help carry things. The area was very remote without electricity or running water, no roads just trails, and no transportation. We used kerosene lamps at night and had to use a river well or just rainwater to take a bath. At first, it was exciting but it got old fast. Johnny continued to preach sometimes late into the night or early in the morning before the sun came up. They were so hungry for God's Word and the love of Jesus.

At one of the tribes' homesteads, there had been no rain, no animals to feed on, and limited vegetation. The tribe prayed for food for us as special guests, and they got a nine-foot-long python.

Johnny helped peel the skin off the snake. They were overjoyed to be able to feed us. I said to myself, "What did I get myself into?" I was not very fond of snakes, on top of that to eat one. "Lord, help me," I cried out. Johnny and Tiffany were

We crossed a bamboo bridge with 100 feet drop to the bottom of the gorge. I was not happy!

anxious to try it out. Reuben and I sat there and stared at the barbecued and stir-fried snake. Johnny and Tiffany gobbled it up, and Reuben and I just tried a little and it was very rubbery. It tasted like spicy chicken, not too bad. However, my mind just couldn't accept enjoying snake. Then there was native dancing celebrating our presence and the Lord's provision of the snake. Johnny and I joined the fun of dancing.

We visited seven tribal churches scattered all over the mountains. Every night I was so tired. By 7:00 P.M., I was ready to pass out. I saw such eagerness on the faces of the tribe to hear what we had to share. My heart was really touched because of their hunger for God's Word. Many of them had never seen white people before. The Lord was faithful to put words in Johnny's heart to preach three times a day. Johnny was a great encouragement to the tribes especially because he could speak their language. God's grace was truly sufficient. Many people's lives were touched as well as ours. The Lord prepared our way to reach them. It was our original vision to work with the tribes in the Philippines. Before Johnny and I were married, God put a burden on my heart for tribal people through a movie I saw on TV and now it had come to pass.the Lord answered my prayers for Reuben and Tiffany to preach at a young age. They both shared the gospel with the tribal children. Reuben would read scriptures and shared what they

meant. Tiffany would sing songs in Visayan to them. They enjoyed their time with them, and they didn't complain about eating rice and fish three times a day.

One of our bathing times

Toward the end of our trip, we arrived at a conference. Johnny told me about an old man who was 86 and dying. He had not eaten for four days. I felt prompted to see him, so I took our friend Jun with me to interpret. I asked the dying man if he wanted to go to heaven and he nodded, "Yes". He was in great pain and couldn't talk. I asked him if he wanted to receive Jesus in his life and be forgiven of his sins. He nodded again. We prayed together for the Lord to forgive and save him. The next morning he went home to be with Jesus. What a close call. No one had ever prayed with him even though he attended church. We saw his body with no life in it.

It had been a temporary vessel for his soul during this short time on earth. I was filled with joy that God used me to lead him to our gracious Lord. I never again questioned the Lord for not using me in the hearing world.

Since our return from Mindanao, Johnny and Jun searched for the tribe on our island Bohol, and Jun found the Aeta tribe by the water in Loay in a week. Jun came over to break the good news, and we were thrilled to hear the good news. We went over to meet the Aeta tribe, and they prepared a feast serving us monitor lizard, roasted fruit bat along with rice. We had to accept the food with gladness. In order for them to accept us, we accepted whatever they gave us, even food was completely strange to us. I skipped the bat without them knowing but ate the lizard. Surprisingly, it was delicious and tasted like chicken. We gave them clothes, rice and encouragement through the gospel. Many of the members had gotten saved including the chieftain of the Aeta tribe Carlos and his family. They were under pressure from the Catholic Church though. Johnny and I taught them every week faithfully. Evan interpreted for me. My heart was filled with the Lord's love for them. It surely blessed me knowing that the Lord knew the desires of my heart as well as the deaf people. However, the deaf had been scattered all over Bohol making it difficult to follow up, so the Lord opened the door to place me with the Aeta tribe for Bible study.

> *To the weak I became weak, that I might win the weak. I have become all things to all people that by all means I might save some. I do it all for the sake of the gospel, that I may share with them in its blessings.*
>
> (1 Corinthians 9:22-23 ESV)

Ging Ging from our prayer meeting joined to help with praise worship which she usually did at her home church. She also helped with the Aeta children's ministry. Evan was faithful interpreting for me at the Bible study. Reuben and Tiffany helped Ging Ging to be part of the children's ministry. Most of all, Johnny was a father in faith to all of the Aeta people; teaching them and being very patient with them. They really looked up to him and respected him even more because he could speak their language.

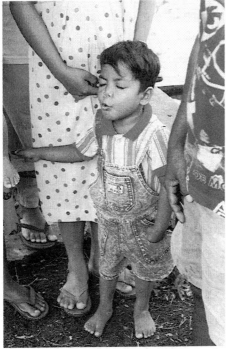

Pepe the Aeta orphan worshipping the Lord, now he is a prophet though only a teenager

...from whom the whole body, being fitted and held together by what every joint supplies, according to the proper working of each individual part, causes the growth of the body for the building up of itself in love.

(Ephesians 4:16 NASB)

I used visual aids and pictures to teach the adults so I was able to keep their attention longer that way. They showed a lot of enthusiasm and really got absorbed looking at the pictures. They didn't have books or pictures so they were blessings to them. Being deaf myself, I always liked visual aids. A picture speaks a thousand words. The pictures helped give a better understanding of what I was trying to teach. The Lord truly was stretching my abilities beyond my handicap for His kingdom and for His glory.

Evonne interpreting for me at the Aeta Tribe bible study

Make your tent bigger; stretch it out and make it wider. Do not hold back. Make the ropes longer and its stakes stronger,

(Isaiah 54:2 NCV)

The Aeta tribe's dinner, a fruit bat.

I Can Only Hear God

Chapter 26

Growing More Faith In God, In Everything

Just around Thanksgiving in 1996, I was making bread as usual and I smelled the rain. It was pouring heavily and caused the water to swell up in the low land where we lived. I continued kneading the bread, and I felt the nudge to check on Reuben and Tiffany as they always ran around in the rain in their bathing suits every time it rained. I saw them swimming in that dirty water that was contaminated with the animal feces that was common in that culture. I yelled at them to get out of the water right then. I had to wash them with soap and rubbing alcohol. I asked them if they had drunk the water and both shook their heads.

Three weeks later, Reuben was throwing up constantly and we took him to the ER in the local hospital. The intern looked at him saying that he had some kind of bug. We took him home, but he continued vomiting and he was dehydrated. We took him back to the ER the next morning. It was a scary time for us. The nurses tried poking the IV needle in Reuben's arms, and they succeeded on the seventh attempt. Reuben was becoming hysterical. We prayed and were at a loss for words when the doctor couldn't help Reuben but sent him to Cebu, the neighboring island. We hired a nurse to help monitor Reuben with his IV. It was nerve-wracking for me. Finally, we got to one of the big hospitals in Cebu City that was Americanized and more civilized. We admitted Reuben, and we stayed with him since the doctor said it was either dengue fever or typhoid. The blood work was taken, and it took a few days to get the results. The doctor told us to immediately begin looking for four to five people with O+ blood to donate and get screened in case Reuben had dengue fever. Johnny couldn't give his blood due to hepatitis. Reuben needed antibiotics if he had typhoid. We called for a prayer chain in the States as well in the Philippines.

On Christmas day about three days after admission, Reuben's red blood count was low. The doctor took immediate action administering powerful antibiotics in an IV. He didn't want to waste time waiting for the results. The next day, Reuben's blood count improved dramatically. The doctor believed it was typhoid before the results confirmed it. Tiffany was upset seeing Reuben with an IV in the back of his hand. The scripture came to me that I taught them and had them memorize in Bible Class as part of homeschooling: *"Remember that I commanded you to be strong and brave. Don't be afraid, because the LORD your God will be with you everywhere you go."* (Joshua 1:9 NCV) I reminded her of that as well as myself. I felt faint-hearted during Reuben's critical condition which lasted four days. I cried out to the Lord to strengthen me so I could stand up strong and be brave. I told Reuben over and over as he suffered so much during that time, "Don't give up the good fight of faith." It helped me, too. Finally, one day he said to me, "Mom, don't worry about me. God is taking care of me!" That swordpierced my heart,

and I knew I had to let
the Lord take control.

While we slept in the room where Reuben was, we hadn't bought anything with us like clothes or toothbrushes because we didn't know how serious it was. I had to wash some clothes as we wore the same clothes for eight days until Reuben was discharged. We saw the gifting come out of Tiffany at the hospital as she continually made gifts and drawings for many patients there. While making her rounds with the nurses, she gave them out. I have never forgotten the sight of four or five lady nurses sitting around Tiffany as she was sharing the gospel of Jesus with them. They were all captivated with her as she was six years old.

Reuben had dramatically improved in a few days and was released on the eighth day. Everyone was amazed at how fast he recovered knowing typhoid could kill a child or cause damage to sight or hearing. We were not allowed to leave the hospital until the full bill was paid. We didn't have the money, and Johnny felt impressed to call our friend Wheaten King in Manila to let him know about Reuben. He quickly offered to pay the bill via phone. We gave all glory to God and thanked Him for His healing power and love as well as the doctor's care. When Reuben was playing or misbehaving as if nothing happened to him, I learned to trust in the Lord in that situation.

I was asked to lead the Bible study with deaf carpenters up in the mountains called Sagbayan which was a two and a half hour bus ride from our place. The Lord truly arranged that for the deaf and me. When I went up there and the deaf carpenters stayed at the deaf dorm with the deaf students, I asked if there was a church nearby because I was not allowed to teach the Bible on any IDEA property. I was led to the Assembly of God church next door. I met the pastor and asked her if I could use their church building once a week. The pastor and her husband were delighted to invite me to sleep over every week. Since the church was not completely done, there was a temporary room. I had to climb a ladder to a tiny, bamboo room that fit only one for sleeping. Some nights when it rained, the water leaked through the roof. I just moved over to avoid getting wet. I had joy when the deaf were strengthened in their faith since they were unable to attend Bible study because of the distance. There were new carpenters from another island who joined the Bible Study class. One of them got saved and had the biggest smile. The others recommitted themselves to the Lord.

Although riding a bus up the mountains was tough, my heart was filled with joy knowing I was meeting spiritual needs and sharing Jesus' love. One night it rained hard all night; my bed was wet. I thought about how I could get home in the morning. There was no pavement on the back roads. The soil there was like clay and when it rained the road become slick just like snow. When I got up and left early to catch the bus, there were more people than usual. Actually, it was packed and I had someone sit by me squeezing me in. Many people were standing up. As the bus was going down the steep hill, a construction truck came down the other side. The bus driver stopped because the road was narrow and the steep drop off had no railing. The bus tires were spinning and slid towards the edge of the road. I yelled to the driver, "STOP! STOP THE BUS!" He stopped driving and the people were standing there like martyrs. I said to myself, "I refuse to die here and be trapped!" I yelled at people, "GET OUT!" Finally, the people were moving to get off the bus. I was so glad to get out of the bus. People were standing not knowing what to do. The bus was stuck. Furiously, I marched

Reuben's monkey pet Solomon

on up the hill to catch another bus. I went down knee deep in muddy water on the side of the road. I was wearing a casual skirt and sandals, and my legs were covered with mud. I didn't care. I wanted to go home. I walked up the hill waiting about ten minutes for the other bus, and it came. I was the only one from the stray bus to get on the other bus. There weren't many people on this bus, and the bus driver looked at my muddy legs with a wondering face. The Filipino people probably didn't understand what an American lady with muddy legs was doing up in the mountains alone. When I got home about 9:00 A.M., Johnny, Reuben and Tiffany greeted me. By that time, I just burst into tears hugging them. They wondered what that was all about. I had to tell them the dramatic story. I will never forget that day. I knew the Lord spared my life. Also, I was there for the gospel's sake.

One day I couldn't walk due to a very sharp pain in my lower back so I got a hold of Johnny's back, and he carried me upstairs to our bedroom. I had to lie down on my bed, and I was in so much pain. Finally, I went to the hospital and had an x-ray. After reading the x-ray, my doctor told me I had a herniated disc that was caused by heavy lifting over the years. He said there was no cure or any way to make it better but to lie down for a month flat on my back. I was awestruck to hear that news, and I had no choice but to lie down for ONE MONTH.

Johnny was due to fly to the States in a few days to speak to different churches for a month. We had someone who helped clean the house, wash clothes and sometimes cook. Johnny thought the helper was sufficient, and he went ahead with his plans. I was just lying down facing the ceiling all day long in the tropical heat. I had the fan going on me for the whole month as I never left the room. My helper washed my hair, washed part of me, and fed me. She was busy doing chores for me and she didn't have time to accompany me. She went to college part time and since she was our helper we also helped with her school expenses. I read the Word, prayed, ate meals, played solitaire and homeschooled Reuben and Tiffany. It was the grace of God. They homeschooled downstairs and followed everything faithfully by themselves, and when they had questions, they came up and talked with me. We discussed and I was able to help them understand what they needed to learn or do. They were very cooperative and I was thankful for that. They even practiced playing the piano for their next lesson with our teacher friend who taught them privately.

On the very last day of the month of lying down on the bed, I was filled with plans for when I got out of bed. However, it ended up a different story. Screaming and crying, Tiffany ran upstairs holding her hands, "I got shocked! I got burned!" Out of impulse, also out of an adrenaline rush, I got up fast and lifted her up as she weighed about 90-100 pounds and carried her downstairs praying in the Spirit. She said that she was trying to move the transformer for the piano plug to be plugged into it. However, the plug for the transformer was unplugged from it, and she touched the live plug by mistake and got electrocuted. She fell backward with force and got released from the plug. It was a good thing that she let go of the plug, otherwise, she would have died especially since she was standing on a cement floor. Her finger and thumb got seriously burned. I took her to the hospital right away, and our doctor looked at her and covered her with bandages. The doctor asked Tiffany if she had any pain and she said, "Not anymore." He was amazed. When I was praying, I asked the Lord to remove the pain and heal her hand, and that's when it happened. The doctor wanted Tiffany to come back in a few days to recheck for infection and encouraged her to move her fingers and thumb constantly as the wound was healing. Otherwise, it would be stiff and immovable. It was hard for Tiffany to move every moment. With my encouragement, she recovered nicely, and now has a scar to be reminded of the Lord's mercy, grace and miracle.

I was in awe about my back that was totally fine even after all the drama and lifting. The very same doctor asked me how I was. I explained to him that it was my last day to lie down, and I was planning to get up the next day. I told him that I lifted Tiffany. He was surprised and nodded that it was somewhat of a miracle. Although he was a born-again Christian, he fully acknowledged that with the Lord anything was possible. A couple of days later, Johnny came home missing all the action of the Lord's amazing grace. After lying down for a month straight, I walked every day to strengthen my back.

Johnny was reading a Basic Youth Conflict character book to Reuben and Tiffany at an evening gathering before bedtime. One time they were on the topic of perseverance. On our day off, we all went to jump off a waterfall with a man-made island nearby where we could take a break. It was a paradise, and there was hardly anyone there. It all belonged to us. We went there often. Since Johnny had been working out and losing weight, his wedding finger was thinner. When he jumped off the small cliff by the waterfall and swam up against it, his ring slipped off. He was freaking out and kept looking for it under the waterfall. It was impossible. We were sad, but we prayed for the Lord to turn up the ring somehow. When we went back home, Johnny was still teaching perseverance when he realized that message was for him. He kept at it and we kept going back every week for three weeks with different experiments like homemade nail rings with a string attached to find the ring in the waterfall and at the bottom of it. There were rocks on the side of the waterfall. Finally, Johnny decided to cut the water flow by putting rocks in the creek to reduce the pressure of the waterfall. Johnny snorkeled and felt the mud that was about a foot deep under the waterfall and found nothing. After the third week, we tried everything again. I was half standing and sitting with my legs against both walls on top of the waterfall. It was exhausting especially for Johnny as his hands were bleeding from scraping the rock walls. I cried out to the Lord, "I am tired. Johnny is tired. We have persevered, and we have faith in you, Lord. Send forth the angel and give the ring to Johnny." I felt impressed to tell Johnny to put his whole arm through the rock wall hole. He agreed and did that, and he grabbed a handful of sand and pulled it out. There was his ring stuck in his hand between the sand. Johnny yelled, "I found it, I found it!!" again and again. He could not let go of the tight clutch of his hand with the ring as we swam to the bank. Reuben, Tiffany and I joined Johnny with the glorious, unspeakable joy of the Lord. It was a REAL lesson of perseverance for all of us.

In May 2000, I had Reuben, Tiffany and other friends joining us to go to the beach in Panglao Island. I was driving the Pajero SUV, and there was road construction going on for a long while close to the beach. In the Philippines, everything took forever. There was a sign that said "Under construction" as I was entering the construction site on the road getting close to the beach. I turned left as there were piles of gravel and dirt. There was a huge bulldozer about 25-feet high backing up towards us. We were trapped, and I honked the horn for a long time; the bulldozer kept backing up and it was ready to run us over. I cried out to the Lord, and it stopped but damaged the left side of the Pajero SUV. The guy was yelling, and I was yelling back and we realized that both of us were DEAF. He lost his hearing as he was getting old. I asked for the owner of the company's phone number. I thanked the Lord that He spared our lives and the damage was minimal. I never forgot that I was able to hear everyone screaming when the giant was about to smash us. I contacted the owner, and Johnny and I met with him. He happened to be one of our neighbors in Tip Tip. He explained that he knew the dangers and submitted to the city to have the roads closed but it didn't go through. He was willing to pay for the damages on the Pajero SUV. Bless that man. The Lord took care of us without any financial burden or injury.

My scooter

Chapter 27

God's Amazing Provisions

When we first arrived in Bohol, we had no vehicles to get around. We used the tricycle taxi service, bus, horse, or we walked. It was not easy to get around, and many times I had to wait for two hours to get a ride. It was very frustrating, and it was hot standing in the tropical sun. Johnny and I prayed and believed the Lord would provide any means of vehicles to get around.

One of the local pastors approached Johnny to let him know that there was an old motorcycle up for sale, and Johnny went to see it and could barely afford it. It was a piece of junk that kept breaking down and it was useless. We had to learn that lesson never again to go ahead of the Lord, and it was always best to wait on Him. It was hard, but we had to wait it out. Then I had a vision that a car was coming to us. Dennis came to us and asked us if we wanted to use IDEA's old jeep that he got from the property he bought for IDEA. It was included. Wow, what a great blessing. We didn't have a vehicle for one year, and it was worth it.

Shortly after, we got an unexpected amount of money that Johnny used to buy a brand new motorcycle so he could go up the mountains to visit the pastors and the Aeta tribe. It was a blessing to be able to have a vehicle around while Johnny was gone.

We believed in the Lord for a piece of property for the training center and a house for us. One day we drove around looking at what was available and didn't find anything appealing. However, Johnny surprised me on our 11th anniversary with a new lady's motorbike since we returned the jeep to IDEA since they needed it back. I was able to get around for food shopping and other errands. The Lord's timing was always on time.

We asked for a contribution to help build the Aeta tribe hall. A couple was touched to give the exact amount of money we needed to build the hall which included a sleeping loft for family members. We were able to hold Bible study two times a week. The Aeta tribe rejoiced in witnessing the Lord's blessings in their lives.

One day in 1998 we got a letter from Rick, our pastor at New Life Christian Fellowship, who took care of our finances and kept in touch with supporters for us. Bless him. The letter said that we got a great amount of money for the land from an anonymous donor. We were filled with overflowing joy and praised God. We immediately got on our bike to drive around looking for property and asked if anyone knew of any property for sale. One lady knew of someone who wanted to sell land in Tip Tip in the country setting of the city. Johnny gave her our phone number, and we waited for a person to contact us. The next day, the lady called and asked us to meet her in a certain place so she could lead us to see the property. We saw the property, and we were not impressed. Johnny looked at the other side of the property and felt impressed with that land. He asked about that property. The lady went to find out, and she came back and told us that it was for sale. We went over to see the owner who was from Mindanao and had stayed for almost a year trying to sell the property. Out of the blue, she proclaimed, "This is the property that God wants you to have." She said that she was about to give up and go back home to another island. We felt great peace and joy knowing that was it. We returned to make an agreement for purchasing, and we bought the two and a half acres in Tip Tip. It was like a promised land with over 50 coconut trees, banana trees, and many other fruit trees that people who lived there for 20 years planted. The Lord's promises to us were real and true. We believed in the Lord to provide land for building the training center in His perfect timing.

We saw the need to purchase a four-wheel drive vehicle and put in the request. Shortly, again the anonymous donor gave us money to buy a used four-wheel drive. We shopped around in the city and couldn't find one. Then a friend informed us that there was one in Cebu City, the neighboring island. Johnny contacted the owner of the vehicle and made an agreement. We got it and it was shipped to our island. We were so blessed to have a four-wheel drive Mitsubishi Pajero with air conditioning and wide tires designed for mountain use. Johnny used it a lot for film-showing all over the island of Bohol and the other big island Mindanao, south of Bohol. It was greatly useful for the kingdom of God.

Finally, we got money to build a center, but it took us two years before the money was provided. The center was finished in September of 1999. With Johnny and Reuben away in the States for two months, Tiffany and I couldn't afford to pay for the visa to get out of the country so we stayed behind. The benefit of that was I was able to be the foreman to finish the training center. We added the bathroom fixtures and tiles with designs for all the floors, plus added the ceilings, painted outside/inside and did the final touch up. I also had the help of an architect.

I Can Only Hear God

That work took us two months. Tiffany, the helper, and I cleaned the whole place the night before Johnny and Reuben came back from the States. Believe me, I was so exhausted from doing all the work in two short months, and it was a miracle that it was finished right on time before they arrived. They didn't know that it was finished, and I wanted to surprise them. We even put up a Welcome Home banner. When we picked them up at the local airport, Tiffany and I tried to contain our joy. They got suspicious and when we arrived, Johnny exclaimed, "It's beautiful!" with awe and joy. He asked me how I did it, and my reply was, "Actually, the Lord did it for me!" The Lord provided us with the specific laborers for tiling, painting, installing the fixtures, and building cabinets in all rooms. I looked back and I ask myself how I did it with no knowledge of building. My architect was thoroughly with me with every thing. I was so grateful for everything especially the Lord's grace and favor in my life.

Chapter 28

Homeschooling Reuben and Tiffany

Johnny and I decided to homeschool Reuben and Tiffany before we moved to the Philippines. We went to a homeschool conference and found the exact curriculum that matched Reuben and Tiffany's needs. I told myself, "How could I get myself into school again? I hate school." I even had nightmares about going back to school and never graduating. I prayed for the Lord's grace and wisdom. Starting with Reuben's kindergarten was fun and easy. He loved school and it was not a problem. He loved reading, even his own children's bible. When Reuben came to first grade, Tiffany was really taking her time with kindergarten. I noticed that Reuben loved reading and didn't care for math while Tiffany didn't care for reading but was good in math. As the time progressed as well their grades, English became a challenge for me. I had always checked with Johnny to make sure that their English was corrected. He taught science, geography, social studies and sometimes math, and I taught the rest. Teaching was fun, but the worst part was discipline and getting them to complete their schoolwork. When they groaned and didn't want to do certain homework or study for a test, I just had them quote the scripture, "*I can do all things through Christ, because he gives me strength.*" (Philippians 4:13 NCV)

There were times I got frustrated and upset with them. The Lord spoke to my heart, "Why are you frustrated and upset?" I had

Our family picture in Bohol

to reexamine myself and ask why, and I realized I didn't like school in the first place. I felt like I was in school all over again as they were moving up in their grade levels. I wanted them to speed up to get it done. Sometimes they didn't get it, and I had to sit down and explain whatever they needed to understand. Also, I had to go at their learning paces, not mine. My character was being built up thoroughly because when I was growing up in school, I skimmed and did not really absorb or understand. So I knew that I had to go through this in order that the Lord could accomplish what he wanted in me.

> *For I am confident of this very thing, that He who began a good work in you will perfect it until the day of Christ Jesus.*
>
> (Philippians 1:6 NASB)

> *We also have joy with our troubles, because we know that these troubles produce patience. And patience produces character, and character produces hope.*
>
> (Romans 5:3-4 NCV)

When Reuben was in 5th grade, he was more determined. I used the Lord's wisdom to deal with him especially in English class. He kept saying that he didn't like to write. I asked him if he liked reading, and he astoundingly said that he loved reading. We always went to the city library to borrow at least ten books at a time. He was a bookworm. So I told him, therefore, he loved writing, too. He didn't know it yet. I always persuaded him to finish writing for his homework. It was an exhausting battle between us. One time, his homework was to write a book report. He chose to write about Abraham Lincoln out of five other easy choices. He picked the tough one. I told him to pick the easy one, and he still didn't budge. So I let him do whatever he wanted. He diligently worked on it, and Johnny corrected it. Reuben finalized it and turned it in at the last minute. He added pictures on about ten pages, and it was very neat. I was shocked and he did an excellent job. Johnny gave him an A+ and I agreed. I told Reuben that he did it. For the rest of his grade, he still said that he didn't like to write. For the rest of the year, I kept responding to him, "Yes, you love to write!"

When the summer came, they had summer vacation. He had a Filipino friend who went to a private school who was very educated. They got along really well. One day I came to pick Reuben up at his friend's house, and I went into the kitchen where Reuben and his friend were. Reuben said, "Hey, Mom, we are writing a book!" I almost fell over hearing his shocking declaration, "I love writing." It was a full year of battling with him to love writing and it had paid off. Whoa, I was amazed at how powerful it was that we could create destiny beyond us.

> *So shall my word be that goes out from my mouth; it shall not return to me empty, but it shall accomplish that which I purpose, and shall succeed in the thing for which I sent it.*
>
> (Isaiah 55:11 ESV)

From day one with Tiffany, it was a challenge to get her motivated in whatever she was learning in English as well as every subject. I had problems dealing with her attention span and her plugging into learning. I discovered that she liked hands-on learning, and she was very visual. Reuben was very abstract. I was able to relate to her because being deaf I felt the same way. It turned out that I had her rewrite in order to memorize as it was more visual. Also, it was helpful when I wrote on the blackboard and showed her pictures. Tiffany changed her mood and started to enjoy the new method of learning. I had to keep at it or I would start over again. It took extra effort and it was worthwhile. She seemed to dread test-taking, so I was able to relate to that. I worked with her closely studying before the test by writing things down or asking her questions. Yes, it was time-consuming but it worked for her. She did very well academically. I could see that she was very bright, and all I needed to do was to tap into her intelligence to be released and used. My teaching style was successful. With all the hard work, it was worth it.

> *Love bears all things, believes all things, hopes all things, endures all things.*

(1 Corinthians 13:7 ESV)

Tiffany and Reuben playing with the piglets

Homeschooling was rewarding, and I learned not only about the subjects but about myself. I homeschooled my children until they were done with eighth grade, so they went to high school after our return to the States. We spent a lot of time together, and they loved to sit down with me and just talk about anything. It was amazing how fast they had grown, and I enjoyed them more and more. I appreciated that I had spent time homeschooling while they were young. There were so many things I had to learn. I am thankful to God that they are able to read and communicate well. Having a deaf mom produced in them much patience and love as they interacted with me. I thank the Lord for Reuben and Tiffany. They have good hearts. They are such a joy as well as a great inspiration.

One of their highlights in the Philippines

Chapter 29

The Last Stage of the Ministry

Upon our return from a couple months of vacation in the States as well as traveling and speaking at different churches, Johnny continued teaching the Aeta tribe. One Saturday, the chieftain Carlos happened to be absent from the Bible study. There were posters of St. Niño plastered all over the tribal hall. Johnny asked the members what was going on. They mentioned the priest who loaned the land to the Aeta tribe demanded their devotion to St Niño, one of their idols (statues) in the Catholic Church. The priest threatened the Aeta to either choose to follow the Catholic ways and forsake the Bible study that Johnny had been teaching or leave the land that was loaned to them from the priest. Johnny explained to them that it was their choice to follow GOD or the priest. He removed all the posters and threw them away. That horrified Carlos when he found out when he returned. He made a vow to hurt Johnny if he stepped on the land where they lived. He was very much afraid of the priest and didn't trust the Lord to work it out. It was the end of it.

However, some members of the Aeta tribe from Mindanao came before that happened. They lived down the hill on different property for a temporary place to stay. They decided to hold a Bible study under a tiny, open bamboo shed. They were hungry for the Lord's word and got water baptized. They were growing up fast in the Lord. It was sad to let go of Carlos' family and some members. We didn't understand but we trusted the Lord to work in the people's hearts.

The Aeta Tribe bible study

the Lord touched a couple from the States to provide finances to buy a piece of land for the Aeta tribe. It was the first time they ever settled down on their own land since they were nomads for years. They were able to build their bamboo homes. They even built a good-sized bamboo hall with a roof, walls and a dirt floor. We continued teaching the Bible and holding the service. They got water baptized and they were growing in faith. More members from Mindanao moved up to live with them.

Johnny had done a lot of film-showing crusades all over Bohol, and many souls were getting saved. The pastors followed up with them. Over eight years, Johnny met with the pastors to teach, disciple and encourage them in faith. He established five churches in an eight-year span: the first church in Valencia, Aeta tribe, the Subanon tribe in Mindanao, the city church in Tagbilaran and the deaf church in Tip Tip.

Johnny built a relationship with Pastor Eddie from Mindanao where the Bible school/church was. He was the guest speaker for the Bible school graduation almost every year. Also, he was teaching at the conferences there.

There was a continuing ladies' prayer meeting every week in our home. I grew close to the group, and the unity was awesome. I was sad to find Evan leaving for Canada. She met the man of her dreams, married him and moved to Canada. We continued having meetings without her.

Every week I taught the deaf Bible study in a rented, tiny house close to where the deaf lived in Dao Diamond. When I had the Pajero, I used to pick up 20 deaf people to bring them to my home for Bible study, then transport them back to their home base. They didn't mind squeezing into the Pajero; they loved it. They were always full of smiles no matter what circumstances they were in. Some of them called me "Mom" as their spiritual mom. I actually watched them growing up in that eight-year span, and they had grown to trust me and my God. Some of them confessed to me that when I first came to Bohol, they didn't trust me, and they thought that I was trying to deceive them. In the long run, they saw the love of Jesus was real. Some had been struggling because of their peer pressure. I encouraged them to stand strong. With the Lord's help, most of them overcame victoriously.

They still experienced much persecution from their classmates, peers and teachers because of their faith in Christ. Some of their parents whipped them or made them kneel on rock salt for many hours and look up at St. Niño, a statue of the baby Jesus in priesthood clothes. Some parents threatened to stop supporting their schooling or disown them. However, some remained strong, were water baptized and served the Lord with all of their hearts.

The new training center was built, The deaf Church was born, 2000

When the building of the training center was finished, Johnny said to me, "It's the Lord's time for the deaf Church!" I was standing speechless and said, "I have no experience starting a church in my life nor have I ever been involved in a deaf church!" Johnny said, "I am here to back you up." It was as simple as that. To be honest, I felt unqualified and unknowledgeable, but again the Holy Spirit was the one who led the way. With Johnny's advice, I decided to announce that we were going to have a deaf church service in the brand new training center/church.

Dennis was the first to respond. He brought 30 chairs the first time he came to our property and to our church. He had never seen it before, and he joined us in the joy of the Lord for our commitment to the deaf church. Dennis gave his life for the deaf, and he made a BIG difference in their lives. Hats off to Dennis. The church was filled with chairs getting ready for the deaf to fill them the next Sunday. The first 40 deaf came; some came out of curiosity. However, out of 40, 15 faithful deaf came every Sunday.

The deaf congregation

About two months before we went to the States for a four-month vacation, the Lord spoke to my heart, "You are not coming back after the vacation." I refused to believe it as I was so attached to the Filipinos. I felt impressed to find a pastor to take my place while we were in the States so the sheep wouldn't be scattered like before. I prayed about who would be pastor for the deaf Church. He impressed Mart on my heart. I met him twice in Mindanao through Evan because she used to live where he was. She knew him well as she was a teacher in the deaf school, and both of them went to the same church. I emailed him but I never heard from him. Evan encouraged me to go all the way down to Mindanao to meet with him. I went with her to have my dress fitted for her upcoming wedding as I was one of her wedding sponsors. When I got a chance to see him, I asked him about taking my place for four months as Bohol's pastor of the deaf church. He said that he grew up with his grandmother, and he felt obligated to stay and help her. Also, she wouldn't let him go. According to his culture, the young respected the elderly and would do anything they asked. I lifted it up in prayer for his grandmother to approve him to go. He said that he asked his mom to talk with his grandmother. When Evan's wedding was over, Mart came to me to let me know that his grandmother gave him permission to go. Wow, everything fell into place. He said that he would come over to Bohol just a day before we left for the States.

The first deaf Church started September 2000

The deaf bible study

I Can Only Hear God

Chapter 30

Back to the States for Good

We were looking for a place to stay. Pastor John said that he just bought an eight-bedroom house with three stories and invited us to stay until the next plans were revealed to us. So we moved into the third floor, and it was like a small apartment for my family with three bedrooms and one bath. It worked out great. We rested then.

On September 11, 2001, as usual, I was the first one to go downstairs to get breakfast ready and I went to turn the TV on. At that moment, I saw the plane crash into the Twin Towers. I turned the TV off thinking how ridiculous that was. I had no live TV for eight years. I just used VHS tapes for movies. I was kind of in shock and refused to believe it was for real. I thought to turn the TV back on to make sure that it was not a joke. Then the news was all over the channel. I ran upstairs to call Johnny, Reuben and Tiffany to come down right away. We watched it with disbelief and shock.

We stayed with Pastor John and his wife and son for almost five months. We didn't have a car to travel on our own as we had borrowed Johnny's parents' old car. We prayed for a miracle for a car. Rick told us about his friend Kim who had connections. We were willing to try, hoping it was really cheap as we couldn't afford much as we were not working. Then Kim called Johnny and said that someone who was from California wanted to give the car to us as the owner no longer wanted it. It was a 1994 Toyota Corolla. We praised the Lord for his goodness.

We continued homeschooling Reuben and Tiffany. We didn't know what to do next. I didn't have the nerve to tell Johnny that the Lord spoke to me two months before we left the Philippines about us not going back. I wanted to see if Johnny heard the same thing from the Lord. Finally, he told me that we were asked to move out the first week of December, and he felt that we might not go back to the Philippines. My heart sank to the floor. I knew it was a confirmation.

We prayed where to move ahead. About three months back, our friends introduced us to Pastor Jeff of Mercy Seat Ministry church. We started going there, and we shared the news that we had to move out soon. Jeff came to us and invited us to house sit their home for the whole month of December. Rick and Joy asked us to house sit their house through New Years for three weeks. It was the Lord orchestrating our lives.

While we were staying at Rick and Joy's in Issaquah where we used to live before we left for the Philippines, Johnny got a phone call from a loan officer. He said that he could help us buy a house. Johnny and I didn't have jobs or any means of income. Out of curiosity, we invited him over to see what he had to offer. He had filled out our application to submit to the bank to see if we were qualified. We were pre-qualified for a house loan up to $150,000. We searched the houses online in Kent and Auburn, Washington, towns south of Seattle. We looked for a cheaper home to match the quote. We called the realtor from the houses we saw online. She led us from house to house. Most of them were dumps. We were discouraged. We kept looking online in the Puyallup area where it was much cheaper. We found the house in Puyallup online that captured our hearts. We knew that was the house for us, but it was $175,000. Johnny called the realtor George. He came over and picked us up, and we informed him that we liked the house. However, he took us from one house to another, maybe nine houses, and we kept asking about that house we liked. He said that the owner of that house would be there when we came to see it. It was the very last house we went to see. The first moment Johnny and I stepped into that house, we knew it was the house. When we went upstairs, I saw a Jesus tapestry, exactly the same one I own. We felt the witness of the Spirit of God in us. It was a beautiful house with a hot tub in a wooded setting on a cul-de-sac. The owners of the house were Christians, and they were selling on their own.

George, our realtor, hesitated to deal with that kind of thing. We had our loan papers processed to submit to the bank for an approval. They turned us down. We tried another bank, and we prayed for His grace and favor. We got approved. We didn't have a job or any savings. We lived day by day depending on Him. When we stayed at Johnny's parents' house for a month before our first move into our new home, I cleaned our home and bought a few things like towels, sheets and blankets. We had nothing to start with except a few boxes of our winter clothes that we left in storage at Johnny's parents' house.

We moved into our new home at the end of February 2002. Mercy Seat church sent furniture and kitchen stuff. The deaf church in Everett where I preached for a few months brought all kinds of furniture for the living room, dining room and bedrooms. We got some from Johnny's family. The house was furnished in one month. We had overflowing furniture that we didn't need and gave away. It was amazing that we put no money down for that house. We still got the mission support to be able to buy food and necessities. All Glory to God. Jesus said, *"I tell you the truth, all those who have left houses, brothers, sisters, mother, father, children, or farms for me and for the Good News will get more than they left. Here in this world they will have a hundred times more homes, brothers, sisters, mothers, children, and fields. "And with those things, they will also suffer for their belief. But in this age they will have life forever."* (Mark 10:29-30 NCV)

Chapter 31

The Beginning of American Life

For a year, Johnny had been looking for any job from odd jobs, waiter to salesman. Not one interview was offered. He worked for a company that sold fire safety equipment, and it turned out to be a scam. As soon as he found out, he quit. It was a frustrating time after being out of work for nine years. He was like a fish out of water. We prayed for the Lord's guidance and nothing happened. Johnny was greatly discouraged, and I had been supporting and encouraging him 24/7 as any wife is supposed to. I felt impressed to fly to California to visit my older brother Jim for his birthday. He wanted to treat me with the flight. While I was gone that week, the Lord did something in Johnny's heart. After my return from California, I was looking online for a healing room in our hometown and found one not far from us. I was in touch with the Pastor's wife and made an arrangement for me to visit with her along with her husband. When meeting with them, I asked for a prayer for a job for Johnny. I was going through a tough time letting go of the fact that we were back in the USA from the Philippines for good and adjusting to American culture that I didn't care for. They prayed with me and encouraged me in faith and love. They invited us to visit their church the following Sunday. It was by divine appointment that after the church service, Pastor Tim invited Johnny for a coffee the next day. He told Johnny about a job for a mortgage company. Pastor Tim worked for the company for a while and introduced Johnny to the job, and he started working there in April 2003. He learned fast and climbed up to be one of the top loan officers of Liberty House Mortgage Company. He was awarded a plaque which said, "The Natural." the Lord gave him favor and blessed him in many ways. Four times, he was awarded special trips from four days to one week at the company's cost. Of course, he took me along, and it was a blessing because I was having a hard time adjusting to American culture. I felt the Lord wanted to pamper me while my heart ached for the missions in the Philippines.

As a matter of fact, the first year since our decision to stay in the States, I cried every day and sat on the couch not knowing what to do. I cried out to the Lord to help me stop feeling that way, so depressed. One day, I searched for counseling that was willing to take the Medicaid (Back then there were just medical coupons for low-income families or unemployed.) I found a lady counselor in Tacoma. I went to see her, and all she asked me was why I was depressed. Although she was not a believer, she had her ears open to listen to me. The Lord definitely used her as I poured out my heart to her, and she asked me if I ever thought of returning to the Philippines to have a good closure. I was surprised by what she said. I felt the witness in my spirit that it was a GO.

As soon I came home, I went to ask Johnny if there was a way for me to return to the Philippines for a month. He said, "Sure, why not?" the Lord's timing for everything was working, and I was able to afford my flight there. I was delighted and went there in September through October 2002. It turned out to be great closure, Mart, the pastor, said it was okay for him to remain in the deaf Church instead of going back to Mindanao. He loved Bohol and its people. After my return from the Philippines for six weeks, I went to see my counselor with my pictures of the Philippines as she requested. She shared the joy I had about the closure and said that I didn't need her as I was doing well. It was God. I thanked the Lord for He used that counselor as His vessel. I was able to move on.

While I was there in Bohol, I felt the Lord speaking to my heart about giving Johnny a cat. He had longed for one since I married him, but I didn't let him have it because of my severe cat allergy. On top of that, I was not fond of cats since I had a fight with one under a bed in England when I was two. One time, I ended up in the hospital while I was on the drama tour due to severe reactions from a cat where we stayed. I didn't want that to happen again as I had a bad experience not being able to breathe. I said, "Lord, You want me to give Johnny a cat then I will die. It's fine with me. You have to take away my cat allergy." After I came back home from the Philippines, I immediately drew him a birthday card with a picture of a cat in a basket. I wrote, "You have longed for this!" Johnny opened the card and had a question mark on his face, "What does it mean? I can have a cat? What about your allergy?" I told him never mind and to just go ahead to the animal shelter to look for a cat for himself. Oh, boy. I have never seen him so excited in my whole married life. I said to the Lord, "OK, now I have faith in You who will take care of me."

We all went to the shelter. One of the kittens reached out to

Johnny and grabbed his heart, and he picked that kitten. He was overjoyed, but not me. Shhh... Once the kitten settled into our new home, with no one in sight, I picked up the kitten named Kitty and rubbed him on my face to see the reaction. I noticed I wasn't bothered at all so I wanted to test my reaction. NOTHING! I couldn't believe that I wasn't allergic to that kitten that eventually got to be a big cat. I had absolutely no reaction to the cat. I looked up to the Lord, "Thank you! You won! You are awesome!"

He said, "Your obedience brought you the blessing of healing!" I humbled myself to Him as He continued to amaze me.

Since I had a rivalry with a cat when I was two, I had ways to "discipline" Kitty. He knew that it could annoy me. I sprayed him with water to keep him off the furniture and kitchen counters. He knew what was off limits. One day, I was coming upstairs to the kitchen/living room, and out of the corner of my eye, I saw him get down from the couch really fast. He pretended that he was lying on the floor. "How cunning he was," I thought.

Another day, he kept going outside and coming in all morning. I said to Kitty, "Enough! You kept going out and in. You keep bringing the dirt and leaves in the house!" Kitty was sitting staring at me until I was finished talking with him. He got up with his tail way up high and his head up too, walking proudly out of the room. About five minutes later, he came upstairs again and looked at me. I mean right at me: eyes to eyes. He threw up his lunch that he had just ate and walked off proudly. OOHH, I was furious and then laughed with the realization of how smart he was.

One day I invited friends and neighbors over for a housewarming and Pampered Chef party at the same time. We had at least 40 people over and had a barbecue. It was a lot of fun.

However, Kitty appeared unhappy so I kept him in our bedroom. After the party was over, he left a big mess (poop) right in the center of our bed. "Wow, how dare he do that!" He knew better and was showing us how unhappy he was with all the people. Who had to clean up the mess after Kitty every time he left a mess? ME. That's why I didn't want the cat in the first place. Anyway, I had to learn to love that cat. Tiffany taught Kitty many tricks and, to my surprise, he did all the tricks even giving me a high five when I asked for it. Of course, he wanted treats after doing the tricks. Kitty did color our lives in a way I had never thought about before. The Lord's gifts to all mankind are animals. They are amazing pets.

I had a great burden for the deaf, and I lifted that up to the Lord. Then the Lord reminded me of that vision of the coffeehouse that I had put on the shelf back in 1986. So I asked for confirmation for me to go ahead. One Sunday morning, Pastor was talking about the coffeehouse out of the blue and I knew it was a "GO" to step in faith for the vision to come to pass. I felt impressed to e-mail all deaf churches and churches that had deaf ministries or interpreted services. I waited for anyone to respond, and no one except for one hearing interpreter who was interpreting at one church in Seattle did. So we invited those from different churches to be part of the brainstorming meeting. Our first meeting was in August 2003 at BCC church in Seattle. I shared my vision to reach out to the Lost with the love of Jesus with no preaching in a safe place where the deaf could meet once a month to play games or chat. It was important to expose who we were in Christ: to love people, listen to them and be an example that they didn't have a chance to get to know otherwise. Some had bad experiences in the past with deaf Christians shoving the Gospel down their throats. I was hoping a new approach to sharing the LOVE of Jesus would win them to the

Lord. We got the date established for the coffeehouse at the deaf center. It was in December 2003, and we used a Christmas event to start the coffeehouse. Sixty came the first time. I was surprised at that number. It was successful on the first night, and we decided to have it the fourth Friday every month in the BCC hall because it was much bigger than the deaf center. We had the ball rolling, and the word got around about that event. On December 2004, we prepared for that big event by having performances of skits, songs and a drama of Jesus. There was plenty of food, and over 200 came. I saw familiar faces that I recognized from the past when we shared the Gospel with them. I was amazed that following up the vision was of the Lord because the interpreter who responded to me about the coffeehouse told me she desperately tried to set up the deaf coffeehouse, but it failed a few times and she gave it up. Then I came responding to the Lord's calling, and it came to pass. It was all the Lord's doing, and all He needed was the willingness of our hearts. That coffeehouse ran for eleven years.

Joya was my friend who had shared the same vision and took my place to serve the Lord through the deaf Coffeehouse. She was behind the whole scene to keep it going and getting it all together. She was a great inspiration to all, and she has continued to live a full life at age 85. I left in January 2005 for Maryland, and Joya took over and oversaw that ministry. When I returned to Seattle from Mexico in 2009, I noticed many deaf people's hearts were sown and some were reaped. I trusted the Lord to finish the rest of the work. In December 2014, the coffeehouse shut down and will hopefully pass on to the willing ones to carry the torch of the Lord's light.

I felt impressed to start another coffeehouse in Puyallup where we lived. So I asked our Pastor if we could use our church building for the deaf coffeehouse. He agreed and gave us a go.

So I called the deaf people I knew and asked them to be part of the coffeehouse. There were two deaf churches, and they jumped on the bandwagon immediately. The first coffeehouse started in January 2005 just before we moved to Maryland. I was able to delegate John and Lance to do the work. The coffeehouse there is still running to this day. Wow. The vision was resurrected and came to pass. I had to move on to the next calling He had for me.

After our return from the Philippines, but before we moved to Maryland in January of 2005. I was invited to speak at the ladies' retreat, ladies' tea, and deaf churches. I had never taught the deaf in America before I went to the Philippines. I had to realize that it was the Lord's timing, not mine.

> *For still the vision awaits its appointed time; it hastens to the end—it will not lie. If it seems slow, wait for it; it will surely come; it will not delay.*
>
> (Habakkuk 2:3 ESV)

We had enjoyed our new home in Puyallup, and the first neighbors across the street brought us cookies to welcome us into the neighborhood. Others brought things, too. Tiffany met Ellen, and they became friends. Connie from across the street welcomed me and found out that I was deaf from the old owners of our house. She told me that she had a deaf daughter, and there was another deaf person a few houses down from us. It was definitely the Lord's divine appointment for us to live there. I discipled to her as a new Christian and shared the Gospel with her daughter Cassidy, and she got saved. It was a blessing to have a neighbor like that, and we grew close.

In the meantime, I was still homeschooling Tiffany in sixth grade and Reuben in seventh grade in a special homeschooling program in public school from March to June 2002. They had a class in portable buildings twice a week in the public school. The class was small so they were able to fit more easily into the public school system and American culture. The following fall of 2002, Reuben skipped the eighth grade to enter Ballou Junior High School as a freshman. I continued homeschooling Tiffany in seventh grade. In the fall of 2003, when the homeschool program closed in the public school due to lack of funds, I had a deaf friend who was a math teacher who was able to work with Tiffany in Algebra. It worked out great. I had to work with Reuben adjusting to public school, as it was totally different from homeschool. He had embarrassing moments, and he grew up fast adjusting to public school. He encountered bullying, and he learned to stand up and walk away from it or speak out in truth. Eventually, he gained respect from his peers. He overcame the culture shock. It has been a long process for both of them to learn American culture that was totally different from the way they were brought up in the Philippines.

Since I love photography, I decided to take a black/white basic photography class at Evergreen Community College. They would provide the interpreter for the deaf if I requested one. I commuted every week for a two-hour class for a whole semester. It was a fun class, and I was able to use a darkroom to develop pictures. I was able to interact with some students. Most of them were young, fresh from high school and some were my age.

One day I was driving my Toyota Corolla on the freeway going home, and it just died. I had to force myself off the road. I realized the mileage was 420,000 with its first engine. It was by the grace of God that we traveled in that car over the pass to Spokane and all over without any problem. "Why did it die on me?" I said to myself. I had a tow truck picking it up and me, too. Its engine just gave out and we decided to donate it. Johnny had a brand new KIA Optima so we just used one car for two months before our big move to the East Coast.

In October 2004, Johnny was nominated as one of the top three loan officers of the Liberty House Mortgage Company since working there for one and a half years. The owner of the company asked Johnny if he wanted to move to Maryland to set up a new branch for that company. When Johnny asked me about it, I thought to myself, "Here we go again. Every time I became comfortable, then the Lord wants me to get out of the comfort zone." In my flesh, I wanted to stay forever, but I had to yield to the Lord to see what He wanted us to do. We prayed and lifted it up to the Lord, and the scripture came to Johnny something like, *"And let the peace of Christ rule in your hearts, to which indeed you were called in one body. And be thankful."* (Colossians 3:15 ESV) We kept that in our hearts, saw it through and knew that the Lord wanted us to move to Maryland.

A part of me was excited because I was able to see my parents and siblings more often, and another part of me was sad to be leaving the coffeehouses in both places and leaving friends and family behind. It seemed to me every time we started something or something was going well, then we had to leave. The Lord reminded me that it was all of His doing, and all He needed was our willingness to accomplish His will just like the blueprint. He saw the big picture while I saw a piece of a puzzle trying to find its way to fit in.

I Can Only Hear God

Chapter 32

Uprooted Again and Again

Our BIG move out East! The company paid for everything: the movers, packers and all the expenses. We had to give half of our furniture and stuff away. We didn't have time for a moving sale. We asked George to sell the house for us, and it was sold a month after we moved out. Before we moved, we looked online for a house to rent in Maryland and we felt quickened that a house was ideal for us. It was a nice big house with six bedrooms and 3 -1/2 baths on four floors. We got approved to rent it, and everything went well. Reuben and Tiffany went to Wilde High School. There was a huge park with a lake in that town, and I loved taking a long stroll especially in the fall colors and the bright flowery spring. I usually gave Reuben and Tiffany a ride to school every morning

I was still without a car when Johnny went to work setting up a branch of the mortgage company from Washington. I didn't know what to look for in a job since I had not been working for seventeen years. I lifted it up to the Lord. Since our house in Puyallup, Washington, was sold in a month and a half, we were able to buy a brand new van which helped us economically. I was able to get around and fell in love with the town, Columbia.

In the fall of 2005, there was a deaf Expo in town. I ran into Cindy and her husband Pastor Tom whom I last saw at their church in Virginia where we, the Hands Extended drama group, performed back in 1984. It was almost eleven years. Cindy recognized me,

Celebrating my parents' 50th anniversary, my siblings

and we chatted and somehow the subject of a job was mentioned. She said that their deaf school was in need of a teacher's aide right away. She suggested that I use her name for a recommendation. I applied for that position as a teacher's aide at Maryland School for the deaf right in the town where we lived. I was called for an interview a couple of weeks later, and I got hired. Little did I know that I was working with three-to five-year-old boys who were more challenging than the "normal" ones. Cindy and I got together outside of work and became good friends. They lived less than a mile from us. It was a divine appointment.

It was difficult not to talk about God at school where it was not allowed. I just talked about what the Lord was doing in my life during our breaks. We worked with a teacher named Kate who was such a great teacher who inspired me. I learned a lot about how to teach the deaf children and get their attention even though their attention span was short.

One thing I hated the most was dealing with K. who was labeled as an autistic child. He was assigned to me. Sometimes at the spur of the moment, he would run inside the school or outside on the playground. There were moving cars in the parking lot and a swamp nearby. Boy, he ran fast, and I just couldn't keep up with him. I always prayed for him to stop or surrender or whatever needed to be done. He was my responsibility and if anything happened to him, I was the one to be blamed. The whole year I always prayed for peace for him and for all that he needed to be in touch with reality. I vowed to myself never to work again in the deaf school, but I accepted it as a character-building challenge.

One morning as usual, I checked my precious gold necklace that I bought in the Philippines the day before we moved back to America. I checked it after lunch and recess. It was gone. I was frantic but I had to calm myself. I asked to be excused to look for my necklace on the playground and I asked everyone in school, even the janitor. I was told that they would look out for my necklace. I prayed to send forth the angels to get my necklace and bring it to me. I rested that faith in Him. Everyone at school kept asking me if I had found it yet. The answer still was no. Two weeks later, I was getting my underwear after taking a shower, and I found my necklace in perfect condition. I wore it to school, and I announced that the angel of the Lord brought back my necklace. They were filled with wonder. Glory to the Lord.

I was able to see my parents and my brother who lived in

Baltimore more often. I also saw my sister who lived only two miles from my parents. It was a blessing to see them often for two years while living in Maryland. Also, we were involved in Immanuel's Church as Johnny knew Pastor Charles from the conference where they met a few years back. It was only a 15-minute drive, and we were so blessed to meet people there. Pastor Charles announced the need for an interpreter for the deaf, and three of them came forward to meet with me. The Lord knew the needs and He provided. I had grown close to them, too. I will forever cherish the people at Immanuel's Church and their great love for us as well for the Lord. We were sad to leave when the Lord called us to move again.

Mart, the Pastor, with Reuben, our trip to Bohol

In the summer of 2005, Reuben wanted to go to the Philippines so we purchased the tickets for Reuben and me to go. I was always delighted to be able to see the deaf in Bohol. It was a special bonding time with Reuben dividing the burden of sharing Jesus with the deaf and the Aeta tribe. We spent three weeks in Bohol. Reuben had a chance to teach and interact with the deaf in the deaf high school (Bohol deaf Academy). It was rewarding for him. Ging Ging came to help me minister to the Aeta tribe as she interpreted for me. I had a chance to preach and teach the deaf all week long. It was a refreshing time for them. Mart, the pastor of the deaf church, had been faithful laboring for the kingdom of God. Bless his heart. Reuben and I were able to get away to the resort island for the day to relax and swim. Panglao had changed a lot, and there were more new resorts. We just loved every moment savoring the tropical climate that we missed so much. I thank the Lord for a special time together before Reuben went off to college.

Johnny had been working hard to keep the business running, and it didn't go well because of the way the system worked. Eventually, the whole company was bankrupted. Johnny had to look for a job as a loan officer. He got one with no problem. He had a good reputation and blessings from the Lord who took care of him. One day he came to me talking about moving to Idaho. I said to him, "You've got to be kidding me, right?" He was serious, and I flatly said, "No." The more I worked as a teacher's aide, the more I realized that it was not the right job for me. I had to drag my feet to work but I had to trust the Lord for His strength and joy of the Lord in me. Again, one month later, Johnny asked me about moving to Idaho. "Oh no," I groaned. We talked more about it. Our good friends who lived there wanted us to move there so we could start a church at our home and work at home with the loan business. The more we talked and prayed about it, I felt my spirit jumping inside, and I finally said, "Okay." I knew our lives were not meant to develop roots but to go from place to place touching people's lives as well as developing a faith connection with people.

I loved the idea of living in a big house with a basement with a pool table. We celebrated Tiffany's sixteenth birthday, and Reuben had friends over from church. That house was very convenient. Also, I had my own darkroom in the basement as I had been taking more advanced photography classes at the community college in town. It was perfect, but the Lord had other plans. We progressed in making plans to move to Idaho even though we didn't know when. In April 2006, we got a letter saying that we needed to move out of the house by July 2006 because the house was put up for sale. What timing it was. I knew that the Lord set the date to push us to get our gears going.

Johnny called a realtor in Boise, Idaho, to find out about a house for sale. He flew over there and looked for a house. One of the realtors led him to home construction, as there was one for sale for a cheaper price even though that house wasn't built yet. The floor plan and materials were already in the package. Johnny asked me about it. I felt at peace to go ahead with it even though we had no idea what it was going to be like. We just put our trust in the Lord to work it out. We sold and gave away furniture and other things. We had the movers pack the truck for us. We took Kitty with us, and it took five days to travel. The miracle was that Johnny was driving the truck along with towing his car. The car's back tires exploded, and we had to pull off the road. No one got hurt. The company covered the expenses and got a trailer to transport the car. Tiffany and I waited for an hour for Johnny and Reuben to go to that company, bring the trailer and pay to replace the new tires. We decided to stay in town overnight after all the excitement and stress.

In the final leg of the trip from the East Coast, we were excited to see the mysterious, new house and when we arrived, we had a surprise meeting our friends waiting at our big home. We were blessed to live in a new home. The climate was so different, and I enjoyed the dry and sunny weather. In the summer, it could get as hot as up to 105. Tiffany adjusted fast and was in 11th grade at her brand new high school that just opened. Reuben adjusted well as he worked for a company for a year seeking the Lord's will about what to do next.

It was hard for Reuben and Tiffany to uproot again. I felt that Wilde High School was not good for Tiffany. She wanted to save the whole high school. She had such a good heart, and she did not realize that there was a different culture. She struggled to be accepted. Reuben handled it pretty well and started Bible study in high school. His studies flourished after he graduated. I realized that Maryland was the worst place for teens, and I thanked the Lord for His grace over them. It was good to get out in time. Both of them still had a hard time adjusting to American culture. With the Lord's grace, they managed very well academically.

I was excited to see our friends who lived one mile from us in Nampa, Idaho (about 20 minutes west of Boise). Rachel and I got together often and walked, cooked and shared the holidays. We met her and her husband Michael back in 2004 when we went to a conference

Rachel, my buddy

in Clarkston, Washington, during our short vacation from the Philippines. They invited us to stay at their house during the five-day conference. Rachel and I hit it off really well and have been friends since then. She has an amazing life testimony, and we have so much in common. Although I was about 12 years older and she was hearing, the Lord allowed us to be neighbors for two wonderful years. She understood me and I understood her. The Lord knitted our friendship for which I am thankful, and He gave me two years to be close to her. It was a special privilege that I will cherish forever.

When we were living in Nampa, Johnny started his own business doing loans. We started a home church with our children and a few people every Sunday. We didn't know anyone to recruit. It went on for five months, and Johnny was tied up with his business, and it was hard to do the church thing and work at the same time. He decided to let the church go and sought the Lord's guidance.

In September 2007, the business was not doing well during the crisis with the housing market. Johnny's friend Jody from Washington offered him a full-time job. We prayed and felt the Lord's GO with the new job and let Tiffany finish her senior year at Columbia High School in Nampa, Idaho. It came with a decision for Johnny to commute back and forth every three weeks via plane. It was by the Lord's grace we pulled through for eight months. I had a video phone so we were able to see each other and communicate.

When I heard about the deaf Club, I showed up and met the deaf people. The president asked me if I could volunteer to take a temporary position as secretary. Unknowingly, I was lured to volunteer for the whole year. I had learned a lot about how to run a deaf board and I was hoping to share the love of Jesus. It was so unspiritual that I was not accustomed to it. I learned to work through it and yet, at the same time, I was able to share my experiences in the Philippines. Eventually, I won the heart of the deaf people in Idaho. A great number of the deaf people were involved in Jehovah's Witness and Mormon faiths. I managed to share my testimonies of what the Lord had been doing in my life hoping to draw them to Jesus.

> *Jesus said to him, 'I am the way, and the truth, and the life. No one comes to the Father except through me.'*

(John 14:6 ESV)

I made an appointment to meet Wes, the director of Idaho for the deaf and Hard-of-Hearing, to see what it was all about. He gave me information about the deaf events and encouraged me to get involved. We have known each other ever since. One time I told him that I had applied for jobs at Costco and Sam's Club but never heard from them. Later on, Wes educated about deaf awareness in the workplace all over Boise and its surrounding areas. He called me one day and told me to go right away to Sam's Club that was close to my house. He mentioned one of the managers wanted to hire me. I met him, and he knew some signs he learned from his deaf brother. He asked me what I wanted to do. I said any opening that was available. He told me that someone quit in the books, software, DVDs, music, and computer games department. I took that position as a sales floor associate. I didn't realize many people wanted that position. I had so much fun doing my job. It took me one month to get used to memorizing which movies or books were on the shelf in case the customer was looking for them. I was amazed at myself when the customer asked me for a specific movie or book, and I could find it quickly and give it to them. I had no problem with most of the customers. I had one or two customers complaining that they didn't understand me or made comments that I shouldn't be working as I was labeled as one of the Mexicans who couldn't speak English. There were a lot of Mexicans where I lived. So I decided to wear a label saying, "I am deaf, but I can lip read." It broke the barrier more easily and reduced the suspicion. I worked at Sam's Club for almost a year until I couldn't work anymore because of tennis elbow from the repetition of putting heavy books on the shelf. I was sad that the doctor's order stopped me from working. That was the first week of June just before I went on vacation for our 20th anniversary.

Since I didn't trust MD doctors because they were trained to give out medications instead of finding the root problem or healthy alternatives, I had no choice but to choose my doctor from the list of names provided by the insurance company. I was given a specific doctor and went to see him. He said that I had tendonitis in my elbow, and he wanted to prescribe medication. I told him that I was super sensitive to any medication and preferred physical therapy. Actually, I argued with him, and he kept insisting on medicine. I told him, "Fine. Watch me and see what happens!" He was prideful knowing everything. I should have had an interpreter in the first place to make it clearer.

Johnny and I celebrated 21st anniversary in Puerta Vallarta, Mexico

After three or four days, the medicine was causing me to have diarrhea. When I was working, I realized that I had to run to the bathroom, but it was too late. It was all over inside my jeans and I smelled terrible. I was furious and had to go to human resources and request emergency release from work. I called my doctor, and he wasn't able to answer but I left an annoying message. He called right back to tell me to stop the medicine right then. I already did that morning. When I went to see the doctor with an interpreter, I blasted him and all he said was that I could see a physical therapist. Of course, I always prayed and believed in healing. So I had to contain myself not to be so in the flesh. I failed miserably by not setting the best example for my doctor.

Wow, he gave me no eye contact ever since I met him. I found out that he was the best doctor in town. I thought it was a JOKE. I realized that Jesus is the only Healer, and we couldn't rely on doctors for our health crisis.

The Lord put me to the test that year. I hurt my knee by falling down on the cement when I worked as a holiday worker in a Fred Meyer store. Then I had a car accident and an elbow injury. He healed me all in that year, and no doctor could.

One day while Johnny was working in the state of Washington, I was supposed to pick up Tiffany from high school. I waited and waited for her to come out. I texted her and asked where she was. She texted me back that she was already home. I was annoyed and didn't want to bother wearing a seatbelt for once even though I heard a little voice telling me to put the seatbelt on. Ah, just once, and I shrugged it off. It was only three miles home. It was a bright blue, sunny warm day in October, and I was driving on a straight, flat country road when I noticed a car approaching a T intersection where it was supposed to stop. I had the right of way. I watched cautiously, and the car unexpectedly went through the stop sign at the T intersection. I could have easily killed the 16-year-old teenage girl as I was driving towards the driver's side. Instead, I turned the wheel and stepped on the brakes all the way. My left leg hit the dashboard really hard. My right arm pressed the arm of the seat all the way. I did hit her car, but I swerved so that I wouldn't hit where she was seated. I yelled at her, "Why didn't you stop?" over and over. I was in a state of shock. I texted Johnny to tell him I was in a car accident. It was my very first and expected to be the last.

I was so upset, and he told Tiffany that I was in the accident. She met me in the emergency room. She was crying and blaming herself. I reassured her it was not her fault. I was in great pain in my left front, lower leg, and it was swollen. The paramedic advised me to take morphine and warned me that it was going to be worse as the state of shock wore off. I said I would take half because I knew my history with medicine. When I took it, it did send me to a strange world. I had the staff, Tiffany and friends who stopped by to help me, laughing at my funny comments from the drug. I drifted in and out of sleep. It went on and on. I said funny things that were so irrelevant. I remember I said really blunt things to a paramedic who took care of me. He was as gentle as possible. I was kind, mean and funny at the same time. It was so weird. Tiffany took me home with the help of our neighbor couple who could watch me while Tiffany went to school.

Tiffany happened to know the girl who was in the car accident. She was in her class, and she told Tiffany to tell me that she was so sorry. What happened was that she was chatting away with her girlfriend and didn't pay any attention to the road or the stop sign. In Idaho, the teens were allowed to drive at 14.

I was really upset that I had to cancel my plans to spend our 20th anniversary at a mountain resort for the weekend. I was in pain for a whole week, and Johnny spent the time with me at home. I was temporarily in a wheelchair then crutches. I cried to the Lord asking why it happened at the wrong time when it was our 20th anniversary. Instead, Johnny and Tiffany took me to

Sam's Club where I worked. In the wheelchair, I was able to greet all my fellow workers. Johnny bought me a beautiful gold necklace with a red, cardinal stone. My co-workers were cheering me on and complimenting me on how awesome and sweet my husband was. It was the Lord's gift to me. I couldn't complain anymore.

I healed and recovered in a short time and went back to work full-time. It was the Lord's grace that my life was spared, and I was much less injured even without the seat belt. You know that I mentioned that my right arm pushed the arm of the seat out of alignment and it never went back again as it was forever bent. Wow, I had a lot of strength like Superwoman to bend that arm of the seat, and it remained a mystery. I am thankful that I was okay.

I Can Only Hear God

Chapter 33

Mission Field Again

In February of 2008, Johnny and I felt stirred about going on a mission field as we had always yearned to serve the Lord in that way. We prayed and asked the Lord to show us the confirmations as we kept it to ourselves, until the prophecy came to us at last in April 2008 at a prophetic conference in Idaho. At first, we thought that He was calling us back to the Philippines, but it turned out to be Mexico. We were a bit surprised as we had never thought we would ever go to Mexico. I never wanted to go there even if it was the last place on earth to go. WARNING. Never say never or no to anything or the Lord will put us in a situation where we said never. It was very humbling.

In May, Johnny surprised me for our belated 20th-anniversary vacation in Puerto Vallarta for one week in June. I flew to Los Angeles to meet Johnny there as he flew from Seattle, and we reunited there then flew together to Puerto Vallarta. AAHH, the tropical climate hit me as we landed. We fell in love with that very authentic Mexican town. I found the Mexicans to be very friendly and very loving yet different from the illegal immigrants pouring into the states. We had a wonderful time, and we saw a harvest just waiting for someone to start reaping. The Lord touched our hearts. I told Johnny that he would work in a hotel, and I would have a deaf ministry there. We just laughed about it and let it go. After our return from vacation, we kept talking about it and lifted it up in prayer. It kept coming back to us. Johnny got laid off from his job and later found out that he got a job working in a hotel in the Vallarta area. Everything fell into place. The Lord had a sense of humor.

We had a garage sale for two weekends, and 98% of everything was sold, from a big commercial printer to a bunch of old coins that Johnny had for years. It was amazing that it was a short period of time. We put the rest of our stuff in storage. Again we were stepping out on faith not knowing exactly where we were going to live or what specific kind of ministry the Lord would open up for us. We were willing vessels to be used by Him in whatever was His will.

Our house was a short sale. There was an interested buyer who wanted us to be out of the house by September 25th, 2008. We went to the realtor's office to sign the papers to release to the buyer. The buyer was not present, and the realtor reassured us with no concern. One month later, we got an email from the realtor apologizing that our home was being foreclosed. We were shocked but we knew it was in the Lord's hands beyond our control. It was said that our buyer went to the bank the day of the BANK COLLAPSE nationwide, and the bank refused to take out loans for anyone. It was the beginning of the housing market collapse, too. It was amazing that we didn't have to experience it, and we just went with the flow of the Holy Spirit who led the way. We didn't lose a penny so it was okay.

Mission Field Again

We spent the night at Wild Rose Bed and Breakfast Manor in the next town and felt very pampered after two hectic weeks. Off we went traveling on the road, and we stopped in Las Vegas for three days. It was a bit too much for me, and I now knew why it was called Sin City because anything goes in that city. It was amazing to see all the splendors and beautiful man-made lights and buildings and its surroundings. We continued our adventures south for seven days and got to see our dear friends, sightseeing the beautiful country of America and mountains of Mexico. We made our first stop in Guaymas and slept in a motel that was an unforgettable culture shock with dirty sheets and exposed windows. I got so mad that I had to smell the gross smell from the sheets. I didn't move and prayed that I wouldn't catch any diseases from it. As soon we woke up around 5:00 A.M., I zoomed to take a shower and scrubbed every part of my body. Johnny did the same. What a horrible experience.

We were surprised that the highway was very nice and comfortable; however, we made sure to fill the tank whenever we saw a gas station as there were only a few in many miles. It was like a desert along with the mountains on the east side in the distance. We stayed in Mazatlan for three nights in a nice hotel. It was a welcome change from that horrible experience. We saw a sunset every night. Johnny surprised me by renting a small sailboat with a captain, and we went to an island to have lunch and relax on a sandy beach. That day was filled with sweetness and love that Johnny expressed to me. I will never forget that day.

Finally, we arrived at Puerto Vallarta and stayed at the hotel for free for three nights as the company paid for it. Johnny went to orientation for his job. Johnny asked his boss if he happened to know anyone who wanted to rent out a place. His boss said to him,

"I have never done this before, but I will do it once. My secretary is renting out a row house in the Mexican community not far from the hotel." Johnny was taken aback and knew it was of the Lord and went ahead and looked at the row house. It was cheap to rent a furnished one-bedroom although the roof was leaking when it rained heavily. It was very small and modest, but it was great for a temporary place to live. We moved in after checking out of the hotel on the fourth day. The Lord actually took care of us just as the scripture said He takes care of the birds and flowers and how much more He would take care of His children.

Since our arrival, I had been settling into our "new" home and finding the local grocery stores. It took me forever to shop for food because I had to read the ingredients in Spanish to see what was in an item. Even the manager of the store didn't know English. I had not known that shopping could be a challenge. I had picked up Spanish and Mexican Sign Language. I felt my brain was cramped with all that learning.

For the first whole month, I prayed to find a church and deaf Mexicans. Our family friends back in Maryland knew a couple who were missionaries in Puerto Vallarta and gave us their contact information. Finally, we got a hold of them, Lee and Carol, and met them at church. They were doing great work. We got together a few times even for Thanksgiving. Lee, the missionary, told me that there was a deaf Bible study at another church on Tuesdays right in the heart of downtown. I went there and found the ladies' Bible study, but no deaf were there. I met the Pastor and his wife who led the Bible study for ladies from different churches. They said there was no such thing as a deaf Bible study and invited me to join the Ladies' group. With hesitation, I did; it was challenging to lip read all the ladies in the circle (average five to eight ladies per group) but to my surprise, they were kind enough to talk slower and clearly. At the end of the study at the time for prayer requests, I asked them to agree in prayer to meet the deaf.

Within a week, Johnny and I ran into a deaf man who was panhandling on the streets where we lived. We asked for his cell phone number and the very same day, he called me to meet his friends. Whoa. I tried to understand Mexican sign language and one of them happened to know ASL as she was educated in the states until eighth grade and moved back with her grandmother. She was a big help in translating and, at the same time, I wanted to learn as much as I could. Naturally, I understood more than I could sign.

I found out that most deaf were self-taught and didn't have diplomas to be qualified for a good job. That's why they tried to make a living through panhandling or selling small items on the busy streets. Anyway, they brought me to the deaf school, actually a one-room building, the following week. I found it very disheartening and disappointing. There were only three deaf present with three teachers. Two of them were babysitting the deaf instead of teaching them. I asked an 11-year-old boy to read a kindergarten level book, and he could not read. It was the year 2008. I found out that there were about 40 deaf attending public school in their hometowns with no interpreters or sign language involved. I was outraged but had to calm down. I realized that the Mexican government was so corrupt and didn't care. I was so thankful that I had a good education even though I didn't appreciate it back then.

Johnny was friendly with the neighbor across the street from our place. Johnny loved to practice his Spanish speaking and greeting people. The old gentleman really liked Johnny and told his son-in-law about Johnny. Around the second week after our arrival, Johnny and Salvador met, then Salvador brought his wife Yesi over to meet me. We all hit it off so well. They said that there was a bigger furnished row house that was vacant right across the street, so we moved in after one month. They adopted us to be part of their family of four.

The Mexican family adopted us

Our new home had two bedrooms, and dining room/living room with an oven. We felt right at home. We were bonding with that precious couple and their children named Chris and Raquel. We were not alone anymore. Yesi was learning English at the same time I was learning Spanish. We used Spanish-English dictionaries to communicate; we also gestured a lot. (She was learning Mexican Sign Language, too.) We knew the Lord's plan was for their salvation because their hearts were so heartfelt and generous.

One amazing thing was that Yesi was drawn to me and wanted to do everything with me. Although she couldn't speak English well and I hardly spoke Spanish, her husband spoke English well since he had been working in the resort where a lot of foreigners spoke English. Johnny and Salvador were amazed at how Yesi and I communicated so well. She was around 28 and I was 54. We cooked together, walked, went to the beach, dipped in the hot springs, and shared picnics. I realized that whomever the Lord sent me to, He wanted me to show the love of Jesus to them. Yesi and I somewhat communicated and I couldn't possibly know how. I knew it was the Lord's doing or anointing.

Reuben started attending Digipen Institute of Technology in Redmond, Washington, in the fall of 2007, and Tiffany got a job as a Certified Nurse Assistant in Boise, Idaho, after her graduation in June 2008. Reuben came down for two weeks for Christmas, and Tiffany was sorely missed. I prayed for direction and grace for Tiffany since she moved out right after graduation. I connected with Reuben and Tiffany through AOL video before Skype was developed.

Johnny felt the Lord's leading to a different job at a different resort because this owner was an incredible expert in scamming people. He knew Johnny was Christian, and he was always trying to put him down. Johnny showed no reaction to the owner's radical impulses. Johnny was able to share the love of Jesus with his coworkers. In that kind of industry, he had a lot of challenges to cheat, lie, scam, or trick to get money from the clients. Johnny had a conscience to remain working openly and honestly until the day he saw his boss scamming the clients. It was so much against his conscience, and he announced that he couldn't continue working there. The workers around him wanted him to stay, but he told them the truth. He couldn't bear the thought of scamming people. He wanted to be off the hook. He gained a lot of respect. Every day he would come home and share the soap opera from his job. The Lord's grace really protected him from all the drama going on.

One day in January 2009, Tiffany called us through an AOL video and announced that she was coming to our home because she felt the Lord's touch to come home to be with us. We had an extra bedroom as the Lord knew of that plan. I was full of joy to see her back and reunited with her. I knew the Lord heard my cry and concern for her welfare. She got a job working for a tour company for a while then worked for Cheeky Monkey restaurant with a perfect open view of the sunset every night. It was our favorite restaurant, and we knew the owner who was from New York City. Tiffany got a favor working for him, and she did a good job. It was a fun job meeting all kinds of people from all over the world. I always prayed for the Lord's angels to protect Tiffany because the town was infested with drug lords and lady seekers.

Meanwhile, Salvador and Yesi were always there for us. We ate at their place often. Yesi was a fantastic cook, and I learned to cook authentic Mexican food. Several times, we went to the hot springs

Tiffany and I with Mexican family on the farm

about 30 minutes away. They took us out to a country restaurant that was amazing. The cooks made their own tortillas and grilled big fish, beef, chicken, and maybe pork. It was phenomenal. We loved going there, and we made sure that we fasted that day as it was very filling. We just loved that family. I know Yesi understood Jesus' salvation for her, and her husband Salvador was open to listening. Their children absorbed everything we had to share. We felt it was the Lord's divine appointment for them to be part of our lives.

Johnny spoiled me by taking me out to different restaurants, and we explored the country. It was so much fun and romantic to be able to be adventurous with my man horseback riding, six wheeling through water, dipping in hot springs, exploring the other cities and countryside, swimming in holes with waterfalls, boogie boarding over the crashing waves, playing in the sand, sunbathing, sharing a picnic with Salvador and Yesi's family, bike riding, taking a long stroll on the boardwalk along the beach in town, watching and enjoying the sunsets from the Cheeky Monkey restaurant. Actually, it was a refreshing time in our marriage. I love him so. Johnny is really GOD SENT. Thank you, Lord.

I kept getting together with the deaf and reaching out to them. One day I saw two groups of deaf arguing and I recognized some of them. I lifted them up in prayer, because some deaf can be very violent because of their lack of education, misunderstanding each other, jealousy and competitiveness over ownership of their turfs for panhandling. Three deaf came over and shared a terrible fight between two deaf ladies over a man.

We started Bible study and shared the love and truth of Jesus with them. More came to join us. Some were surprised that they were welcomed to our place for a meal and they felt unworthy. It was a matter of time reaching out and hoping someday they would come to know the truth of the Lord's love for them.

Johnny couldn't find work. Since SARS spread, the planes

stopped coming and some hotels shut down. Actually, America's bad economy was finally felt in the Mexican tourism industry. So Johnny met a guy from work saying that there was a job opening in Los Angeles. I said to myself, "NO WAY!" I expressed my concern to Johnny, and he said that we had to go and check it out. Here we go again traveling back to the U.S.A. We had been in Mexico for eight months. We had a hard time getting a visa because our passports were never stamped upon our entering. The Border Patrol and Immigrations had told us to go ahead and enter Mexico without stamping, but we didn't understand why. We were living in Mexico illegally. When we arrived at the USA border and the immigration person looked at our passports along with the letter, she laughed and said that the papers were worthless and let us into the U.S.A. Wow, the Lord was in control and took care of us. If you want proof that we were in Mexico for eight months, our passport wouldn't tell you that but our pictures do.

Deaf outreach outside of Puerta Vallarta, Mexico

Chapter 34

Back to the State of Washington After Years of Moving

We stopped at a workplace where Johnny had an interview in Van Nuys, in Los Angeles, California. We stayed overnight at his friend's house nearby. We went to visit Jack Hayford's church and after the service, Johnny asked around for housing information, but we were brushed aside. We were taken aback and tried not to take it personally. Maybe it was the Lord's hand pressing to prevent us from moving there. We traveled back to Washington to stay at Johnny's parents' empty house. At that time, they were building their new home in eastern Washington. Johnny and Tiffany went to Idaho to get some things from storage and dropped Tiffany off at college.

Then Johnny headed for California to try out working for a loan company. He was there for one day, and he didn't have peace all day working. So he quit and came back to Washington. It was the longest drive he had ever driven in a short time, and he got home exhausted. I was relieved and knew it wasn't meant for us to live there. We looked up for His guidance and direction every day.

As we were sitting at Johnny's parents' house, Johnny and I discussed what to do next. His parents asked us a favor to stay at their house until it was sold. Meanwhile, we sought His direction. Jody, Johnny's friend and old boss, called him to come back to work for him. He didn't have to travel to work but stayed at home to work. He went to see Jody once in a while. Oh boy, the house was so big and cold. If we used the

Johnny's parents' 50th anniversary

heat, the electric bill would run up between $600.00 and $700.00, and we didn't have the money yet to pay. So we found free wood on Craigslist and went to the nursery and found planks piling up and some old lumber. We salvaged all the wood and Johnny had a chainsaw to cut it up and put all of it in the van. It was hard labor but we felt great and had a wood stove going that kept part of the house warm. We blocked it off with a curtain from downstairs. The only thing was that in the morning, it was freezing cold when getting out of bed. We put the wood in the wood stove and it took an hour to warm up the house. It was like in the old days. I was not complaining because at least we got warm and had shelter. We stayed until the house was sold in March 2010. Johnny got laid off again, and we didn't have the money to move into an apartment right then. We lifted up in prayer and stepped out in faith.

Johnny went to help his dad with the new house, and I went to stay with a friend at her apartment for two weeks. I looked for an apartment all over the place. Johnny found a possible job and was waiting for their call during that time. The people from the office at City Church were willing to help us with the move-in expenses but hadn't approved it yet. I scanned all apartments in Bellevue, Kirkland and Redmond. I was so exhausted. I cried out to the Lord that I couldn't do it anymore. I never liked apartments because of their smell, and they felt cramped. However, I received about five e-mails from Redmond Reunion. That lady was persistent and I was thankful. I called her up and made an appointment to see the apartment home. It was for people over 55 so I went to see it. I liked it as it was brand new, spacious with open space and up in the country. I told Johnny about it. He brushed it off because it was five to ten minutes from the town. I had to cancel the appointment for us to see it. Then we went to see the apartment in Bellevue, and it was way too small and more expensive. I had to convince Johnny to take a look at Redmond Reunion where we had just cancelled that appointment. Johnny called to see if we could go see it, and he was told that we had only five minutes to see it. We zoomed over there and looked around. Johnny said that he was surprised as it was a very nice apartment home. We signed our contract by faith and said that we could put down $200.00 to hold it for the next two days as we didn't have money to put down for move-in fees. The very same day, we got a letter from City Church with a check with the exact amount of money to put down. Also the very same day, Johnny got a call that he got a job at a mortgage company and had to fly to California for training for three days the following week. We were able to get a lot of help from Reuben and his friends with moving into the apartment the next day. Wow, the Lord's timing was all in one day. He is an amazing God we serve. He blessed us so much because he was pleased with our faith in Him.

> *Faith means being sure of the things we hope for and knowing that something is real even if we do not see it.*
>
> (Hebrews 11:1 NCV)

> *Without faith no one can please God. Anyone who comes to God must believe that He is real and that He rewards those who truly want to find him.*
>
> (Hebrew 11:6 NCV)

In June I was asked to start a Bible study for the deaf ladies from the Seattle area. I was surprised that His timing was perfect for me to teach the deaf. I loved every minute of it. It was more challenging because I was dealing with intelligent ladies. I encouraged them always to go by the Word of God as the final authority. I had been teaching them for a year, and each of them had a place in my heart, and they were precious.

Shortly after, I flew over to visit my friend Rachel in Idaho for ten days as she just started her summer vacation from teaching second grade. We walked every day, shared things of life and God, cooked, and relaxed. I just loved being around her, and she was so precious to me.

As soon I got back home to my sweet husband, I couldn't walk because my leg/hip was inflamed for one year. I went to see natural and other alternative doctors. Nothing worked. They didn't know what to do. Finally, I lifted it up for prayer and I slowly got healed. It was a painful year and a time of testing. Jesus was always the source of healing and wisdom. I changed my diet, and it helped reduce the inflammation.

Preaching at Christmas deaf Ladies Breakfast

Tiffany felt the calling to go to Bible school at City Church, and she came home to be with us. Eventually, she moved into a dorm on campus. It was good to see Reuben and Tiffany pressing through seeking the Lord and growing in Him. It blessed my heart, and I will always continue praying for them to have Godly lives and have Abraham's blessings especially their great revelation of the hope of God's calling in their lives.

> *I do not cease to give thanks for you, remembering you in my prayers, that the God of our Lord Jesus Christ, the Father of glory, may give you the Spirit of wisdom and of revelation in the knowledge of Him, having the eyes of your hearts enlightened, that you may know what is the hope to which he has called you, what are the riches of his glorious inheritance in the saints, and what is the immeasurable greatness of his power toward us who believe, according to the working of his great*

might that he worked in Christ when he raised
him from the dead and seated him at his right
hand in the heavenly places...

(Ephesians 1:16-20 ESV)

Since our move back to Washington, it had been a very frustrating time finding a church where we could fit in. I realized that our hearts would forever be in the mission field, expecting more. In that the American culture had been a challenge for us, we wanted to be examples of the love of Jesus by reaching out. I noticed that Christianity in America had been greatly compromised, and I hardly saw any move of God. So I pressed myself believing in miracles and signs of wonders in my life to be a living example of Jesus' love and the supernatural. We did land in City Church for two years and needed to move on to a smaller church. We had our own service at home for one year until Johnny's friend led us to New Hope International Church. We went there for two years, and we have been there since then.

In summer 2010, I had been praying for us to go to the Philippines as I wanted to be part of the ten-year anniversary of the deaf church there. The Lord knew the desire of my heart. Dennis, the director of IDEA as well as a dear friend in Bohol, emailed me inviting me to train the leaders of the deaf church. Also, there was a great need for the children's ministry since many deaf got married since we left in 2001. All expenses were paid for and covered while we were there. The church was growing but there was no children's ministry then. I was eager to go, but first I asked Johnny to see if he was in agreement. He was hesitant at first, but after a week of prayers and discussion, he had peace to release Tiffany and me to go to the Philippines for three months. Our primary goals were to provide leadership training, encouragement, teaching, and also to start a children's ministry. My daughter Tiffany came with me to pioneer the children's ministry for all the children of the deaf parents in the church. Though she grew up in Bohol, she had not been back since we returned in 2001 when we lived there for eight years.

We were so excited and thankful to the Lord for opening this door of ministry. We both went expecting miracles, divine appointments, and a refreshing time at the deaf church. My first impression when we first arrived was that I was greeted by a great blanket of humidity and warmth, a welcome change from the cold Seattle weather. It was good to see so many familiar faces and meet even more for the first time.

When I first saw Nick Cadiz, the associate pastor, he appeared totally downcast and hopeless. Even worse, he had stepped down from being the associate pastor two years prior without my knowledge while still continuing to be the caretaker of the land where the deaf church is located. Normally, he would be overjoyed to see me, but the years of isolation on the church property and even lack of encouragement from other leaders had left him in a state of depression. I made it a priority to specifically minister to him, encourage him, and restore his leadership involvement during the course of my stay. By the end of our time in Bohol, he was fully restored; even his countenance radiated with the joy of the Lord.

Also, at the beginning of our stay, Dennis loaned us a multi-cab to get around. Dennis did so much for us. Bless his heart. Tiffany and I shared a cute, small two-bedroom cottage on Bohol deaf Academy campus. We met the deaf students and the teachers there. I became good friends with one of the deaf teachers, Maria, who was from Manila. The funny thing was that I knew her deaf best friend personally at the Maryland School for the deaf in Columbia, Maryland.

Small world. Naomi, the deaf teacher's aide, grew up under my wing and discipleship, and she became a woman of God. She and Nick got married two years earlier and couldn't get pregnant. Before we left, the leaders and I laid hands on them and prayed for a miracle of having a child. A few months after our return to the U.S.A., Naomi informed me that she was PREGNANT. It was a miracle indeed.

I was preaching on 10th anniversary at the deaf Church in Bohol 2010

While we were there, I found out that there had not been a prayer meeting for two years. I challenged Pastor Mart with the basic scriptural fact that the church cannot survive without prayer. I challenged each of the deaf leaders to commit themselves to pray daily every week as well as corporately in prayer meetings and pre-service prayer. It was a humbling recognition for each leader to see how important it is to simply worship Jesus, lay down any prayer requests, and believe in a breakthrough in the church and deaf community as well as around the world. Every time we met for prayer after that, the Lord moved powerfully in each meeting, growing their faith as well as their maturity.

On October third, we celebrated the tenth anniversary of the deaf church. When we arrived at the church early Sunday morning, there was no power which meant no lights, no fans, and no water. Why now on the biggest Sunday in the history of the church?

Pastor Mart joining the celebration

Tiffany, the leaders, and I prayed together in faith and believed the Lord would bring the power back on and also for the Holy Spirit to work in the people's hearts. Normally in the Philippines, it can take all day for the power to come back on. Just as we were about to begin the service, the power came back on. Praise the Lord. What an answer to prayer.

Being a deaf church, there was no music; we had worship, as well as a visual performance that combined worship song lyrics with choreography. I shared a message called "the Lord is Faithful." I talked about how the Lord is always faithful to us using the history of the deaf church as an example, even including the power outage that morning. Counting everyone, there were about 115 deaf adults and 15 children. Tiffany and Ging, my prayer partner for five years when I was living in Bohol, were teaching and taking care of the children. This was the beginning of the children's ministry. Creating this ministry allowed the deaf parents of the children to come to church with peace of mind knowing that we

Deaf congregation

would be caring for and ministering to their children. After the service, many old friends that I knew back when we were living in Bohol shared their stories about how I had impacted their lives. It was so humbling and wonderful to hear their testimonies, to see the fruit of my labor, and to know that God deserves the glory.

One of the other big things that happened while we were in Bohol was a retreat for the leaders of the deaf church. It was an intimate time of worship, study, and fellowship that strengthened the unity of the leadership as a whole. One of the activities we did was to take a test that revealed what kind of spiritual gifts had been given to us according to 1 Corinthians 12. Everyone was amazed and became so excited at the realization that they all have special gifts given to them specifically by God. After other team-building activities and teaching, Ging Ging and I challenged the leaders to not only continually work together in the body of Christ, but also to start home groups that reach out to the lost people in the deaf community. I encouraged them to begin teaching and stepping out as leaders in the five-fold ministry pattern instead of simply receiving at church and Bible studies. I reminded them to keep each other accountable. Tiffany and Ging Ging were such servants assisting wherever they could in teaching and in activities as well as cooking for everyone over the course of the whole retreat. The Lord showed up again and again throughout our worship, teaching, and activities' time, and by the end, every one of the leaders was truly transformed.

130 deaf people celebrating church 10th anniversary

After the retreat, we established six home groups, all of which are still active and bearing fruit today. One of the most important fruits that came out of our visit to Bohol was the establishment of home groups. Many deaf adults, who are also leaders in the church, had begun to meet in informal home groups to build strong Christ-centered relationships. The purpose was not only to grow closer to God but also to demonstrate Christ in their lives by sharing each others' burdens and joys.

Ging Ging and I prayed to find volunteers to help the children's ministry. The Lord led us to the Spirit of the Word Bible School in town, and we found four volunteers who were willing to learn sign language and help out with the children's ministry after we left. Tiffany and Ging Ging trained the volunteers and handpicked one of them, Jesa, to be the head teacher of the children's ministry as well as slowly getting her involved with the deaf leadership as she learned sign language. Mission accomplished. We praise the Lord that we accomplished all the objectives that we set out to do in such a short time. I could not have done it without Ging Ging's help and unfaltering devotion. Lord, bless her. Truly, it was all by His grace that we were able to accomplish anything at all, not to mention the sleepless nights, the heavy heat and humidity, and many trips to finish the legal work for the Aeta tribe's land.

We celebrated the ten-year deaf church anniversary, had a leadership retreat, established weekly leadership and prayer meetings, equipped and encouraged leaders, established pre-service prayer Sundays, established six home groups as outreach, established the children's ministry in church and celebrated the first baby dedication.

Tiffany and I managed to get away to Panglao to rest, sunbathe and swim at the resort. I will forever cherish the special time we had for three months. I thanked the Lord for allowing us to be together for that period of time.

Tiffany said, "When I first left to go to Bohol, I thought I had a lot to offer, but when I came back I realized the children and the church family gave me something much more than I could have imagined. God has known the two main things in my life that I have wanted since I was four: to get married and have children. When I came back to the States, I realized I was simply content with Jesus, and that God had filled an ache that I had in my heart. Proverbs 13:12 says, 'Hope deferred makes the heart sick but a longing fulfilled is a tree of life.' My heart was sick from the hope for children that was being deferred, but I came back a whole woman with the knowledge of who I am in Christ as well as that longing was satisfied in me."

Tiffany helped start the children's ministry in the deaf Church

I Can Only Hear God

Chapter 35

Walk in the Supernatural

Before I went to the Philippines in the fall of 2010, the Lord specifically told me to stop the deaf ladies Bible study. Since my return from the Philippines, my friend Jenny and I had met once a week to pray for the deaf in the Seattle area as well as Washington State for two years. We prayed for the deaf/blind community as well as the deaf community strengthening and equipping the deaf Christians.

One day, a friend of mine encouraged me to work with the deaf/blind people as a support service provider (SSP). I applied online and was notified to attend the training for three days in December 2011 at the deaf-Blind Service Center in Seattle. I started working shortly after. It was a completely new world. I felt for the deaf/blind as I couldn't imagine being blind and not hearing. It's so unimaginable. Then I remembered that Jenny and I had been praying for laborers for them. He sent me there. At first, I was very awkward working with different clients since each of them had different eye problems. I picked up fast as I enjoyed meeting people, and I was very sociable. My first client on the very first day of the job said to me, "I know that you are Christian. Are you against gays?" I was taken aback not fully prepared for that comment. I prayed and asked the Lord for wisdom because I was not supposed to become personal since it was confidential. I didn't say anything. After two years working with him, I finally asked him how he knew that I was Christian. He replied, "Because of the way you react to things, and I am familiar with the good attitude you have."

I did a lot of sowing the seeds of Jesus' love with my clients and sharing who I was in Christ. I worked as a communication facilitator after my first year as a support service provider. It was fun, too. I just loved my clients, and I hoped that I added joy to their lives when I made them laugh. To carry their burden eased their lives, and I prayed for them to receive the love and peace of Jesus.

One day I was in a hurry to meet my client at the hospital who got injured on the job right in Capitol Hill. Getting out in a hurry without thinking, I left the van running with the keys in it and the doors unlocked. I was with the client for one hour or so. When it was time to bring the client home, I couldn't find my keys in my purse. With horrified surprise, I found my van intact still running. I thanked the Lord that no one stole it. The van was right in the heart of Seattle and was in plain sight. Whew, I haven't told Johnny about this yet. Bless his heart for putting up with my irrational human errors.

Another time, I was in south Seattle and it was pretty far for a SSP job. I took the deaf/blind client out food shopping, and I was asked to drop the food at the house before running other errands. I stopped at the house and got out of the van quickly to guide the client out of the car on the busy street. Without thinking, I locked the doors with the keys in the ignition, and the van was running. I couldn't open the locked door. I didn't know what to do as I was in a panic. I forgot to cry out to the Lord. I texted Johnny and asked him if he could come, but he said to try to get help if I could. It was far away for him to travel. So I tried calling 911 a few times through video relay on my iPhone. The signal was bad. I let it go and my client said that I could use the TTY to call the police to get help. I prayed for help to be sent. I got through and I was told that the police were on the way. Finally, the police showed up. I sensed something different about him. He approached me in a very gentle way and asked me what he could do for me. I was trying to shake off being so upset with myself. He asked me if the client had a long stick. With permission, we went to the shed looking for a long piece of wood and found one. He put it through the sunroof and pressed the electronic doorknob, and it popped open. I cheered, thanked him and even hugged him. I had the van running for more than an hour with almost an empty tank as I planned to fill up on our next errand. I asked the police where the gas station was, and he said it was one mile down the street. I thanked him again. He waited for me to go ahead of him, and he followed me all the way to the gas station. I kept looking to see if he was following me, and he did out of courtesy. As I was nearing the gas station and looked in the rearview mirror to see him, he disappeared. I kept looking for him, and it was a mystery. I knew that I met an angel of the Lord. No wonder he was so calm, so peaceful and willing to help. He was so kind. I thought it was strange, so it figured. I thanked the Lord for sending him to help with my time of crisis. I asked for forgiveness for forgetting Him in the first place when I was in a panic.

As soon as I got home, Johnny asked me why I called the police who came to our apartment. I said I had no idea then I realized that I did call 911 through the voice relay service although I was unable to connect due to low signal in that area. The relay service already had my home address in case I couldn't get through. The police still responded to my urgent call and double-checked to see if we needed help. Johnny said that the policeman came and knocked on our apartment door and asked where I was. Johnny had no idea what he was talking about and said that I was working. The police officer didn't believe him so he asked permission to look around the apartment in case I was there. Johnny let him in. I wasn't there since I was in south Seattle struggling with my locked out van with its engine running.

Exploring Scotland and its several castles

The Lord's amazing provision was more than enough when we asked for it. Johnny and I had been discussing what we wanted to do for our 25th anniversary. My heart had been yearning to see Scotland since I was born there. We were in prayer for that and decided to have faith in the Lord to go to Scotland at the end of August 2012.

Johnny's work was slow and we didn't have any savings. I said to the Lord, "As you know that we have been married for 25 years and I want to share our testimony with everyone in the troubled world, I believe that you would want to bless us." Time was running out, near the end of July. Johnny said that there was no money coming in from his work. We agreed together and believed in the miracle of the Lord's provision. The first week of August, there was unexpected dump load of money from Johnny's loans. We got $6,000 in one day! I hurriedly reserved plane tickets for both of us to Glasgow, Scotland and rented a car for 2 weeks starting at the end of August. We traveled from Glasgow to Prestwick where I was born. Then up north to see Skye, the mountains, then the Hebrides, the islands up north, then south to Sterling, and finally back to Glasgow. We stayed in bed and breakfast inns, everywhere we went. There are more of them than motels or hotels. We got to meet the real people, the Scottish people. We fell in love with the romantic town called Inverness. There were countless magnificent castles!! The weather was just great! We thanked and praised the Lord for His unwavering promises!

We lived in our Redmond Reunion apartment for three years.

Scotland's beauty

I was so fed up with commuting to storage as we didn't have room to put the rest of the stuff in our 920 square foot apartment. It was a real pain to go there for winter clothes, camping stuff or tools that Johnny needed. Anyway, we arrived at the point where we wanted to live in a house. I longed for a vegetable garden. We lived on the fourth floor so far from the earth, and I had to be patient until I was able to reach for real earth. We prayed and asked the Lord for the house of our desires. We prayed for a three-bedroom house with garages and a garden. We looked all over Redmond and Kirkland for a house or apartment. I told Johnny I was not moving to an apartment again. I needed a house to live in so I could have a garden.

We saw many run-down homes that matched our income. Kirkland is very expensive and a popular place to live because of its

Our 25th anniversary trip to Scotland, a real piper with kilt

location and activities. Johnny wanted to live in Kirkland since he had a new job there, and it was hard going through 30 traffic lights especially in the rush hour. We decided to ask our realtor to look for a house, and we found out that we were not qualified to buy a home because we had no stable, steady income. We just kept looking for a house to rent. Finally, we were up

to our necks scouring all over Kirkland and some in Redmond. We just gave up our house search and planned to stay at our apartment for another year. I had already informed the apartment management not to renew the lease beforehand, in case we found a house. However, we ran out of options finding a house that we could afford so we were ready to pay April's rent for our apartment which was due in a few days.

The very next day, the realtor called Johnny to let him know that a house just came up as a new rental listing that day and sent us the link to look it up. Immediately we looked it up. We felt quickly that was the house for us. The rent cost was just right. Right away we filled out the applications online and notified our realtor that we had turned in our applications. We waited and waited for the realtor to let us know when we could look at it. Finally, she called us Saturday night and asked us why we didn't go to the open house. Johnny told her that no one contacted us about it. She realized that she actually forgot to let us know. The property manager called to advise us that we were the very first applicants for that house, and it didn't matter if we didn't attend the open house. She said that there were many people looking at the house who filled out the applications. Johnny made an appointment to sign the lease. We had never seen the house but we put our faith in our God. It was time for us to see the house and sign the papers for lease agreement. Wow, what perfect timing.

We saw the house that was perfect for us, and the garden was waiting there for me to plant. This past year we had the best harvest of raspberries, and I froze them. I had a garden with varieties of vegetables. It was April 15. I kept thanking the Lord for many months. I kept aiming and wanting to buy the house if it was for sale. Then I realized that it was the Lord meeting our needs and not to go overboard. I had to pull the reins to hold my emotions and live a day at a time.

I talked with the property manager about the strong dog odor in the house that I couldn't stand, especially in our bedroom. She said that she would have it professionally carpet cleaned right away. Otherwise, I would have the carpet ripped away. After professional carpet cleaning was done, the strong odor was still lingering. Oh man, I couldn't stand it. I put baking soda and all kinds of natural stuff on the carpet. It still smelled. I was trapped. Johnny and I cried out to the Lord and asked Him for a miracle to remove the strong odor. We forgot about it for a while. Later, we realized that there was no longer a powerful dog odor. The Lord did it. Wow. Praise His most wonderful name.

Settling into our new home seeing how the Lord blessed us at the last minute was amazing. I noticed His pattern that He wanted to make sure that we were willing to press through until the last minutes to see our faith being stretched or tested. He wanted to make sure that He got the credit. He is all powerful, very timely and never late.

My mom's 80th birthday and family reunion 2011

I Can Only Hear God

Chapter 36

Closure

The last two years before I reached 60 in April of 2014, I faced several trials. I was challenged by my relationships with some people. I realized that I had enabled some unhealthy relationships and gave them to the Lord as I trusted Him to work in their lives as well as mine. It wasn't easy for me to do that, and I truly believe that the Lord is shaping me to be more like Him.

As my 60th was approaching, I asked Tiffany to be the master of ceremonies for my birthday party. I felt it was important for me to get together with people I loved before we moved on to whatever the Lord called us to do. It really blessed my heart seeing 40 of them unexpectedly get up individually to share funny or touching stories about me. I had an opportunity to share some testimonies and that I was writing a book. I thank Tiffany, Johnny, Reuben and some girlfriends for making it happen.

Here I am. I have finally arrived at my milestone. I look back at what the Lord has done for me as I couldn't have done it without Him. He shaped me greatly; a lot of times it was painful. *"We do not enjoy being disciplined. It is painful at the time, but later, after we have learned from it, we have peace, because we start living in the right way."* (Hebrews 12:11 NCV)

You might think it is easy for us to move again and again. No, it is not. I want to follow the pillar of fire and cloud like the Israelites did. I don't ever want to leave the Lord's presence in our lives. Obedience brings blessings.

I want to summarize an allegory about a young man who was born in a cave and had never been outside of the cave through an attached tunnel. He heard stories that whoever escaped had never returned. People who lived in caves didn't believe that anything existed outside of their cave. There was a campfire with torches that had been burning ever since they remembered, and they thought it was the only light they would ever see. There was a wise man by the fire who said that no one could survive outside of the cave. The tunnel was long and it would take days to get through.

The young man, Seto, was full of curiosity wanting to know what was beyond the dark tunnel. The wise man noticed his restless, curious behavior and said, "Beware, whoever has gone through the tunnel has never returned!" Seto wanted to find out the truth. Why not risk it rather than die in the cave never knowing what was beyond the tunnel? One day, he decided to venture on his own to go through the pitch-black tunnel. It was discouraging but deep inside he wanted to move on close to the truth. He kept going for days, and it seemed endless and endless. He was scared but he would rather die in the tunnel than the cave. He kept going and going and, at times, he took rest or sleep. He kept fighting the doubts and didn't give up.

Finally, one day, he saw a tiny, glimmering light peeking through. He was delighted and hopeful and kept moving on. It took days, and he noticed when there was no light, he rested. When the light was glimmering, he kept at it until it got dark again. The light got bigger and bigger. He was running and scrambling to see where the light was coming from. The light got brighter and brighter and it made his eyes blink and squeeze from too much light. He rested and tried to get used to the light, and it took him a while. He kept on sometimes with eyes closed, adjusting to the light.

Finally, his eyes were beginning to adjust, and he could see the tunnel and its formations and noticed the path that people were on. He was full of excitement and hope reaching the end of the tunnel. It was unbearably bright, and he got to the end with his eyes closed. Slowly, he was able to open his eyes seeing the sun shining over the valley. He saw a meadow covered with wildflowers with a fresh creek running through it. He was blown away by the breathtaking beauty. "How could people live in the cave where they have been in the dark forever?" he was saying out loud. He ran down to the meadow and smelled the wonderful scent of flowers, grass, and fresh air. He saw the birds playing around in the sky and heard their chirping and singing coming from the trees. It was overwhelming to contain it all. He ate some berries and fruits and drank refreshing water. He slept on the moss carpet and had the best sleep he ever had.

He woke up feeling refreshed, thinking about the people back in the cave, saying out loud, "Hey, what about picking the flower and berries and bringing them to the people and the wise man to prove that there is life outside the cave?" He went back with flowers and loads of berries to give energy. He finally arrived and announced that he was back. People were frowning, and the wise man spoke up, "You were very foolish to leave. I am glad that you are back and alive!" Seto said, "Hey, look at these flowers and berries." They were dried up. Everyone looked at them and shrugged with disbelief. Seto tried to convince them that there was beautiful nature with sun on the other side of the tunnel. They were not convinced. Seto said that he wanted to go back and asked if anyone wanted to join him. No one made the move. Seto said his farewell and left the flowers and berries there. Seto went back to the wonderland hoping someday some of them would decide to follow after him.

How do we relate to this allegory? In a spiritual way, I found Jesus as the Light of the world. I have wonderful experiences with Him and what He has done for me. How can I contain the joy and keep from sharing it with the others I love? I want to share the Good News with you and not preach. I long for you to see the Light of the gospel of Jesus Christ. He has never failed me ONCE. I am sharing the truth like Seto with unspeakable joy. I understand that some of you reject the enlightened truth. I challenge you to give Jesus a try once and for all.

I speak to you, brothers and sisters. There is always risk when stepping out like Seto did. Never give up following the Light who is Jesus. He gives you strength, empowers you, loves you, accepts the way you are now, gives you challenge, trains you, heals you, comforts you, counsels you and does anything that you ask Him in faith, and you shall be blessed.

> *Then Jesus again spoke to them, saying, "I am the Light of the world; he who follows Me will not walk in the darkness, but will have the Light of life.*
>
> (John 8:12 NASB)

<u>*Closure*</u>

*My family on Resurrection Day enjoying cherry blossom trees at the
University of Washington campus*

My 60th birthday party

About the Author

Veronica was born deaf. She has never heard the voices of her parents, family or friends. But that never stopped God from speaking to her! Funny, painful, and always poignant, her autobiography shows us how the Lord wants to have a relationship with us and be our heavenly Father throughout every season of life. Her dramatic adventures, funny anecdotes, and relevant stories let us follow her journey with God from childhood through middle age, and encourage us that though we may not want to hear Him, God is always speaking to us.

Veronica likes cooking healthy foods, researching alternative health, reading, traveling, bike riding, photography, board games, and exploring new places. She likes people and enjoys spending time with people. She likes being challenged to try something new, and enjoys finding joy through her adventures. She loves tropical climates, spring flowers, and warm summers. She especially loves spending time with her treasured children, Reuben and Tiffany, and their spouses. Finally, she loves to serve the Lord.

For more information about Veronica's present ministry, and opportunity to be contacted and to contribute, visit Veronica's Facebook page.

Made in the USA
Lexington, KY
01 May 2018